WITHDRAWN Praise for *YOUNG MONEY* APR -- 2015

"Roose has something new to contribute, it's in concentrating not on the 'masters of the universe' but on the 23-year-olds who stay up all night prepping their PowerPoint slides."

—*New York Times Book Review*

"Roose's prose is snarky, satirical and antipathetic to Wall Street. At the same time, he evokes sympathy for his informants, five of whom managed to escape finance." —*Washington Post*

"As a cautionary tale for aspiring 'masters of the universe'—and really just anyone looking for a quick and easy glimpse into the 1 percent—it's quite compelling. As for the vortex of douchebaggery, it seems safe to conclude that it exists, but is eminently escapable."

—*NPR*

"Kevin's conclusions present a fascinating reality and perspective of young Wall Street life today that I think everyone will find intriguing. It's also a great case study on entitled Millennials, or Generation Wuss, as Bret Easton Ellis has recently described them."

—*Business Insider*

"Vigorous and vivid."

—*New York Magazine*

"This is not a sponsored me dorsement, and to prove it times. Fuck fuck fuck. Anyw

"A colourful taxonomy...Roose triumphs."
—*The Financial Times (UK)*

"A great new read that doubles as a post-crash update to Michael Lewis's *Liar's Poker*." —*Mother Jones*

"Sharp and witty...his prose is crisp and colorful. Recommended." —*The Fiscal Times*

"Highly entertaining and impressive...Roose's captivating read is sure to appeal to readers young and old who are interested in the zeitgeist of Wall Street since the crash."
—*Publisher's Weekly*

"A compelling glimpse of Wall Street in the post–2008 recession era...thought provoking, excellent book." —*Booklist*

"[YOUNG MONEY] captures the daily indignities to which the junior capitalists are subjected." —*Kirkus Reviews*

"If Martin Scorsese's film *The Wolf of Wall Street* is about the finance industry's greediest adults, Kevin Roose's YOUNG MONEY is a look at those wolves as cubs...a surprisingly sympathetic portrait." —Amazon.com

"Roose is an excellent writer and fine storyteller, who succeeds in making us wiser about an important but amorphous subject."
—*The Motley Fool*

YOUNG MONEY

Inside the Hidden World of
Wall Street's Post-Crash Recruits

KEVIN ROOSE

GRAND CENTRAL
PUBLISHING

NEW YORK   BOSTON

Grand Central Publishing
Hachette Book Group
1290 Avenue of the Americas
New York, NY 10104

www.HachetteBookGroup.com

Printed in the United States of America

RRD-C

Originally published in hardcover by Grand Central Publishing.
First trade edition: February 2015

10 9 8 7 6 5 4 3 2 1

Grand Central Publishing is a division of Hachette Book Group, Inc.
The Grand Central Publishing name and logo are trademarks of Hachette Book Group, Inc.

The Hachette Speakers Bureau provides a wide range of authors for speaking events. To find out more, go to www.hachettespeakersbureau.com or call (866) 376-6591.

The publisher is not responsible for websites (or their content) that are not owned by the publisher.

Library of Congress Cataloging-in-Publication Data
Roose, Kevin.
   Young money : inside the hidden world of Wall Street's post-crash recruits / Kevin Roose. —First edition.
      pages cm
   ISBN 978-0-446-58325-1 (hardcover) — ISBN 978-1-4789-2542-2 (audio download) — ISBN 978-1-4555-7232-8 (ebook) 1. Stockbrokers—New York (State)—New York. 2. Investment bankers—New York (State) —New York. 3. Investment advisors—New York (State) —New York. 4. Financial services industry—United States. 5. Global Financial Crisis, 2008–2009. I. Title.
   HG4928.5.R656 2014
   332.64'273—dc23
                                        2013032580

ISBN 978-0-446-58326-8 (pbk.)

To my parents, who taught me about money and its limits.

The eight young financial workers profiled in this book allowed me into their lives to an astounding (and, frankly, ill-advised) degree over the course of the more than three years I spent interviewing them. Despite Wall Street's tradition of tight-lipped secrecy, they told me everything. They spoke candidly about their struggles and shortcomings, made me privy to confidential information about their work, and, in some cases, turned over their private diaries, photographs, and e-mails.

In doing so, they took an enormous risk. All of them violated rules set by their employers that forbid them from speaking to the media without permission, and most breached boundaries of personal comfort as well. If they had been caught talking to me, they could easily have been fired—a possibility that escaped none of them.

In exchange for their openness, these young financiers made only one request: that I keep them anonymous. As a result, most names in this book have been changed, many personal details have been altered or obscured, and a few events have been re-ordered chronologically or given minor tweaks to make them less recognizable to the people involved. In some cases, the description of a person's job function has been changed to that of a related job, and the names of some financial firms have been replaced with the names of similar firms. (I've left in place the names of prominent executives, as well as people who allowed me to use their real names.)

With these necessary exceptions, the stories in this book are true.

INTRODUCTION

IF YOU WANT to succeed as a young banker on Wall Street, there are some fairly strict preconditions. You have to be pleasant, polite, and attentive to detail. You have to be able to work three consecutive twenty-hour days without having a nervous breakdown or falling asleep on your keyboard. You have to know how to calculate the net present value of future cash flows, how to make small talk about the Yankees, and, ideally, how to write a coherent memo to your boss after your third Jäger Bomb.

But most important, you have to be handy with an Excel spreadsheet. Not just handy, actually. You must be an Excel wizard—a grandmaster of the XLS file format. Which was why, on a weekday afternoon in 2010, I found myself sitting in a cramped conference room on Broad Street while a statuesque Russian woman named Valentina pitted me against thirty brand-new Wall Street recruits in a spreadsheet-formatting competition.

"On your mark, get set...go!" she cried.

All at once, the room filled with the machine-gun *cli-cli-cli-click* sound of fingers flying over laptop keys. I looked down at my unformatted spreadsheet—it was a mess. Rows 14 and 18 should have been bolded but weren't. There was an empty row between row 11 and row 12, and the years in row 5 were formatted to the first decimal place, so instead of saying 2007, 2008, 2009, and so on, they said 2007.0, 2008.0, and 2009.0. In all, there were about fifteen errors standing between me and the kind of pristine, organized Excel spreadsheet that would make a senior banker swoon. The all-time record for total beautification was thirty-five seconds, set by a freakish junior analyst from an investment bank called Moelis and Company. I'd be lucky if I was done in ten minutes.

I looked up at the other students in the room—a crew of eager young finance cadets who had been sent to a five-day boot camp, run by a company called Training the Street, to learn elementary accounting, basic financial analysis, and other skills they'd need at their new jobs on Wall Street. Most of them were in their early twenties, the ink still drying on their college diplomas. Some were lifelong bankers-in-training. Others were liberal arts majors who didn't know bonds from bananas. And in a matter of days, all of them would be let loose on the markets. Armed with Bloomberg terminals and can-do attitudes, they'd get to work selling stocks, building models for billion-dollar mergers, and giving business advice to corporate executives old enough to be their parents. They were just entry-level analysts—the lowest of the low in Wall Street's pecking order—but the fact that they had managed to get hired by some of the world's most powerful investment firms meant that they were on the rise. Soon, they would officially become card-carrying financiers, and they would be invited to take part in a giant, globe-spanning moneymaking operation that controls the fates of companies, governments, and millions of ordinary people around the world.

I, too, was a twentysomething living in New York, but that was about where the similarities with my fellow Excel grunts ended. I studied English in college, took a grand total of zero business or economics courses, and paid no mind to the corporate recruiting circus that came to campus every year. Neither my upbringing in small-town Ohio nor my schooling had helped me understand or sympathize with what went on inside Wall Street banks. And during the economic collapse of 2008, every story I read about the financial sector's implosion seemed to be describing a cartoonish fictional universe—one that seemed as distant from my everyday life as reading about Scientology or the mob.

But when I moved to New York after college, I started getting curious. The economy was still in shambles, and the world's anger toward Wall Street banks was still burning blue-hot. Politicians and pundits fulminated on the greed of bailed-out bankers, and many called for them to be prosecuted and jailed. HBO talk show host Bill Maher quipped about executing Wall Street higher-ups; one online clothing vendor sold "I Hate Investment Banking" T-shirts for $18.99 apiece; and a new arcade game called "Whack-a-Banker" was introduced in the United Kingdom, in which players used mallets to take their aggression out on pinstriped financiers. (The game became so popular in its first location, the BBC reported, that the worn-out mallets had to be replaced.)

Watching Wall Street incur the world's wrath, I often found myself wondering how the financial crisis was affecting young bankers and traders—the people my age who started their jobs in 2009 and 2010. They had nothing to do with the crash, of course. They had been in college while banks like Bear Stearns were loading up their books with mortgage-backed securities and increasing their leverage to dangerous levels. Still, as a result of the work they'd chosen, they were experiencing the financial industry's pariah status right along with their elders.

Being young on Wall Street has always been a bizarre combination of glamour and masochism. On one hand, you're a budding Master of the Universe—an apprentice at the feet of some of the world's most talented moneymakers. You earn significantly more than your peers in other industries, get to witness billion-dollar deals unfold, and have a prestigious launching pad for the rest of your career. On the other hand, the work itself is often repetitive and boring, and the long hours and hellish lifestyle associated with the job can wear down even the brightest and most ambitious recruits. After the crisis, Wall Street recruits also had to cope with their industry's new stigmatization. Many of the young people who came to Wall Street expecting champagne and caviar got dirty looks and ignominy instead.

I first realized how far the financial sector had fallen during a dinner party held at the home of a friend's parents in Manhattan, shortly after my graduation. During dinner, an acquaintance mentioned that she'd just gotten a job in finance.

"Where?" a parent asked.

"Downtown," the acquaintance replied.

"At a bank?" the parent prodded.

"Yeah," she said.

"Which one?"

The young woman blushed, cast her eyes downward, and sheepishly croaked out: "Gold...man...Sachs?" The topic of conversation changed quickly, and for the rest of the night, she looked ill, as if she'd spilled wine on the host or hip-checked a family heirloom.

If one bank recruit felt this way, there were doubtless others. For years, thousands of graduates of the world's most prestigious colleges and universities have gone to Wall Street, most only halfway knowing what they're getting themselves into. At Harvard in 2008, 28 percent of seniors who had jobs at graduation were headed into the financial services sector. At Princeton in 2006, it was a staggering 46 percent. At Brown, my alma mater, about one in eight employed graduates typically went to Wall Street immediately after graduation—not as many as at some schools, but still a larger chunk than went directly to law school or medical school combined.

These numbers struck me as being incredibly important. After all, the junior bankers who flock to Wall Street every year are some of the nation's most credentialed young people—the kinds of people who will make up the financial and political elite for decades to come. They are the next generation of American capitalists, and they're coming of age in an era of tremendous shock and upheaval. I realized that if I wanted to understand what Wall Street, and America, would look like in the future, I had to figure out who these people were, and how the crash was changing their initiation process.

So, in 2010, I began embedding myself with the young finance world. I read a waist-high stack of books and articles on investment banking. I signed up for workshops to learn how to do the work of an entry-level banking analyst. I spent time at banker bars, got myself invited to parties and networking events, and snuck into the ones that wouldn't invite me.

I considered applying to become a banker myself, but I'd written a book in college that involved going undercover at an evangelical Christian university, and I worried that Google would blow my cover if I tried a second infiltration. Instead, I tried to find as many entry-level Wall Street workers as possible who were willing to talk to me. Over drinks, at charity galas and quiet dinners in restaurant backrooms, and on sofas in their apartments, I asked them to teach me the secrets of the young finance life, and show me inside their cloistered world.

Over the course of the next three years, I interviewed dozens of Wall Street workers in every conceivable function—bankers, traders, salespeople, risk managers, executive assistants, and many more. Of those multitudes, I singled out eight young financiers to follow closely. The hours I spent with those eight—Arjun, Chelsea, Derrick, Jeremy, Samson, Ricardo, Soo-jin, and J. P.—were my clearest window into the day-to-day realities of working in finance as a young person. Their stories are the primary focus of this book.

When I wasn't shadowing young financiers, I reported on the financial industry for the *New York Times* and *New York* magazine. In the process, I learned about the deal makers who plotted and executed huge transactions, the relationship between big banks and the broader economy, and what makes Stock X safer or more risky than Bond Y or Credit Derivative Z. But I also learned that despite its forbidding structure and impenetrable jargon, Wall Street is and always has been a human endeavor. People, not machines, run the financial sector. And that basic humanity is more pronounced in young financiers, who haven't fully made the cutthroat, technocratic ethos of Wall Street their own yet.

"There's a generation gap in finance," one middle-aged hedge fund manager told me at the outset of my investigation. "Young people have their own risk models. They look at their place in the world completely differently than we do."

I wanted to learn to see the world in the same way they did, even if it meant spending five days plugging formulas into Excel under the supervision of a Russian drill instructor.

"Okay, time's up!" Valentina said, when the clock had run out on our formatting competition. Her announcement provoked a mass of groans from the students, including me, who hadn't yet finished. "Congratulations to the winner," she said, pointing to an incoming Credit Suisse analyst in the second row. "And congratulations to the rest of you, too. I've seen some very impressive work this week, and you're all on your way to becoming excellent financial analysts."

Or in my case, close enough.

CHAPTER ONE

ARJUN KHAN STRAIGHTENED his tie, brushed a lint ball off the charcoal gray suit he'd bought for $179 at Lord and Taylor to wear to his high school graduation, gave his hair a final pat, inspected his teeth for food in the bathroom mirror, and bounded out the door of his apartment and into the elevator of his downtown high-rise.

A confident, bright-eyed twenty-two-year-old with an aquiline nose and a slight belly paunch, Arjun was on his way to his first day of work as a mergers and acquisitions analyst at Citigroup. His neck muscles were tense and his stomach was turning over, but those were just surface nerves. Mostly, he was filled with the flinty resolve of the newly emboldened. After thousands of hours of preparation, dozens of interviews and expertly crafted e-mails, and one extremely lucky break, he had finally become a junior investment banker at a major Wall Street firm—the job he'd been chasing for years.

Nine months earlier, Arjun's plans had been derailed by the financial crisis. The Queens-born son of a data engineer father and a social worker mother who had both emigrated from India to New York as young professionals, he headed into the fall of his senior year with a prestigious job offer at one of the best banks on Wall Street: Lehman Brothers.

Arjun felt lucky to have gotten Lehman's attention in the first place. He attended Fordham University, a Jesuit school in the Bronx that, while strong academically, wasn't among Wall Street's so-called target schools, a group that generally included the Ivies, plus schools like Stanford, New York University, Duke, and the University of Chicago. That meant he had to work harder to get his foot in the door—joining the Finance Society at Fordham, attending lectures at Columbia Business School, spending his free time watching CNBC to pick up the cadence of the investor class. And his strategy worked. He secured a junior-year internship at Lehman, and he did well enough that at the end of the summer, he was offered a full-time job beginning after his graduation. His recruiter told him, sotto voce, that he had been the only Fordham student to get an offer from Lehman that year.

During Arjun's internship, things began to go south. Ever since the Bear Stearns collapse earlier that year, industry watchers had been speculating that Lehman would be the next bank to fail. The firm's stock price had tumbled, thousands of workers had gotten laid off, and one well-regarded hedge fund manager jolted Wall Street that summer by proclaiming that Lehman wasn't properly accounting for its real estate investments. Still, Arjun assumed that Lehman would be fine.

He was wrong, of course. In September 2008, while Arjun

was starting his senior year at Fordham, Lehman filed for bankruptcy. (Most of its U.S. operations were bought several weeks later by Barclays Capital, the investment banking arm of the large British firm.) The same day, Merrill Lynch, which had also been pummeled by the housing collapse, announced it was selling itself to Bank of America for $50 billion. AIG, an insurer weighed down by towering piles of credit default swaps, had to be given a massive $182 billion bailout, and Goldman Sachs and Morgan Stanley, the last freestanding American investment banks, turned themselves into bank holding companies in order to give themselves better access to the Federal Reserve's emergency lending window. Congress passed a $700 billion bailout package that gave a lifeline to banks and kept the markets afloat, and the entire country sank into a recession that would cost millions of jobs, engulf every sector of the economy, and…well, you can probably fill in the rest.

From the Fordham campus, Arjun watched reports about Lehman's bankruptcy with a knot in his stomach, knowing that it would probably cost him his job. And several weeks after the bank's sudden death, he was in chemistry class when he got a call from an unfamiliar number with a 212 area code. He let the call go to voice mail, then checked it in the hall after class.

"Hi Arjun, this is John from Barclays Capital," the voice on the message said. "Obviously, you know why I'm calling. I just wanted to let you know that I'm very sorry, but we're not going to have a seat for you next summer."

After the bankruptcy, Barclays Capital's human resources department tried to help Lehman's spurned analysts find new jobs. But that just salted the wound. One human resources staffer pointed Arjun to a job at a small private wealth management firm in Miami—the financial sector equivalent of being cut from the Yankees' starting lineup and offered a bench-warmer spot with the Toledo Mud Hens.

"I'm just interested in investment banking," Arjun told the staffer. "I don't care what city it's in."

Arjun knew that Wall Street operated on a strict power hierarchy. Within every firm, there were so-called back-office workers who cleared trades, maintained the firm's computer systems, and performed all other kinds of technical and administrative work. One step up was the middle office, which comprised lots of disparate jobs that were important to the functioning of the bank but were not revenue-generating in their own right: legal, compliance, internal risk management. And then there was the promised land: the front office. The front office was what everyone pictured when they thought of Wall Street—pinstripe-clad deal makers and red-faced traders, making millions and getting their work on the front page of the *Wall Street Journal*. And when he decided to pursue a job in finance, Arjun decided he would accept nothing less.

But now, everything had changed. With the failures of Bear Stearns and Lehman Brothers and the sale of Merrill Lynch, the so-called bulge bracket of top-tier American banks was whittled down to just five firms: Goldman Sachs, Morgan Stanley, Citigroup, Bank of America Merrill Lynch, and JPMorgan Chase. And even those firms looked to be in jeopardy. All around the financial sector, the markers of success and failure were shifting. Tiny boutique firms were weathering the changes better than global financial conglomerates. In some cases front-office bankers were being laid off while back-office IT workers were being promoted. Up was down. Down was up.

That year, as the crisis unfolded, the message boards at Wall Street Oasis, a popular finance-industry website, filled with posts from confused young finance aspirants, wondering what the industry's changes would mean for them:

Reconsidering Wall Street?

Will banking recover? How long?

Are banks really not hiring for the fall?

In September, one poster summarized many of the fears about what would happen to the financial industry: "I think it'll be a long time, if ever, before the swagger returns to Wall Street. The 'Masters of the Universe' image has been shattered."

Newly jobless, Arjun spent the rest of his senior year looking for work. He applied to financial internships on Craigslist, sent out dozens of résumés and cover letters, and pressed on every finance-industry connection he had. But nothing materialized—nobody was hiring. Finally, in late spring of his senior year, Citigroup contacted him about a last-minute opening in the bank's mergers and acquisitions division, where they needed another analyst to help with a bigger-than-expected workload going into the summer. Citigroup, like most banks, had been battered by the financial crisis, losing billions of dollars and being saved only by a massive government bailout. But the bank was alive, and it was doing deals again. Arjun knew that with the year's recruiting cycle already over, it was likely to be the only front-office offer he would get. So a few weeks before his college graduation, he accepted.

Throughout college, Arjun had drawn inspiration from the lives of people who had made it big on Wall Street despite not having the advantages of privilege or pedigree. The most famous example was Sidney Weinberg, a working-class Jewish kid from the slums of Brooklyn who started as a janitor's assistant at Goldman Sachs in 1907 and eventually worked his way up to become the senior partner of the firm. But there were more recent role models, too. Arjun knew, for instance, that there had been a Lebanese-American executive who had gone to Pace University—not exactly a finance feeder school—yet had become the vice chairman of Bear Stearns and one of the most powerful deal makers on Wall Street. Even Citigroup's CEO, Vikram Pandit, was an Indian-born outsider who had trained as an electrical engineer before breaking into finance. On Wall Street, he thought, it didn't matter whether you were a blue-blooded WASP with degrees from Exeter and Harvard or, like him, an Indian kid from Queens with no family connections. If you were talented, if you could make money, and if you were willing to kick down every obstacle in your path, you could qualify as what is known in certain parts of the financial world as a "PHD"—a "poor, hungry, and driven" worker—and, eventually, you could make it to the inner circle.

But now, as he surveyed the wreckage of the crisis, Arjun felt even less sure than ever that the old social compact still held. After all, who knew what would happen to Wall Street in a year? More banks could go under. Entire lines of business could be wiped out by new regulations. There was no telling whether New Wall Street would look anything like Old Wall Street, or whether the traits that had mattered in American finance for the better part of three hundred years—hard work, hustle, and commercial instinct—would still be rewarded in the future.

As he got ready for work on his first day, though, Arjun's anxiety was trumped by excitement. In the worst Wall Street hiring climate in a generation, he'd finally gotten a seat at the table.

He was proud of how far he'd come. He knew he'd made his parents proud, too, by getting a job at a prestigious bank they recognized by name and reputation. And he was determined to prove to his new colleagues that he could work every bit as hard as they did, even if he didn't have an Ivy League degree behind him or a trust fund lying in wait.

As he walked out into the brightly lit Manhattan streets that morning, Arjun gave his building's front desk attendant a smile and a wave. Then, he walked through the open door, pointed his cap-toe shoes toward the bank, and started to strut.

CHAPTER TWO

As THE SUN shone down on her, Chelsea Ball lifted her red Solo cup, chugged the six or seven ounces of beer inside, then placed it on the picnic table, with the bottom hanging an inch off the edge. She hit the cup from below, flipped it so it landed upside down on the table on the first try, and shouted "Go!" to the next teammate in line, who also happened to be the oldest managing director in her group.

Chelsea, a freckle-faced redhead who grew up in a middle-class Connecticut suburb, was intimately familiar with this game—"flip cup," it was called—from the dozens of nights she'd spent playing it in college, mostly with the other members of the Georgetown women's soccer team. Flip cup was a favored pastime in her group of friends, and over time she'd developed the light touch required to land the cup properly on the first or second try. But she'd never imagined playing it in a setting like this—at the annual field day of the public finance division of Bank of America Merrill Lynch.

The field day, which was held at a posh New Jersey country club, was a corporate outing the likes of which Chelsea had never seen. There was tennis, softball, volleyball, and a giant tug-of-war pit. A cornucopia of food—burgers, wings, hot dogs, chips—and a keg of beer at each activity station rounded out the scene.

Chelsea drank it all in, more figuratively than literally. It was her first week as a full-time analyst, and she was still stepping cautiously to maintain peace with her new colleagues. She'd spent her summer internship the previous year in Bank of America's structured credit department, and she had barely understood any of what was going on. She was determined to get her mind around this new assignment.

A lot had changed since Chelsea's internship. The previous fall, while she was starting her senior year at Georgetown, Bank of America had acquired Merrill Lynch as Merrill—one of the oldest and most venerated banks on Wall Street—flirted with death. The government had stepped in with $45 billion in bailout money, but even that hadn't been able to keep the new Bank of America Merrill Lynch's stock price from sliding to historic lows. There were shareholder lawsuits, congressional hearings, and unexpected losses. To make matters worse, Merrill CEO John Thain was revealed to have spent a Croesus-like $1.2 million renovating his office while his firm was dying, buying antique items including an area rug costing $87,783 and a "commode on legs" costing $35,115. All told, the plots and subplots surrounding the merger looked bad enough that the *Wall Street Journal* had christened it "a $50 billion deal from hell."

Chelsea had felt sure that she would get screwed out of a job. She'd accepted Bank of America's offer in early September, just a few days before the Merrill acquisition, and she and her fellow interns had been e-mailing each other with panicked queries about whether their offers were still valid in the wake of the news. Luckily for Chelsea, Bank of America and Merrill Lynch eventually agreed on a deal that would allow all the new hires from the class of 2009 at both firms to keep their jobs. The combined firm would have more first-year analysts than it needed, but it would save the bank from having to rescind offers.

Chelsea arrived at the Crowne Plaza in Manhattan in June for her first day of training. There, for the first time, she saw how slapdash and hastily assembled the new Bank of America Merrill Lynch really was. There were hundreds of analysts, startlingly few managers, and an obvious shortage of supervision. There was also a culture clash that was unmistakable. Bank of America, the country's largest commercial bank, employed more than two hundred thousand people, and had retail branches and ATMs spread out across the country. Merrill Lynch, on the other hand, was a white-shoe firm with a proud history of elitism. Its investment bank was blue-blooded in temperament and composition, recruited primarily from Ivy League schools, and did only the more lucrative work of advising corporations, issuing securities, and managing money for ultra-wealthy individuals. In fact, many at Merrill Lynch considered commercial banking—the business of taking deposits, issuing mortgages, and giving loans to regular people—a lower form of commerce.

Chelsea quickly found she could scan the room and pick out the Merrill kids. They had expensive ties, jutting jaws, and looks of mild disgust on their faces. They had been recruited to work for one of the most prestigious firms on Wall Street, but now found themselves working for what they considered a lesser enterprise. To them, it was as if Tiffany had merged with Costco, and now they were stuck selling pristine jewels next to freezers of chicken cutlets.

The new analysts spent four weeks in the ballroom of the Crowne Plaza, being put through their paces in a Finance 101 course that taught them the basics of equities, fixed income, corporate valuation, and other skills they would need for their jobs. Most of the job openings in the highly sought-after groups had been filled by Merrill kids. For the people who had originally been hired by Bank of America there were a few positions open in mortgage sales, a rate sales job or two, and a handful of openings in something called public finance.

Of the open groups, Chelsea decided she liked mortgage sales the best. She'd worked in marketing before, and she figured that once she learned about mortgage derivatives, selling them would be like selling anything else. She listed the group first on her preference card, and waited until the last day of training, when an HR representative gathered the thirty-odd first-years in sales and trading in a conference room and gave out assignments.

"Chelsea, you'll be in public finance," the HR woman said.

Chelsea blinked back tears. She had wanted to find an assignment she could sink her teeth into, in a division where she might eventually prove her worth. And now, in a matter of days, she would be doing something she barely understood yet again. That night, she went out to a bar with friends and drank until the world blurred.

"They made a mistake hiring me," she told me a few days

later. "I'm the dumbest person here, I don't understand any of this, and I'm just so overwhelmed by the lingo and everything else."

Now, three days later, things were looking a little brighter. A boozy corporate field day was hardly the worst way to start a job, and as Chelsea looked around the country club grounds at the men in her group—and they were mostly men, with a sprinkling of female analysts and support staff—she found her mind opening. They looked happy enough. A little worn out, maybe, and way too excited to be outdoors during the daytime, but at least they weren't moping.

When she returned from field day, Chelsea settled into her cubicle on the ninth floor of the World Financial Center, in a windowless bullpen with ugly neon lighting, and went to work. She quickly learned that her new group paid much more attention to detail than the group she'd interned in the previous summer. Her first few projects came back marked up with changes from her boss, who would do things like cross off her 2s and write in the word *two*, and realign her cells so that all the first digits lined up instead of the last digits. For Chelsea, who had always gotten by on her charisma, the new detail orientation required of her was maddening. But she'd devoted herself to being a good student, and she'd told her boss early on: "I just want to work hard and learn." True to form, she rarely left the office before midnight.

Chelsea was still dating her college boyfriend, a Georgetown sophomore named Anton. They'd met the previous year, when Chelsea was a senior and Anton was a freshman. And even though the three-year age gap had seemed crazy at the outset, it worked. Anton was kind, thoughtful, and mature, and he didn't seem to mind her long hours at the bank. He was still in school, so the actual contact he and Chelsea had was limited. They Skyped late at night, and every third or fourth weekend, she would board a Megabus for the four-hour trip to Washington, D.C. There, she would work remotely and, once in a while, pry herself away from her BlackBerry in order to spend time with him.

As summer turned into fall, though, Chelsea became deeply lonely. Her roommate was an accountant and worked the same long hours she did. Their schedules meant that they rarely saw each other, and even more rarely saw their other friends. Her relationship with Anton was becoming more distant and detached, and her long hours made it hard to keep up her normal gym routine. She'd started out with a half-hour morning commute, but eventually, Bank of America Merrill Lynch moved her group to the giant office tower it had purchased at One Bryant Park. Soon, the extent of her daily exercise was walking the three avenues and six blocks from her Forty-Eighth Street high-rise to the tower and back.

Chelsea didn't mind working hard. She had come to Wall Street for the money, and she knew that long weeks and grueling projects were part of the deal. College had left her with more than $100,000 in student loans, and she hoped to save most of her $70,000 base salary and all of her bonus in order to begin paying them down as quickly as possible. Still, she missed the intellectual stimulation of college, when she'd taken quirky classes, read stacks of good books, and written long papers on topics that actually interested her.

During the darkest moments, when Chelsea felt herself spiraling into work-fueled depression, she thought about her older brother, Josh. He had graduated from Tufts in 2008, with a degree in economics and a cushy job offer at a boutique investment bank. Just as he was scheduled to begin, the financial crisis struck and the bank rescinded its offer. He'd spent the next six months jobless and depressed before getting an equity research job at a second-tier firm that paid him a fraction of what he'd expected to make.

At least she had avoided Josh's fate, Chelsea thought. She had a prestigious, high-paying front-office job in an industry that was shedding them left and right. And even though the job wasn't the perfect fit for her, she felt comforted by the fact that it existed at all. In 2009, a bit of stability was all a twenty-two-year-old on Wall Street could reasonably ask for.

CHAPTER THREE

AFTER MY EXCEL boot camp was over, I decided to back up a bit and try to answer a more basic question about young financiers: namely, how do they get to Wall Street in the first place? So I booked a ticket to a place where the vast majority of financial careers are born—the campus of an elite university—and went to see the finance recruiting machine in action.

I wound up in Philadelphia, on the campus of the University of Pennsylvania. On the day I arrived, it was raining buckets, but a biblical flood wouldn't have kept a small army of students from making their way to Houston Hall. There, in their ill-fitting suits, their leather padfolios clutched tightly to their sides, hundreds of eager Penn sophomores, juniors, and seniors filed into a recruiting session for Morgan Stanley, where they would hear a one-hour pitch for the bank's virtues and, hopefully, score a business card or two.

When most of the seats were filled, the lights inside the room dimmed, and a Morgan Stanley recruiter pressed Play to be-

gin a promotional video. Upbeat pop-rock music played as the
screen filled with text banners:

> IN THE FINANCE WORLD, EVERY DAY IS A NEW DAY.
> SOME DAYS, FORTUNES WILL BE MADE. OTHER DAYS,
> HISTORY WILL.
> THE STORY OF A NEW GENERATION OF LEADERS.
> FROM THE FIRM THAT BROUGHT YOU GOOGLE, UPS, AND
> JETBLUE COMES THE OPPORTUNITY OF A LIFETIME.
> BOUNDARIES WILL BE SHATTERED.
> EVERY VOICE WILL BE HEARD.
> AND THE FUTURE WILL BE BRIGHT.

When looking at schools to visit, I singled out Penn for a
reason. Like all Ivy League schools, Penn sends a chunk of
its graduating class into the financial services industry every
year—about 30 percent in 2009. But Penn's link with Wall
Street is particularly tight because its Wharton School, a business program that contains both graduate students and undergrads, is considered America's primo farm team for budding
young financiers—a sort of West Point for Wall Street. More
than half of Wharton's six-hundred-person undergraduate class
typically heads to banks, hedge funds, private equity firms, and
other financial services companies after graduation. Among the
celebrity financiers the school has churned out are SAC Capital billionaire Steven A. Cohen, the junk-bond impresario
Michael Milken, and real estate megagoon Donald Trump.
Wharton's list of famous alumni, and the fact that its graduates
emerge armed with advanced finance training, has made it a
place where recruiters are prone to drooling.

"Penn, and especially Wharton, is in a league of its own," one hiring manager at a top Wall Street firm told me. "It's the only place where you go to campus and it's already done and dusted—it's a matter of *which* financial services firm students want to go to, not *whether* they want to go into finance." (Patricia Rose, the head of Penn's career services department, gave a slightly milder diagnosis: "To come to Penn is to, at some point in your undergraduate years, ask yourself the question, 'Should I think about investment banking?'")

These days, financial firms—as well as top-tier management consulting firms like Bain and McKinsey—court Wharton students in a manner reminiscent of very polite stalking. They barrage students with information sessions, interview workshops, lavish restaurant meals, "sell days" in New York City, follow-up calls, and follow-up calls to the follow-up calls. At Wharton, these firms behave less like faceless corporate entities than like insecure middle schoolers, desperately fishing for clues about whether their favorite students like them back.

Getting a job at a top firm on Wall Street, even with a Penn degree in hand, is never easy. But it's especially hard when the financial industry is in turmoil, since a similar crowd of applicants competes for fewer spots. (In one recent year, Morgan Stanley received 90,000 applications for 1,200 full-time analyst positions—an acceptance rate of 1.3 percent.) And most banks draw between 50 and 90 percent of their full-time hires from the previous year's pool of summer interns, meaning that competition for the best offers is often all but locked up by junior year.

The race for Wall Street jobs is so cutthroat that an entire cottage industry has sprung up to give aspiring bankers a boost.

You can now buy the "Investment Banking Interview Prep Pack" for $79.99 from Wall Street Oasis; the "Ace the Technical Investment Banking Interview" webcast and PDF guide for $99 from Wall Street Prep; or, if you're really playing catch-up and don't mind shelling out, a four-day "Intern Core Skills" workshop from Adkins Matchett and Toy for $3,000.

Wharton students generally don't need these study aids, since they already learn advanced financial skills in their classes. Still, in an attempt to garner offers from their financial firms of choice, they spend months burnishing their résumés, practicing their interview skills and elevator pitches, and poring over the Money and Investing section of the *Wall Street Journal* in order to arm themselves with sufficient knowledge to impress the recruiters. And then, every year, they head off to information sessions to begin closing the deal.

It wasn't always such an ordeal. For many years, Wall Street banks recruited like any other corporation—hiring a handful of graduates from top colleges to fill their junior ranks and employing them indefinitely. But in the early 1980s, banks began instituting what became the modern Wall Street recruiting program, in which college seniors are hired for two-year stints as analysts. After their two years are up, analysts are expected to find work at a hedge fund or private equity firm, or, in a few cases, get an offer to stay on for a third year of banking. The ones who don't are gently shown the door.

This new plan, nicknamed "two and out," was a brilliant tactical move. Selling Wall Street jobs to undergraduates as a temporary commitment rather than a lifelong career enabled banks to attract a whole different breed of recruit—smart, ambitious college seniors who weren't sure they wanted to be bankers but could be convinced to spend two years at a bank, gaining general business skills and adding a prestigious name to their résumés in preparation for their next moves. The strategy also created a generation of accidental financiers—people who had graduated from elite colleges with philosophy or history degrees, had no specific interest in or talent for high finance, yet found themselves still collecting paychecks from a big bank three decades later.

At Penn, though, most of the enthusiasm was genuine.

"Finance is a great industry filled with great people," one revved-up student told me.

"Traders are probably the coolest people you'll ever meet!" raved another.

Morgan Stanley's actual recruiting pitch was a fairly unremarkable collection of corporate banalities ("culture of excellence," "world-class mentoring opportunities") and promises of prestigious "exit opps" once the analyst years were over. But few words were given to describing the actual, day-to-day work of being a first-year analyst. And nobody from the bank mentioned the biggest reason a college senior might be attracted to Wall Street—namely, the fact that first-year analyst jobs pay a starting salary of around $70,000, with a year-end bonus that can be upwards of $50,000.

The lack of overt focus on money surprised me, though perhaps it shouldn't have. As strange as it sounds, a big paycheck may not in fact be central to Wall Street's allure for a certain cohort of young people. This possibility was explained to me several weeks before my Penn trip by a second-year Goldman Sachs analyst, who stopped me short when I posited that college students flock to Wall Street in order to cash in.

"Money is part of it," he said. "But mostly, they do it because it's easy."

He proceeded to explain that by coming onto campus to recruit, by blitzing students with information and making the application process as simple as dropping a résumé into a box, by following up relentlessly and promising to inform applicants about job offers in the fall of their senior year—months before firms in most other industries—Wall Street banks had made themselves the obvious destinations for students at top-tier colleges who are confused about their careers, don't want to lock themselves in to a narrow preprofessional track by going to law or medical school, and are looking to put off the big decisions for two years while they figure things out. Banks, in other words, have become extremely skilled at appealing to the anxieties of overachieving young people and inserting themselves as the solution to those worries. And the irony is that although we think of Wall Street as a risk-loving business, the recruiting process often appeals most to the terrified and insecure.

"It's incredibly risk averse," the Goldman analyst told me. "Think about it: if you go to a bank, you make as much money as anything except hedge funds, private equity, or possibly a tech startup. Those things are wildly more risky and a lot harder to do. So if a bank comes to me with an opportunity to lock down a good, high-paying job in September of my senior year without working too hard for it, I'm going to privilege that over anything else I might be thinking about doing."

After watching Penn students line up to nab precious seconds of face time with Morgan Stanley recruiters that night, I couldn't help feeling like not much had changed since the financial crisis. Whether because of the structured, well-timed nature of recruiting or simply Penn's finance-centric campus culture, the fact remained that these jobs were still objects of intense desire. Even a financial near-Armageddon, it seemed, hadn't been able to dislodge Wall Street from its pedestal. And I wondered: if students at Penn couldn't be swayed from their synchronized march to big banks by the worst economic crisis since the Great Depression, was the financial sector's allure simply irresistible?

CHAPTER FOUR

DERRICK HAVENS LOOKED down at his cell phone, suspecting and fearing what was coming. "I can't do this anymore," the text message read. "You have to choose what's more important to you—this job or me."

Derrick winced—not only was he still at work after midnight on a Sunday, but he had just been given an ultimatum by Erica, his girlfriend of four years, in a text message. "*Fuuuuu-uuuck*," he groaned, rubbing his forehead and leaning his desk chair as far back as it went.

Erica had spent that weekend in Chicago, where Derrick lived and worked as a first-year analyst at Wells Fargo. She was a senior at the University of Wisconsin—Madison, where they'd met and started dating, and it took her two and a half hours to get from Madison to Chicago, driving along the cold, desolate stretches of Interstate 90.

In the beginning, going long-distance had been a no-brainer.

Derrick and Erica had similar values, similar left-of-center politics, a similar sarcastic sense of humor. They even looked good together. Erica, a shapely brunette with a toothpaste-commercial smile and the innocent look of a teen catalog model, was exactly the kind of girl you'd expect to fall for Derrick, a tall, lean high school basketball player with a tousled head of dark brown hair and the cocksure charisma of a one-time homecoming king. They'd fallen deeply in love, and they had been talking about getting married after Derrick's two-year stint at the bank was up.

That weekend, Derrick knew he would have to work. He always did. Life was brutal as a first-year analyst at an investment bank. He knew that the same qualities that make first- and second-year analysts successful at their jobs—willingness to work long hours, obsess over small details, and be constantly on call—also make them bad romantic partners. And he'd heard other analysts refer to the "seven-week itch," since seven weeks of interrupted dinners and last-minute cancellations was about all most bankers' significant others could handle before threatening to break up with them. But Derrick had counted on making his relationship work.

On Erica and Derrick's weekends together, they typically spent late Friday night and early Saturday morning together, and played Sunday by ear. Erica usually spent the rest of the time doing homework or watching DVDs in Derrick's empty apartment.

Derrick could tell that Erica was getting impatient with the routine, and so on this visit, he had floated the idea of a Sunday night dinner. One dinner, with no interruptions, and no emergency trips back to work. That much, he said, he could promise.

His plans were stymied on Sunday morning, when he arrived for what he thought would be a quick check-in at work. He had planned to meet an intern at the office to work on a "buyer ID," a memorandum that was used to pitch a company on several other companies that might be interested in an acquisition. Derrick had offered to help with the project, but when he got to the office, the intern was nowhere to be found. Eventually, the intern e-mailed Derrick apologetically, claiming that he had food poisoning and wouldn't be able to make it into the office. (Derrick knew that "food poisoning" was code for a hangover.) So Derrick e-mailed his associate—the slightly older, business-school-educated banker who was his direct supervisor—and told him that without the intern, he wouldn't be able to finish the project. The associate called back immediately.

"Listen," he said. "I've been pretty amenable to your schedule, and I've been flexible with all the things you wanted to do this weekend. But we have a client needing this information, and I'm sorry he didn't show up, but this is your responsibility."

Derrick sighed. "Got it. I'll get it done."

Then, with a heavy heart, he called Erica. "Hey, I've got to deal with something. I should be done in an hour or two. I love you."

Erica had heard this tune before, and she offered to leave.

"No, no, this should be quick," he said. "Just hang out, and I'll be there as soon as I can."

But Derrick had overpromised, and the buyer ID quickly got entangled with problems. After two hours, he called Erica again to ask for another hour. Two hours after that, at around 10:00 p.m., he called to deliver the news she had been fearing.

"Look," he said. "I'm so, so sorry, but I'm going to be here for a while. I don't think I can do dinner."

Erica burst out crying. She knew that bankers worked hard, and she'd done her best to accept that for the next two years, Derrick would only be partially hers. She'd shrugged off God knows how many interruptions in the middle of movies, weekend brunches, football games. But the grace period had elapsed. After months of playing second fiddle to Derrick's job, she couldn't take it anymore.

"This always happens to me," she said through her tears. "And it hurts."

She drove home from Chicago in a rage, and stopped midway through to text him with the ultimatum. After receiving it, Derrick sat at his desk, head throbbing. This wasn't how things were supposed to go. Investment banking was supposed to be tough, but it wasn't supposed to jeopardize the things that mattered most to him.

Derrick knew that if aired anywhere outside the banking world, his complaints would set off a symphony of the world's most minuscule violins. He understood that, objectively speaking, he was no pity case; that he was *insanely* lucky to have such a stable, high-paying job in a time when many people he knew were struggling to pay the bills. Still, it felt at times like he was being tugged in two irreconcilable directions—between the girl he loved and the career he wanted to build.

Derrick didn't consider himself a banker at heart. He was born and raised in Waupaca, Wisconsin, a town of six thousand that was famous mostly for its annual strawberry festival. His father, who owned a small grocery store chain, had convinced Derrick to study economics in the hopes of someday recruiting him to take over the business. While in college, Derrick had been inspired by watching Barack Obama run for president. He had always believed in free markets, but he also believed that the government should help lift up the least privileged. Obama's pragmatic progressivism struck a chord with Derrick, and so, as a sophomore, he'd decided to follow in the president's footsteps and go to law school.

His plans changed during senior year, when he was invited to interview for an investment banking job at the Chicago office of Wells Fargo, the giant San Francisco–based bank. Derrick knew a few things about entry-level banking jobs. One, they paid well. Two, they were good preparation for law or business school. Three, the jobs were highly desired by the BBAs, students who were getting their bachelor of business administration degrees at Wisconsin's undergraduate business program, many of whom were self-serious protofinanciers who walked around campus in bad suits and patent leather shoes, hauling copies of the *Financial Times* and holding investor committee meetings. And lastly, if he got one of these jobs and the BBAs didn't, it would absolutely kill them. He cherished the thought of waving an offer letter in front of them, watching their faces redden as they veered into apoplexy.

Derrick had always been tempted by money. His family was either middle- or upper-middle-class, depending on how his dad's grocery business was doing. His mom was a nurse, and he'd been raised with the values of Waupaca, a town where people prized hard work and thumbed their noses at big-city millionaires. But, for some reason, he still dreamed of being rich, of owning a sports car and a summer home, and never having to look at price tags when he went shopping for clothes.

When he was fifteen, Derrick watched *John Q.*, a Denzel Washington movie about a father whose son is diagnosed with a fatal heart disease. In the movie, the father goes postal when he finds out his insurance won't cover a transplant, and he takes the entire hospital hostage in a last-ditch attempt to save the son from certain death. The movie is supposed to be a sort of liberal caricature about the moral turpitude of insurance companies, but it hit another note with Derrick. At the dinner table the next night, he shared with his parents the lesson he'd learned: "It just, like, makes it pretty obvious how important money is."

At this, Derrick's mom stopped chewing and narrowed her eyes.

"Listen to me, Derrick, this is important," she said. "Money shouldn't define who you are. It just makes certain things easier."

Her lesson stuck with him. And it kept him grounded even during his senior year—when he applied to Wells Fargo on a whim, got a second-round interview, then went to Chicago for a SuperDay (the all-day sessions at which banks grill their final-round recruits) that culminated in a job offer, and decided on taking it. Along the way, Derrick had convinced himself that making money wasn't the goal of going into finance. The goal was to build the skills he'd need to take over and expand his dad's grocery business someday, and to send a message to the people who had doubted his ability to make it in a prestigious, high-pressure industry.

"I want to make my dad proud," he told me. "And I want all those people in high school who thought I was stupid to fucking suck it."

Derrick moved to Chicago and started at Wells Fargo a

month after his college graduation. He had now been working
for several months, and he had built a reliable if unexciting routine. Most days, he'd wake up at 7:30, be in his cubicle by 8:30,
spend the next sixteen or seventeen hours hard at work, then
head home for a beer and an episode of *The Wire* before bed.
It was a lonely life, but Derrick liked being productive. And he
was getting real experience. He'd already earned several "deal
toys"—clear Lucite hunks, roughly the size of a tea saucer, that
were given to the entire team that worked on any major transaction, as recognition of their work. He kept his deal toys lined
up on the desk in his bedroom, and he liked looking at them
before bed. There was always a little line on them, set in etched
type, that made him smile: "Advised by Wells Fargo," it read.

In the regional offices of Wells Fargo, the work was largely
the same as it was in New York or San Francisco. But the environment felt different. The young bankers in Chicago weren't
blue bloods with Ivy League degrees. They were kids who had
gone to Indiana, Michigan, Notre Dame. And while most of
them were highly accomplished, they didn't flaunt it. They
drank domestic beer, talked about cars and girls, and spent late
nights tossing a football around in the "bullpen," as their cubicle farm was called.

Derrick had been to New York once before for a trip during
college, and he'd fallen in love with the city. He had flirted
with good-looking girls at the W hotel bar, looked over the water in Battery Park, seen the giant bull statue on Wall Street,
and gone dancing at a club on the Lower East Side. Manhattan, he saw, had an energetic hum to it that Chicago
could never match. It was the city where power was forged,
where social and economic capital accumulated, and where,

in the course of an average day, you could see dozens of cross-sections of humanity.

But he knew Erica would never agree to move to the East Coast. She was planted in Wisconsin, with friends and family and ambitions all centered within a fifty-mile radius of her hometown. Aside from good food and shopping, the big city had little to offer her.

"Why do you need to go to New York?" she said, when he'd brought up the possibility. "I'm here. Our families are here."

At the time, Derrick had consoled himself with the fact that being with Erica was more important than living in New York. But part of him had been disappointed. He didn't know quite what could happen to him in the big city, but he dreamed of throwing himself in and finding out.

Maybe, he thought, a breakup could be the spur he needed.

CHAPTER FIVE

OVER THE NEXT year, as I spent more time interviewing young Wall Street workers, I felt the mysterious nature of their work coming into sharper focus.

Investment banks, I learned, are vast collections of different money-related functions, all jammed somewhat haphazardly under one roof. There are, of course, the true investment bankers—men and women who tour the country helping large companies raise money, acquire smaller firms, and in all other ways serving as paid advisors to the corporate elite. And there are the junior analysts and associates who do the grunt work for those bankers. But there are lots of other people at investment banks whose work has nothing to do with investment banking. There are traders, who buy and sell stocks, bonds, futures, options, and other financial products. There are salespeople, who work in tandem with the traders, and match up buyers and sellers of those financial products. There are "quants" or "strats," a bank's math geeks, who build complex computer programs that analyze and trade on market data. There are research analysts, who churn out detailed reports on various topics and companies. There are prime brokers, who provide basic services for hedge funds and other investment firms, and structured finance divisions that devise and package complicated derivatives. There are media relations people, political lobbyists, HR managers, and private wealth bankers. And there are lawyers and compliance officers, who help keep everyone else out of trouble.

Most of the young Wall Street workers I was shadowing were first-year analysts in the investment banking divisions, or IBD, of major banks. IBD analyst jobs are typically considered some of the most prestigious positions for new bank hires, but they also have the longest hours. Today, as before the financial crisis, it's not uncommon for a first-year IBD analyst to work one hundred hours a week—the equivalent of sixteen hours a day during the week, then a mere ten hours on each weekend day.

Which is not to say that these twenty-two-year-olds are actively doing one hundred hours' worth of work every week. In fact, many sit around idly for hours a day, listening to music or reading their favorite blogs while they wait for a more senior banker to assign them work. (These drop-offs are never pleasant, but they're worst when they happen at 6:30 or 7:00 p.m. as the senior banker is leaving for the day, giving the analyst a graveyard shift's worth of work before he or she can go home and sleep.)

Most of a first-year IBD analyst's work revolves around gathering, organizing, and presenting financial data. If a bank is trying to convince one of its clients (say, Apple) that it should buy another company (say, Microsoft), the bank's analysts first have to gather every available nugget of financial information about Apple, Microsoft, all of Apple's and Microsoft's competitors, and the entire consumer electronics sector. Revenues, expenditures, margins, buybacks, dividends, secular trends, ratings changes, large buyers and sellers of stock—all of this information, and much more, must be pulled from subscription services like FactSet, Bloomberg, and S&P Capital IQ. Once the data is pulled, it gets corralled into a "model," a big Excel spreadsheet that is used to calculate the specifics of the deal being proposed. For an Apple-Microsoft deal, the model would be able to come up with a reasonable estimate of Microsoft's present and future worth, as well as helping show how best to acquire it, what the risks are, and what the benefits to Apple's long-term finances and product lines might be. Once the model is made, the most important information in it is put into tidy, organized charts and graphs, inserted into a template, and turned into a "pitch book"—a professionally bound, attractive-looking book that, over the course of several hundred pages, tells Apple a detailed story about why, exactly, it should buy Microsoft and how much it should pay.

Investment banks are ruthless about making sure models and pitch books—both called "deliverables," since they get delivered to clients—are perfect, down to the last comma and decimal point. And that's where the analysts come in. Every day, a Wall Street analyst works at the mercy of the associates, vice presidents, and managing directors above him or her, any of whom can request changes to any deliverable at any time. An MD wants a bar graph instead of a line graph on page 63 of a pitch book, and it's 3:00 a.m.? A good analyst will wake up and snap into action. A VP finds a broken cell reference in cell L57 of an Excel model on Christmas Day? The analyst had better wait to open presents.

"Until you get older, you're not setting your own pace," one Wall Street executive told me. "You're on call. It's much more like a doctor's life in that regard."

At-will scheduling is the bane of the young analyst's existence. It means that every evening activity is subject to last-minute cancellations, that stress-free vacations and personal trips out of town are impossible, and that work-issued phones function as permanent third limbs.

"It's not the hours that kill you—it's the lack of control of the hours," one first-year analyst told me. "My life doesn't belong to me anymore."

Unflagging loyalty is taught to analysts early. In the *Vault Guide to Finance Interviews*, a short book used by many analysts to prepare for Wall Street work during college, would-be bankers are told to answer this question:

> It is Friday afternoon. Tomorrow morning you have to catch a flight to Boston for your best friend's marriage, and you are in the wedding. You have informed your deal team well in advance and they know that you will be gone. Just when you are about to leave, you find out that a client wants to meet with the banking team tomorrow. What will you do?

The correct way to answer, according to the Vault guide, is to "express the fact that you understand the hardships that an I-banking career would involve, and that you have endured such sacrifice situations previously." In other words, you are expected to say: "Yes, sir, I will absolutely miss my best friend's wedding to sit silently in this half-hour meeting, where I will say nothing and have no discernible impact on anything."

Banks try to mitigate the effects of the nonstop lifestyle they force on their analysts by giving them some institutionalized perks. Many banks have gyms inside their buildings, and all firms provide dinner allowances for analysts who stay at the office past a certain time. Analysts at many firms are given vouchers for luxury town cars, which they are allowed to take home after a late night at the office. But often, these perks function more as incentives to work more and later.

Karen Ho, an anthropologist at the University of Minnesota who has studied the culture of finance, writes that young bankers are "oriented into a culture of instability and competition where they must hit the ground running." Part of that orientation, she writes, is learning to conceive of their work differently from the work done by nine-to-five employees in the "real" economy, who clock in and out, who can leave work at the door, and who don't live in constant fear of being called in on an urgent project. This sanctified status, which Ho calls the "cultural geography of segregation," is bequeathed to analysts during the training process as a point of pride, and a rite of passage to which all analysts must subject themselves. And it works. In bullpens across the Street, young analysts play games of "misery poker," in which they proudly—and often, with some exaggerated details—complain to each other about how overworked they are. ("I'm staffed on three deals, and haven't left the office before 1:00 a.m. in a month." "Oh, yeah? Well, I'm staffed on *four* deals, and I pulled three all-nighters last week.")

Young Wall Street analysts aren't victims, of course; they all choose this path voluntarily, and they are well compensated for it. But as I heard more of them describe the everyday frustrations and boredom associated with their jobs, it occurred to me more than once that some right-thinking people would be unwilling to do this work for *any* amount of money. Wall Street, more than most industries, makes its workers feel expendable; many entry-level bankers conceive of themselves as lumps of body mass who perform uncreative and menial work, and whose time can be exchanged for labor at any moment. The banks themselves reinforce this people-as-assets view, referring to their flesh-and-blood employees in purely transactional terms. (At Goldman Sachs, for example, what used to be the human resources department is now known as "Human Capital Management.")

For first-year financiers—who just months earlier were happy, autonomous college students—the process of becoming human grist for Wall Street's labor mill can be a blunt trauma. Among the young bankers I interviewed, I saw disillusionment, depression, and feelings of worthlessness that were deeper and more foundational than simple work frustrations. And at times, while listening to analysts nearly in tears describing how much they despised the mindlessness of making Excel models, or meeting a banker at a bar at 11:00 p.m. on a Sunday because it was the only free time he had available for an entire month—my thoughts drifted. I recalled those statistics about how many graduates of top colleges end up working in finance, and the massive allocation of the nation's social and economic resources toward the functions of Wall Street banks. And I thought, with more melancholy than anger: *We're giving all that to* this?

After one analyst spent most of a late-night interview describing his anxiety and ennui, I reflected on a passage from *The Financiers*, an early book about Wall Street investment banks. The passage was written in 1976, a decade before Tom Wolfe coined the term *Masters of the Universe*, and it spoke of investment bankers as if they were a newly discovered superhuman species:

> Their offices are furnished with expensive antiques and original works of art. They dress in conservatively cut $500 suits, and are as quick to place a telephone call to Rome or Zurich or Frankfurt as most Americans are to call their next-door neighbor....They engineer multi-million-dollar transactions and, although they render middleman services only, enough money remains in their hands to make them the richest wage earners in the world. They are the investment bankers of Wall Street; the men who raise billions in cash for America's giant corporations.

That passage may have been true of senior bankers in 1976, but it bore no resemblance to the life I'd heard so many young bank analysts describe in the post-crash era. Today, a more accurate version would read:

> Their offices are covered in moldy takeout containers and pit-stained undershirts. They dress in whatever is left in the clean laundry bag from last week, and haven't seen sunlight in two months. They make pitch books for clients who will never read them, and get yelled at

for improperly aligning cells in Excel, all in hopes of a year-end bonus number that won't make them want to jump in front of the 4 train. They are the young investment bankers of Wall Street, and they just want some sleep.

CHAPTER SIX

"IDs," THE BOUNCER grumbled.

Jeremy Miller-Reed and Samson White, two first-year sales and trading analysts at Goldman Sachs, fished into their wallets, pulled out driver's licenses showing that they were, respectively, twenty-two and twenty-one, and handed them over for inspection. After a once-over, the bouncer nodded, and waved them into the Frying Pan, a floating bar and lounge built into an old ship docked on the west side of Manhattan. The bar served as young Wall Street's favorite summertime haunt, and all around the boat, fresh-from-college bank analysts were drinking and mingling, their dress shirts still creased from the store packaging.

Jeremy, a lithe, golden-haired crew rower from San Francisco who wore black-framed glasses and dressed like an assistant professor, had picked out Samson—a pudgy prep from northern Virginia who favored polo shirts and Sperry Top-

Siders—as one of the most like-minded people in his intern class at Goldman Sachs the previous summer. They had both been rising seniors at Ivy League colleges (Jeremy at Columbia, and Samson at Princeton), and their elite educations had given them the ability to fit in with the fratty, beer-chugging bros who populated places like the Frying Pan. But they'd both considered themselves less high-strung than the average Goldman intern, and their easygoing demeanors had made them fast friends on the trading floor.

Now, in the summer of 2010, the two were back in New York to start their full-time jobs. They were in the second week of a ten-week training program that was supposed to turn them from know-nothing college kids into hotshot Goldman employees.

Jeremy, who was working on the firm's commodities desk, was learning about all the different kinds of commodities Goldman dealt in—oil, gas, corn, wheat, precious metals, and more. And Samson, who worked in the firm's mortgage department, was being schooled in the many complex and esoteric mortgage-related products and derivatives Goldman packaged and sold to clients.

First, they had to endure all-day sessions of mind-numbing training in an auditorium at Goldman's Jersey City office, most of it on topics they'd never need to use on their desks. (On one of the first days, they'd spent several hours playing a business-themed board game that involved buying and selling yachts. Nobody had been able to figure out how it related to working at Goldman.) Then, after learning about a host of other boring securities topics, they began studying for the Series 7, an examination required of all incoming analysts at large Wall Street firms, and the Series 63, a more specialized exam required for

incoming traders, salespeople, and some capital markets workers. Only after passing both exams would they be allowed to do
anything resembling an actual trade.

Jeremy never expected to end up on Wall Street. He was interested in sustainability, urban planning, and politics, and he
had been planning to become a mechanical engineer since he
was a teenager, when he spent six months and several thousand dollars of his lawn-mowing money turbocharging his car.
But talking with older members of the crew team at Columbia
had convinced him to apply for banking internships. He knew
that the skills he would learn at an investment bank would be
applicable to any number of other jobs. And he knew that Goldman's internships paid around $15,000 for ten weeks of work, a
tidy sum that would give him plenty of spending money for his
senior year.

So he pursued a summer internship offer, then, when he got
it, spent the next few months reading financial blogs like Dealbreaker and Wall Street Oasis, buying a navy blue suit (with
his parents' credit card) at Macy's, and skimming Vault career
guides for tips on how to impress his new corporate overlords.

At Goldman, the hierarchy of prestige was shifting rapidly.
Before the financial crisis, the big money and status had been
located in proprietary ("prop") trading units, where traders had
made millions of dollars a year making big, leveraged bets with
the firm's own money. A group called Goldman Sachs Principal Strategies had popped up to focus on proprietary trading,
but there had been others, including prop-focused commodities and mortgage traders, and an elite team of investors known
throughout the bank as SSG—the Special Situations Group.
Jeremy had heard these groups spoken of in reverent tones, but

he had also heard that they were on the way out of vogue. The Volcker Rule (named after former Federal Reserve chairman Paul Volcker), a much-heralded piece of the Dodd-Frank financial reform act that cracked down on proprietary trading, was moving toward implementation, and the days of glory for prop desks all across Wall Street seemed numbered.

Now, Jeremy was in the sales and trading side of Goldman, which had its own layers of power and prestige. There were "hot" desks like credit trading, mortgage trading, and commodities trading—the areas in which real money was made, and in which a successful trader with several years of experience could easily make $500,000 or $600,000 a year if he played his cards right. Then there were "cold" desks, like equity sales, prime brokerage, and internal risk management, which supported other desks and initiatives within the firm but were not big revenue producers themselves.

Goldman's sales and trading internships were famous for the "desk scramble," a ten-week cutthroat competition that in many ways resembled a fraternity rush process. At the beginning of the summer, all of Goldman's roughly 120 summer sales and trading interns were assigned to three-week rotations on three different desks, the idea being that rotating among desks would give them the flavor of various parts of the bank. The interns, of course, saw it as a competition for spots on the hot desks, and spent all three rotations sucking up to the managers of the desks they coveted. In August, after the final rotation, managers got together to decide—via a voting process that resembles a professional sports draft—which interns would get the full-time offers on hot desks, which would get stuck with less desirable assignments, and which would not be invited back at all. For many incoming Goldman analysts, who spent their lives acing standardized tests and excelling in varsity sports, the desk scramble represented the first time they ever struggled to measure up.

Jeremy had started the scramble with a rotation on Goldman's prime brokerage desk, a group that provided basic services for hedge funds who held their money at the bank. It was a cold desk whose work amounted to little more than acting as bank tellers to hedge fund managers, and he'd quickly grown bored of it. His second rotation, in equity sales, was slightly better, but still something a trained chimp could do. But his third rotation, in the commodities division, had redeemed the failings of the first two.

Commodities was one of the two or three hottest divisions at Goldman. It was known within the firm as a rough-and-tumble place, where huge risks were an everyday occurrence and where adrenaline ran nearly as high as bonuses. And Jeremy knew immediately that it was where he wanted to be.

The commodities division's prestige could be traced to 1981, the year that Goldman bought J. Aron, a large commodities brokerage. The merger was rocky at first; J. Aron had been known for an aggressive, take-no-prisoners trading culture, which didn't mesh well with Goldman's buttoned-up civility. (For years, J. Aron had its own set of elevators within Goldman's headquarters.) But in recent years, J. Aron had gone on to colonize Goldman from the inside. One J. Aron worker, Gary Cohn, became Goldman's president; another, a Harvard Law School graduate turned commodities salesman named Lloyd Blankfein, was named the firm's CEO. As a result of its success, J. Aron took pride in its legacy, and still considered itself a sort of VIP cluster within the firm. Thirty years after the initial acquisition, it was still not uncommon for a Goldman trader to introduce himself as "John from J. Aron."

Jeremy liked the swagger of the J. Aron guys, and he quickly sidled up beside their desks during his rotation, learning the lingo and getting to know some of the more colorful characters. The most intriguing figure was Graham Campbell, who ran the firm's energy desk. Graham was a born-and-raised Texan who had turned his oil-country pedigree into a lucrative gig selling oil and gas products to some of the world's largest companies. He was brilliant, charismatic, and handsome, with perfectly cut suits and a full head of hair that was graying at the temples. He looked the part of a central-casting politician, which explained his nickname among the analysts in the group: "the Senator."

The Senator had first impressed himself upon Jeremy at a commodities cocktail hour, when he stuck out his hand and introduced himself.

"So, how's the summer going?" Graham asked.

"It's great!" Jeremy raved. "I'm learning a ton, and—"

"Let me stop you before you continue to blow smoke up my ass," Graham interrupted. "I know this sucks for you. I did it as an MBA intern, and I know it's a shitty dance."

Jeremy laughed. He was impressed by Graham's straight-shooting personality and his willingness to forge an actual connection. Not every Goldman executive pulling in $4 million or $5 million a year would have taken the time to joke with an intern. After they had talked a bit more, Jeremy decided to cut to the chase.

"I want to work in the commodities business," he said.

Graham chuckled. There were a few things standing between Jeremy and an actual commodities trade—namely, getting a full-time job and passing the Series 7 and 63 exams. But for the next ten minutes, they talked about the job—what it entailed, what kinds of risks were involved, and what the market for different kinds of products was like.

"Look," Graham said eventually. "Just so you know what you're getting into: We're not here to save the world. We exist to make money."

Jeremy nodded along. And after another few minutes of conversation, Graham decided he liked the kid's gumption. So, at the end of the third rotation, when the sales and trading executives made the list of interns they wanted as full-time workers the next year, the Senator made sure to put Jeremy on his list.

And now, ten months later, Jeremy was here, on an anchored ship in the Hudson River, looking up at the jutting, gleaming towers that composed the skyline of his new city. He hadn't even properly started work yet; still, he couldn't stop dreaming about what was in store for him. He hoped he would one day learn to throw millions of dollars around the oil market before lunch. He hoped he would be able to impress Graham, who seemed to have a zero-tolerance policy for bullshit and fudging. And he hoped that eventually, he would find a way to make Goldman Sachs feel like home.

* * *

Sitting beside him at the Frying Pan, Samson also wondered how he'd come to this point.

The well-bred son of a lawyer and a playwright, Samson had taken an introductory economics course out of curiosity during his freshman year at Princeton. Later, he'd been inducted into an eating club—Princeton's version of a fraternity—where he'd overheard some older students talking about finance. On their recommendation, he picked up *Liar's Poker*, a memoir by Michael Lewis about Wall Street in the 1980s, in an effort to learn more.

Like Lewis, who worked as a bond salesman at Salomon Brothers after his Princeton graduation, Samson had no specific connection to the world of finance, except that he happened to go to a school that sends a phenomenally high proportion of its graduates to Wall Street banks. But after reading Lewis's account, Samson was intrigued. The idea of working on Wall Street sounded slightly hollow to him, but the challenge and the prestige appealed to the same competitive part of his psyche that had landed him near the top of his class. He knew that as a Princeton student with good interview skills, he would likely have his pick of investment banks. And he knew that if he put in just two years at a bank, he would have amassed valuable skills that would serve him well in any industry.

His Goldman internship interviews, conducted in Princeton's career center, were a breeze. The first Goldmanite pitched him softballs like "Why do you want this job?" and "Tell me ten financial headlines over the past year that were interesting." The second round was a little tougher, and included the following brainteaser:

Here's a game I've just invented. The rules are that I flip a coin, and if it comes up heads, you pay me a dollar and the game is over. If it comes up tails, you flip again. If it comes up heads the second time, you pay me two dollars, and the game is over. If it comes up tails again, you flip again. Third time, you pay me four dollars for heads and the game is over, and you flip again for tails. And so on and so on, each time doubling the payout for heads, and flipping again on tails. How much would I have to pay you up front to play this game?

The question was a version of the Martingale, a French gambling strategy. The purpose of asking it was to test a candidate's understanding of tail risk—the chance of low-probability, high-impact outcomes. The idea is that, while the theoretical expected value of the game is a small negative number (because the coin will probably land on heads within a few flips, ending the game and limiting your losses), there is a tiny possibility of a catastrophic result, in which tails comes up again and again until you owe millions of dollars. There was no right answer, but the way a person replied could shed light on what his thought process might be like as a trader; a candidate who said he'd need only a dollar to play probably wasn't thinking through the tail-risk scenarios carefully, while a candidate who answered with too big a number was being excessively cautious. Tail risk was an important idea for someone working in finance after the crisis, since one of the biggest mistakes financial institutions had made during the inflation of the subprime mortgage bubble was ignoring the small chance that the entire interconnected mess would collapse.

Samson knew something about gambling—he'd read books on card counting and been to Las Vegas a handful of times with friends. But he'd never thought about the Martingale strategy as an interview question for a finance job. He talked through the possible outcomes and managed to convince the interviewer that he knew something about game theory and probability. Two weeks later, Samson got an e-mail telling him that he'd gotten an internship in Goldman's fixed-income, currencies, and commodities division. Known as FICC, the division houses all of Goldman's bond trading, mortgage sales, and other types of fixed-income transactions. It was also one of the most profitable areas of the firm, and accounted for anywhere from 50 to 70 percent of the entire firm's revenue in a given year. In the moneymaking theater that was Goldman Sachs, he'd been invited to sit in the front row.

That summer, Samson had crushed it. He had done his best rotation in mortgage sales, a top-tier desk with no shortage of competition among interns. He had dedicated himself to the task, printing out pitch books and making Excel models with attention to minute details, and maintaining an upbeat attitude. As a result, he had become beloved by the MDs and partners on his desk, and he had guaranteed himself a full-time position the following year.

Samson also met Jeremy that summer. At first, Jeremy struck him as bristly and unfriendly, but soon the two had warmed to each other, and were sitting together at Open Meetings, Goldman's weekly Q&A sessions for interns. Both of them had gotten to Goldman more or less accidentally, and neither one had fully bought in to the mystique or the aura of self-importance that surrounded the place. One night, after a taxing day at the firm, Samson pulled out the small Moleskine notebook he used as a diary, and wrote:

> Typically, I'm comfortable in situations where personality is the defining factor in what makes you successful.

But what makes me uncomfortable is that if you take 120
kids who have succeeded in life basically on work and intellect and not personality, and if you say that personality
is how you're going to succeed, there's just going to be a
ton of masking and falsifying and people trying to finagle
and adapt their personalities to what they think is right.

Despite his reservations, Samson stuck it out and got rewarded
with a job offer on the mortgage sales desk. Now, nine months
later, he was back in New York, with a head full of hope and a
job at the most prestigious investment bank in the world.

Samson was excited to start work on his new desk, which was
on the fifth floor of Goldman's brand-new building. The building, located at 200 West Street in Battery Park City, was a $2.1
billion monument to Goldman's financial prowess. The bank
had spared no expense, and had outfitted its new headquarters
with a gym, a cafeteria, an espresso bar, a state-of-the-art conference center, and hundreds of expensive pieces of art. (The
painting in the lobby alone, a 23-by-80-foot mural by the artist
Julie Mehretu, had cost $5 million.)

As Samson walked through the trading floor, everything
looked vaguely similar to 85 Broad Street, Goldman's old building, where he'd done his internship the summer before. There
were the shoulder-to-shoulder trading desks, connected in rows
spanning the room, each with two, four, six, or eight computer
monitors in front of it. There were the phones, which never
stopped ringing during the trading day, the flat-screen TVs overhead tuned to CNBC, and the digital clocks hung from the
ceiling, showing the current time in not just New York but
London, Tokyo, Hong Kong, and other global financial hubs.

There were the glass-walled offices on the periphery of the floor, where the partners sat. And there was the pantry, a walled-off area where Goldman traders could get coffee and snacks without wandering far from their stations.

But as much as 200 West Street seemed familiar, it also had an odd sterility to it. Samson wasn't sure how to characterize it, but something about the building felt fortified—as if the entire place had been sanded down to make it a little more secure and a little less welcoming. The new building felt designed to keep employees and information securely inside, while keeping outsiders at a total remove.

Maybe it was in his head. In the nine months since his internship, Goldman had undergone a massive transformation in the public imagination. Once a relatively anonymous investment bank, it had taken on the image of a global financial villain—a firm whose name was shorthand for unrepentant greed and vice.

The popular backlash had started in the summer of 2009 with a *Rolling Stone* story, written by Matt Taibbi, that accused Goldman of being "a great vampire squid wrapped around the face of humanity, relentlessly jamming its blood funnel into anything that smells like money." Then came a series of stories about Goldman's crisis-era misdeeds, which centered on the firm's creation of mortgage-backed collateralized debt obligations (CDOs), some of which Goldman was selling to its clients while simultaneously betting that they would tank. In April 2010, Goldman's image problems boiled over when the Securities and Exchange Commission sued the firm, along with a midlevel mortgage trader named Fabrice Tourre, for defrauding investors in one such deal—a mortgage-backed CDO called

Abacus 2007-AC1. Goldman's mortgage trading desk, the same one Samson was slated to work on, was at the center of the scandal. It was the desk that had marketed the Abacus deal, and where the firm's massive bets against the housing sector had originated. And as such, it quickly became the center of attention. Incriminating e-mails from many of the four-hundred-person desk's executives surfaced in the SEC's suit, including ones in which a top executive referred to a specific mortgage-backed CDO as a "shitty deal" and others privately gossiped about the fact that the entire housing sector looked ready to collapse. If Goldman was a vampire squid, the mortgage desk appeared to be the part doing the sucking.

That April, when the Senate Permanent Subcommittee on Investigations called on a number of Goldman executives to testify about their bad behavior, Samson and his friends gathered to watch the hearings on C-SPAN in his Princeton dorm room. It was the day of his eating club's annual spring party, and the group was pregaming with cups of orange rum punch. They were already a little tipsy when Samson saw a few familiar faces cross the TV screen.

"Holy shit!" he said. "I've had dinner with that guy!"

Samson had never met Fabrice Tourre, the baby-faced trader at the center of the Abacus scandal. But he had spent time with Michael Swenson and David Lehman, two of the executives who ran the structured-products group, and both of whom had shown up to testify that day. He recognized their looks of discontent from bad days on the floor, and wondered how annoyed they were to have to explain themselves to a bunch of underinformed elected officials.

Despite all the fraud and villainy Goldman had been accused of, Samson was still proud to be working on the Goldman mortgage desk, which he thought was filled with upstanding and ethical people who were being wrongly treated as scapegoats. He had spent weeks after the Abacus story came out defending Goldman's behavior to anyone who would listen, using talking points he'd cribbed from friends at the firm.

"Mom, don't worry," Samson had told his mother, when she asked him if Goldman's mortgage traders had acted unethically in the run-up to the crisis. "Obviously it's bad that people lost money, but they were sophisticated investors who should have known about the risks. There's nothing unethical about what we did."

In April, as he watched the firm's executives getting yelled at by red-faced senators, Samson felt a different worry grow in the pit of his stomach—namely, that Goldman would bow to public pressure and shrink its mortgage division or shut it entirely, putting him out of a job. It was a natural worry. Even if the firm had done nothing wrong, would anyone want to buy complex mortgage products from Goldman after the Abacus deal?

"You're not going to be fucking trading any mortgages anytime soon," one of Samson's friends said, chuckling, while they watched the C-SPAN proceedings.

But the friend was wrong. A handful of Goldman traders left the bank in the wake of the Abacus scandal, but the group was still standing in May, when Samson graduated from Princeton with honors. And now, he would be there, as its newest member, when it licked its wounds and tried to move on.

After graduation, Samson moved into an apartment in TriBeCa with two of his college friends, pulled his suit out of storage, and prepared for the massive amounts of work that lay ahead of him. Oddly, the troubles of the past months hadn't dented his eagerness to start his job. In fact, they had made it stronger. If the mortgage desk could survive the Abacus scandal, he told himself, it could survive anything. Since his internship, he had become a true believer in the integrity of Goldman Sachs, and now he was ready to go to war for the firm as a full-time employee.

Over the summer, Samson sat down again and distilled his thoughts in his journal:

> So on to the next chapter—NYC. Nice TriBeCa apartment w/ two of my best friends from school. Working at the most profitable firm on a desk where I love the people. That's the real next chapter—a brand-new set of relationships. Should be exciting. Real life starts now. Looking forward to it.

Several weeks later, he continued:

> About a month into real life and loving it. Though my obligations are greater than they were in college, I realize I only have responsibility to myself—that is, my only responsibility is to make enough money for rent and my lifestyle, and so the job and doing well at it is just a means to that end. Which is good, because if, over the long-term, I realize I'm unhappy with the job, I will hopefully have the balls to quit and find a different way to fulfill that responsibility to myself.
>
> That said, I do really expect to like my job. My job is the perfect application of my skills. Additionally, I

hope to gain some modeling experience in order to have a transferable skill set to other possible careers. After a while, I expect to be a complete expert on risk— managing it, structuring it. And that general skill is something worthwhile in every industry.

Enough about the actual job. That hasn't started yet. I'm actually liking the city more than I expected, and I think it's because I've found fun friends, the best of which don't try to have something to prove, whose company I enjoy, who can have good, candid conversation. Hopefully this continues. We'll see once training's over and the real work starts. 'Til then, loving it.

Those had been more sober thoughts. Now, as he sidled up to the bar at the Frying Pan for another beer, Samson had the same thought that had been running through his mind since the first day of his internship:

I just hope I survive.

CHAPTER SEVEN

SEVERAL MONTHS INTO my finance industry immersion, I began noticing signs of change in the young financiers I was getting to know.

Some of the changes were minor and cosmetic. A few started showing up in expensive suits and using finance jargon like "delta" and "top-tick" in casual conversation—the marks of Wall Street culture on their impressionable psyches. Others insisted on drinking during our interviews, no matter where or when we held them. And several began using the communal "we" to refer to their firms—"we closed a deal on Monday," "we're bullish on housing," and so on.

But others seemed to have undergone complete, 180-degree personality shifts in a matter of months. One of the most profound changes I saw was in a guy named Ricardo Hernandez.

I'd met Ricardo shortly after his graduation from Cornell, where he studied biology in the hopes of becoming a doctor.

Ricardo—a first-generation Mexican-American who grew up in San Antonio—was diligent and bright, but not overly self-serious or haughty. He was just as happy playing basketball in the park with off-duty cops as he was going to expensive clubs with velvet ropes and bottle service.

Ricardo had been pulled onto Wall Street during his junior year, when he came back from a summer internship at J.P. Morgan with stars in his eyes. He put his dreams of practicing medicine on hold and started working in the bank's mergers and acquisitions group after graduation.

The pay for first-years at J.P. Morgan, a $70,000 starting base salary with a bonus of about the same amount, had been a draw. But more than that, Ricardo liked the idea of spending two years after college *doing* something, not just learning about neural pathways and antigens. He saw himself spending two years doing M&A at J.P. Morgan, then changing careers entirely.

"This is not my be-all end-all, but I am looking forward to the intellectual stimulation," he said of his banking gig.

But five months into his first year, the culture of finance was clearly making an impression. He'd gained fifteen pounds, owing to a sedentary lifestyle and seven days a week of restaurant meals eaten at his desk. (On Wall Street, this is called the "Seamless Belly," after the website that is used to order restaurant meals on the company dime.) His eyes were tired, his skin was sallow and pale, and his calm, nonchalant manner had been overtaken by the machismo of the finance industry.

"Last year, some first-year bonuses were about twenty after tax," he complained to me one night, sipping a beer at a bar in the Meatpacking District. "That's an insulting number. A guy busts his balls all year, works his ass off, and gets a $20,000 bonus? You've got to be kidding me!"

It didn't help that Ricardo couldn't get away from Wall Street, even at home. He lived in Windsor Court, a massive apartment complex in Murray Hill that took up an entire city block and was known as the banker dorm, owing to the huge number of young Wall Street types who lived there. The building had a gym, laundry rooms on each floor, and a roof deck where, in summer, you could find analysts from every bank in Manhattan smoking hookahs and drinking Bud Lights.

Ricardo missed a lot of things about his prefinance life—going to dinners and movies with his girlfriend, reading books, getting out on the basketball court without checking his BlackBerry at every time-out. He cherished his autonomy, and he hated the way a managing director could ruin his weekend with a project.

But he liked the prestige associated with J.P. Morgan, and he liked being part of an analyst class that was made up of like-minded twentysomethings. Ricardo had become part of a group of first-year guys that went out for drinks after work, sent around blog links and funny videos on the firm's instant message system, and played pranks on each other. That summer, they had started "icing" each other—a game in which one analyst hides a bottle of Smirnoff Ice somewhere in the office that, when discovered, must be chugged immediately by the person who finds it, while kneeling on one knee.

Those new friends allowed Ricardo to feel at home at J.P. Morgan, even though the substance of the work was still not all that captivating.

"Here's the thing," he told me one night over drinks. "The

vast majority of people at the bank are great, hardworking, nice people. There are some psychopaths, but most people are just trying to keep their heads down and avoid messing up."

In some ways, Ricardo's Wall Street education reminded me of the kinds of transitions I'd seen while writing about evangelical Christianity. Wall Street, like a religion, had its own rules, regulations, and enforced cultural norms. And being new, you were expected to blend in as quickly as possible.

One difference between religious conversion and college-student-to-banker transformation is that religious conversion, in Christianity at least, happens in a single, swift step. Wall Street, on the other hand, converts new employees over the course of a two-year cultural baptism that encompasses every aspect of their lives.

The first part of blending in on Wall Street is learning a slightly different language. On Wall Street, analysts are quickly taught to say "equities" instead of "stocks," use "leverage" as both noun and verb, and speak in long strings of insider acronyms and abbreviations: DCF, CIM, LBO, VIX, and hundreds more.

Incoming analysts are expected to adopt the mannerisms and behavior of financiers, including the proper dress. For men, navy suits and white dress shirts with dark, plain ties are considered standard issue. For women, conservative is the watchword—no low-cut tops, skirts well above the knee, or dresses that show too much skin. For both genders, it is important to avoid two pitfalls: outdressing the boss (no Patek Philippe watches, Gucci loafers, Hermès bags, or other too-big-for-britches signifiers) and trying to appear overly fashionable with bright colors or offbeat patterns. One analyst at a major bank told me that a male classmate of his had shown up for the first day of training in a tan hound's-tooth coat with a black turtleneck underneath, and was humiliated by the snickers and shaming glares of his peers.

Wall Street also imbues its new analysts with a sense of where they are supposed to live, eat, and spend time outside of work. These rules are less hard and fast, but generally, neighborhoods like Murray Hill and Hell's Kitchen are considered the terrain of the first-year analyst, and bars like Joshua Tree (nicknamed "J-Tree" by a generation's worth of analysts) and the Patriot Saloon are considered first-year watering holes. A second-year analyst might live in the East Village or Chelsea, and hang out at slightly better bars like Brass Monkey and Penny Farthing. Not until he or she reached the associate level, and began making $200,000 or more a year, was a Wall Street worker expected to shack up in a chic neighborhood like the West Village or SoHo, and age out of dive bars altogether in favor of finer establishments.

At the same time the analyst is being educated in the ways of Wall Street, he or she is also being slowly separated from the outside world. Most large investment banks block Facebook, Twitter, Gmail, and other social media services in their offices, meaning that other than using a personal cell phone, an analyst has no easy way to keep in touch with nonfinance friends and family members. Meals, gym workouts, haircuts, dry cleaning—many of these things now take place inside the building, lessening the need for outside contact. Corporate perks become subtle narcotics, and the result is more time spent at work, and less desire to leave the finance bubble.

"I basically didn't have time to talk to people for two years," one young banker told me. "I felt antsy or guilty whenever I took any time off. And frankly, some of my friends were making the same exact amount of money I was in other industries. So a lot of nights, I sat there in the office trying to rationalize why I possibly decided to subject myself to this."

Eventually, the changes to a first-year analyst start taking place deep in his psyche. Strange nomenclature starts becoming normalized. The id-driven, testosterone-filled culture of the bank makes him a little sharper and more direct when he's talking to his parents, roommates, and friends. Money goes from being something that is infrequently discussed to being the primary subtext to everyday life. Social relationships start to feel transactional. And the world inside the capital markets starts to appear bigger and bigger, while the world outside it shrinks to a distraction.

One Goldman Sachs analyst told me about the change that had befallen him during his first year on the job. "You sort of lose your nonfinance friends," he said. "My friend might be in Teach for America, and they can't afford to go out to the places I go out. It's shitty, because for the first time, it's almost like money matters. In college, you're all living in that dorm. Here, there's hierarchy. And that level of spending, all the time, means that you just naturally grow away from people who don't work in the industry."

A recent academic study of young bankers by a University of Southern California business school professor named Alexandra Michel underscored the vital, even bodily, nature of the transformation that is taking place during a banker's first years. Michel wrote:

During years 1–3, bankers construed their bodies as objects that the mind controls. They worked long hours,
neglected family and hobbies, and fought their [bodies']
needs in order to enhance productivity. They suppressed
the need for prolonged sleep, taking "naps at 11 p.m.
and then again at 1, 3, and 4." When I asked, "Aren't
you worried that this will affect your health?" most responded like this Bank A associate: "For the next few
years, work has priority. I'll worry about my health then."
To my question, "What if you do irreversible damage?"
many answered, "I am willing to take that risk."

Over and over again, as I spoke to Wall Street veterans and
newcomers alike, I heard that the financial crisis had fundamentally reshaped the industry. Bonuses were smaller. Jobs
were less secure. The culture of Old Wall Street had disap-
peared. ("The bosses who do lines of coke off a stripper's ass
don't exist anymore," is how one banker put it to me.) And
banks themselves were still struggling to recover from the upheaval the crisis had caused.

But although banking had certainly changed in the post-
crash age, the process of *becoming* a banker seemed to have
changed very little. Cultural norms and institutional knowledge
were still transmitted from old to young, and the list of expec-
tations of a first-year analyst was largely a carbon copy of an
earlier era's list. The post-crash generation of analysts was expected to work hard, drink liberally, dress like Brooks Brothers
mannequins, and put the concerns of their firms above all else,
just like the pre-crash generation had.

Near the end of one of our interviews, Ricardo Hernandez

gave a time-honored response to a question I asked about his months on Wall Street so far, one that would have been just as at home in 1987 as in 2010.

He said, simply: "Banking is the best thing you never want to do again."

CHAPTER EIGHT

SOO-JIN PARK LOOKED around the Sheraton ballroom and saw pantsuits. Lots of pantsuits. Black and navy ones, mostly, but also the occasional red, which she figured must indicate the presence of a very senior executive. In finance, you didn't wear a red pantsuit unless you had amassed real power and were unafraid to convey it.

Even though she thought of herself as confident, it was hard for Soo-jin, a risk analyst at Deutsche Bank who stood five-two in heels, not to feel intimidated by her surroundings. She was at the Women on Wall Street Conference, an annual gathering put on by her firm to draw attention to the concerns of women in the financial sector. Two thousand women came to the Manhattan Sheraton from nearly every bank in New York to nibble on cake pops, drink Chardonnay, and listen to a panel of high-ranking women that included private equity executives, bank bosses, and entrepreneurs. And most of them, she thought, seemed to have their shit together.

A few minutes earlier, Soo-jin had finished hearing Deutsche Bank's male investment bank chief, Anshu Jain—who would later become the bank's co-CEO—give a fairly harsh condemnation of Wall Street's boys'-club legacy. "From a national origin standpoint we're effortlessly diverse," Jain said. "And yet our industry's track record when it comes to gender diversity is a long way from what we'd like it to be."

Sitting halfway back in the ballroom, Soo-jin nodded knowingly. She'd come to Wall Street from the all-female Wellesley College, where she majored in economics. She had hoped to land a front-office banking job at a major firm after graduation. But those were the dark days of the financial crisis, and investment banks were hiring only the bare minimum number of first-year analysts necessary to do business. Instead, she'd been steered by a career counselor to risk management, a division that was considered middle-office but, on the plus side, was hiring.

The starting compensation in risk management was still good—a $60,000 base salary, with a bonus of about $15,000 at year's end. And the hours were better than in the front office—9:00 a.m. to 6:00 p.m. on an average day. Soo-jin decided she was willing to give up some of the money and prestige of the front office for the sake of having a job at all.

Having come from Wellesley, Soo-jin was attuned to the challenges she might face as a woman in a male-dominated industry. And she'd arrived at Deutsche Bank feeling optimistic. She had pored over the firm's recruiting materials, which looked like brochures for liberal arts colleges, filled with happy-looking multiracial crowds and testaments to diversity and harmony. To her untrained eye, the bank looked like a place where being female would be, if not an asset, at least a nonliability.

But she had quickly discovered that her risk management group was still a man's world. The unit was run by an ex–military officer who ran it in the rigid, disciplined style of an Army platoon. Soo-jin was the only woman in the group who wasn't an administrative assistant. And for years, anyone getting promoted within the division was put through "risk college," an orientation program that included several boot-camp-type physical challenges. Military culture, in fact, seemed to set the tone for the entire bank—from the chief executive's office (he, too, was a veteran) right on down to the uniformed officer, out-fitted in military fatigues, who stood outside the bank's 60 Wall Street headquarters every day and greeted employees as they entered.

Soo-jin got friendly with some of the other women on her floor, who were sales analysts, administrative assistants, and brokers. They were nice enough, but they weren't exactly icons of female empowerment. A typical day's conversation in the pantry might cover the subjects of celebrity gossip, hair stylists in Manhattan, and fashion. One woman, an older assistant in an adjacent group, had once asked Soo-jin for a favor. "After you get your bonus, could we go purse shopping together?"

Soo-jin cringed at that, and at many of the other social niceties of the bank's female clique. She was used to Wellesley, where women sat around the dining hall discussing politics and international affairs, planning careers in the halls of power. And she suspected that being seen discussing shopping for purses with administrative assistants wasn't helping her career prospects.

The cause of female advancement on Wall Street was a perennially thorny issue that only got thornier during the years leading up to and including the crisis of 2008, when several of the most senior women in finance—executives who had served as role models for young women across the sector—lost their jobs. Zoe Cruz, the number two executive at Morgan Stanley, was fired in late 2007 by CEO John Mack. Erin Callan, the CFO of Lehman Brothers, was fired in 2008, shortly before the bank went bankrupt, and Sallie Krawcheck, a high-ranking Citigroup executive, was forced out of her bank two months later. Krawcheck, who was later hired (and ousted again) by Bank of America Merrill Lynch, later made a compelling argument that these weren't accidents—that women had fared worse than men during the depths of the crisis. "On a case-by-case-by-case basis, as promotions are decided, they choose the known entity, who tends to be someone who looks and sounds a good bit like those already in leadership roles," Krawcheck wrote of male executives, "and this seems to be particularly true when businesses are under stress."

According to Melissa S. Fisher, the author of *Wall Street Women*, the number of women working in finance fell by 2.6 percent between 2000 and 2010, while the number of men in finance grew by 9.6 percent in the same period. Fisher blames the loss of female bodies, in part, on the crisis. "Many believed that a woman from their generation was poised to break through the ultimate glass ceiling in finance and become a CEO," she wrote. "But instead of crashing triumphantly through the penultimate gendered boundary, these women, like the economy writ larger, were in freefall."

Of course, compared to women of a previous generation, today's Wall Street women have made significant progress. Thanks to diversity hiring efforts at major banks, mentorship programs, and the rise of gender parity in corporate America more generally, today's incoming analyst classes are more diverse than ever before, and many first-year cohorts are nearly evenly split between genders. No longer are job applicants to Wall Street firms asked, "When you meet a woman, what interests you most about her?" as applicants to Merrill Lynch's 1972 brokerage trainee class were. (The answer the bank was looking for was "her beauty.") And banks now give their incoming workers lengthy sexual harassment seminars and strictly prohibit behavior that is deemed hostile to women, like holding client meetings in strip clubs.

But women's progress in finance has been somewhat shallower than it appears. A 2006 analysis conducted by the *New York Times* found that 33 percent of first-year analysts were women, but only 25 percent of incoming full-time associates and 14 percent of managing directors. There are very few C-suite executives at Wall Street's largest firms, and no female CEOs at all. At Deutsche Bank, where Soo-jin worked, women represented 44 percent of all staff, but only 16 percent of senior managers.

Just weeks before the Women on Wall Street Conference, both Goldman Sachs and Citigroup were hit with class-action lawsuits from female former employees, alleging gender discrimination. The former Goldman Sachs employees alleged that men were "viewed more favorably, receive more compensation, and are more likely to be promoted" than women at the firm. Citigroup's former employees alleged that "the outdated 'boys' club' is alive and well at Citigroup," and said that women had been disproportionately targeted by layoffs during the financial crisis.

Soo-jin had hoped to use the Women on Wall Street Conference to sort through some of these issues, and hear from women who had successfully navigated them on the way to successful careers. But she found, to her chagrin, that real gender inequality was only given a light gloss, and most of the women on the panels seemed to cherish bragging about how *little* discrimination they'd faced. (Presumably because they wanted people to think that they were so competent at their jobs that they had overcome gender altogether.) During the panel, one female Deutsche Bank executive said, in response to a question about being treated as a social equal as a woman, that she "never felt that there was a boys' club that I couldn't join. If people went out for a drink, I always went, too."

The executive's nonchalance was troubling to Soo-jin, since even if it had been true in her specific case, it ignored some of the very real barriers that faced women in finance. Yes, she had often gone to drinks with her male colleagues. No, they had never said anything misogynistic to her face, or tried to sleep with her, or any of the other more common situations women on Wall Street had faced through the years. But there were a hundred subtle, insidious ways in which her experience as a woman in finance had been less than ideal. She felt trapped—in the middle office, in a division where there were few female role models for her, in a bank that seemed to give lip service to the idea of gender diversity but had few mechanisms in place to ensure that female analysts were actually being treated equally. And for the rest of the conference, she sulked, knowing the event had been mostly a waste of her time.

Several months later, Soo-jin saw something even more troubling. During a press conference, in the midst of a European

debate about whether Germany's government should set gender quotas for German corporate boards, Deutsche Bank's
then-CEO, Josef Ackermann, said that he hoped to add women
to the bank's executive committee in order to make it "more
colorful and prettier." The apparent joke landed with a thud
in the European press, and caused a backlash among Germany's political leaders, who accused Ackermann of tone-deaf
sexism. (One leader, consumer protection minister Ilse Aigner,
responded, "Whoever wants it to be more colorful or prettier
should go to a flower meadow or a museum.")

After reading about Ackermann's comments and the outrage
that followed, Soo-jin decided to take action. She wrote a
lengthy e-mail to the female Deutsche Bank executive who,
months earlier, had made the comment at the Women on Wall
Street Conference about never feeling left out by virtue of her
gender. As politely as she could, Soo-jin thanked the woman for
her presentation, but suggested that "unfortunately, I think what
you said threatens to undermine the steps you are taking to correct the gender issues that exist at Deutsche Bank." To Soo-jin's
surprise, the executive replied, and pasted in a statement that
seemed to have been written by a lawyer or a PR expert. (The
statement touted Ackermann's "concrete endorsement together
with that of his colleagues on the Group Executive Committee
of greater gender diversity in the bank's management positions,"
which showed that "he and the bank support a performance-
driven promotion of women [and men].")

Soo-jin read the statement with a sigh. Officially, the bank
was still essentially claiming that all women at Deutsche Bank
needed to do in order to advance was work as hard and perform
as well as men—that there were no barriers in place that kept

them from moving up the ladder, except the limits of their own talent and ambition.

She hoped that was the case. And, deep down, she didn't know if Deutsche Bank was truly an openly hostile place for women or was simply mired in the past. But she found the executive's response flimsy and trite. It completely ignored the structural challenges that have existed for females on Wall Street for decades. And that night, Soo-jin found herself getting paranoid and fearful about her professional future. After all, if a top female executive wasn't willing to stand up for young women like her, maybe nobody was.

CHAPTER NINE

IT WAS A slow afternoon in the Goldman Sachs commodities division, and Jeremy Miller-Reed was finishing up a conversation with one of the vice presidents in his group. He spun around to go back to his desk, and ran with a thud into a passing colleague.

"Ah!" he said. "Sorry, man."

Jeremy looked down, and was horrified to see that the man dusting himself off was none other than Lloyd Blankfein, the firm's CEO, who had been making the rounds on Goldman's trading floor. Jeremy was mortified. He'd always wondered when he would run into Blankfein, who by virtue of his position was generally considered the most powerful man on Wall Street. But he hadn't meant it literally.

Luckily, Blankfein had a sense of humor about the collision.

"Security, get this kid out of here!" he said, a broad smile on his face.

It was a rare misstep for Jeremy, who was quickly distinguishing himself as one of the most promising first-year analysts at Goldman.

Jeremy was in the energy group within commodities, meaning that most of his job consisted of acting as the middleman between buyers and sellers of oil and gas derivatives. The bank's clients—typically large airlines, shipping companies, and refineries—used these derivatives to protect themselves against fluctuations in the price of fuel caused by a production shortage, a major geopolitical event, or a natural disaster. Goldman's traders would run the numbers and decide the right price to offer, and salespeople—who worked right beside them—would execute the actual transaction and take a commission on the deal.

At first, Jeremy's work had consisted of booking trades made by more senior members of his team. But he soon advanced to making deals of his own.

Energy sales and trading, like most jobs in finance, involved a huge amount of jargon and shorthand, and Jeremy had quickly learned to decipher most of it. He'd learned the difference between NG (natural gas) and HO (heating oil), and between Nymex (the New York Mercantile Exchange) and the IPE (the International Petroleum Exchange). He'd learned about options, enhanced-value swaps, swaptions, costless collars, and something called a three-way, which sounded kinky but was in fact a complex kind of derivative trade.

Several times a day, clients would call the desk asking for some exquisite beast of a trade, and Jeremy would get to put his newfound knowledge to use.

"Can I get an offer on the 70-by-110 collars in Cal 15 for 50 lots per month?" a CFO of a large airline might say. (Translation: "How much will it cost me to buy a collar trade—a trade that allows a buyer to effectively take out insurance against rising oil prices without paying a large up-front premium by simultaneously buying call options and selling put options on the same security—that has a put option struck at $70 a barrel and a call option struck at $110 a barrel, that settles based on where oil prices end up in the calendar year 2015, and that covers 50,000 barrels of oil per month?")

Jeremy would put the client on hold, and use Goldman's proprietary options pricing software to figure out the correct price of the trade. Then, once he had the price, he would take it back to the phone.

"I can do that structure at $4," he'd tell the client, meaning that the trade would cost $4 per barrel in option premium, or $2.4 million in total.

"Okay, let's do that," the client would say.

Before closing the trade, Jeremy would stand up from his chair and yell to Magnus, the senior trader who sat several rows away, to make sure that the $4 price was still valid.

"Hey Magnus!" he said. "Are you still there on that 70-by-110 collar in Cal 15?"

"Yep!" Magnus would yell back.

"Okay, we're done on that," Jeremy would tell the client before hanging up and entering the trade in his log.

Making a trade took five minutes, at most. But it would leave Jeremy with an adrenaline rush for hours. He loved the quick thinking and sharp analysis it required, and getting to stand up and yell on a trading floor made him feel like he was acting in a Wall Street movie set in an earlier, more exciting era.

Jeremy was still a long way away from being a rainmaker. The trades he executed might generate fees of $100,000 for Goldman on a good day—a far cry from the haul some senior traders pulled in. But he still felt proud. He had no formal financial education—hell, he'd never heard of most of this stuff until the previous summer—and yet, in a matter of months, he'd been able to assimilate himself into the Goldman Sachs machine and act as an official representative of Wall Street's premier investment bank.

Compared to the bankers upstairs, the salespeople and traders on floors 3, 4, and 5 of 200 West Street lived lives of leisure. Unlike bankers, who work around the clock, traders and salespeople generally work from 6:30 or 7:00 a.m. to 5:00 or 5:30 p.m. They generally aren't tethered to their phones outside of market hours, and many don't even think about coming in on the weekends. (The exceptions are traders who deal in foreign markets and who often work hours that correspond with the time zones they trade in.)

Traders also define success differently. Banking is a client-service business, and being able to schmooze for new business is part of the job. But trading is a meritocratic exercise in execution. As a trader, it doesn't matter whether you're charming, whether you dress well, or whether you went to Harvard or community college. All that matters is what your P&L, your running "profits and losses" tally, looks like at the end of the day. (Salespeople, too, focus on P&Ls, but they have to be slightly more polished, since they interact with clients.)

That emphasis on results over charm made Jeremy's job highly volatile and gave him a smaller margin of error than a banker might have. He'd found out how small the margin was when, during his first-ever solo trade—an options contract for jet fuel that he sold to a major airline—he'd made the mistake of rounding the number in the fourth decimal place down, instead of up. The error only cost him a thousandth of a penny per gallon, but given the huge volume of the trade, those thousandths added up—to more than $8,000 in total profits given away. By getting one number wrong, he'd cost the bank the equivalent of a Rolex. Sheepishly, he told his boss, the Senator, what had happened.

"Well, that was pretty fucking stupid!" the Senator replied with a laugh.

Despite his early mistakes, Jeremy had grown to appreciate his desk. The Senator was a tough boss, but he was fair and always made sure to offer help when it was needed. Jeremy liked most of the people in his immediate group, and he respected the way they did business. He had halfway expected to discover fraud and wrongdoing after the Abacus scandal and the bad press of the last few years, but he found, to his pleasant surprise, that the bank treated its clients fairly and decently most of the time.

Which is not to say that Jeremy's experience had been boring. Every day, things happened on the fifth floor of 200 West Street that seemed to have originated inside a Wall Street cartoon. There were the European analysts who had come over to New York for training and had bragged about going out to exclusive Manhattan clubs thirty-six nights in a row. There was the head oil trader, a former Ivy League wrestler named Fred, who once bet his colleague $200 that he could hold a plank position for five minutes straight. (Fred won the bet and used the winnings to buy pizza for everyone on the floor.) There was the endless lighthearted mockery of analysts by older traders and salesmen, which simultaneously flattered the analysts and made them fear for their lives.

And there was the endless, relentless pursuit of money. In Jeremy's little corner of the trading world, all that mattered was a person's P&L and a related number, called "gross credits" (or just "GCs"), which measured revenue generated by a single employee. Workers used both their P&L and their GC count to estimate their likely bonuses the following year.

Jeremy had gotten a sense of how little else mattered early in his first year, while sharing a drunken cab ride back from a group outing with several of his colleagues. During the ride, one colleague — a third-year associate — put him on the hot seat.

"So, Jeremy, why did you come to Goldman?"

Jeremy, who had downed a few drinks too many, slurred out the closest thing he could to an explanation. He told the associate that there was a lot of economic value in the work the desk did — that helping companies hedge their energy costs was a legitimate function of the capital markets, and that Goldman was the best place on the Street to do it. The associate took a moment to contemplate, then said, "You know, helping the world is great and all, but you need to be motivated by money."

He'd said it so bluntly that Jeremy attributed it to the booze, but the next day, as he came down from his hangover, he couldn't help but think that the associate might have been telling the truth.

Jeremy was no milquetoast. He knew banks like Goldman existed to make money for their shareholders, and that any societal benefits of the work they performed were mostly a coincidence. But he'd always been able to justify the moral dimensions of his specific role within the bank's profit machine. Trading oil derivatives *did* seem like a useful function, and a well-timed trade could in fact create massive cost savings for a client—savings that, he imagined, could eventually be passed on to customers. Jeremy wanted to believe that a bank didn't have to exist solely for its own preservation and enrichment— that all that stuff he'd heard in recruiting about being a "trusted advisor" to clients wasn't just marketing fluff.

But now, he was starting to wonder whether he'd been fooled.

*   *   *

While Jeremy was being schooled on the commodities desk, Samson was plowing ahead in mortgages.

Samson's group was a subset of the mortgage division that helped Goldman's clients unload complex piles of mortgage assets they no longer wanted, and lined up buyers to take those assets off the clients' hands. Samson typically got to work around 7:00 or 7:30, just in time for his group's daily all-hands meeting. At the morning meeting, the heads of the group would discuss market events, outline a strategy for the current day's trading, and announce the "axes" for the day. "Axes," in Goldman-speak, were the trades that executives wanted to give the highest priority. Executing an axe might be getting rid of sovereign bonds that were expected to decline in value, or buying oil futures that were expected to spike later in the day. As a trader, it was in your interest to take care of as many axes as possible. Traders who came through on big axes would often get congratulated in the morning meetings, and often found their year-end bonuses increased as a result.

Three months after Samson joined the desk, he saw the biggest axe of the quarter unfold. One day, an associate in his group confided in him that Goldman had just closed a deal with another investment firm, whereby the firm had agreed to buy billions of dollars' worth of mortgage-backed securities off the other firm's books. This huge pile of mortgage-backed securities were much like the ones that had gotten banks in trouble during the crisis, but now that prices had stabilized, Goldman's traders knew they would be able to resell them to clients at a markup. Over time, those bonds would likely produce more than $200 million in pure, unadulterated profit for Goldman. The deal was an "elephant," in Goldman-ese—one so big that it could change the fortunes of the entire group.

Most days weren't that exciting, of course. On a normal day, Samson might spend the early morning meeting with his VP about an insurance deal the bank was pitching. He might spend the late morning listening in on a conference call with a regulatory agency, outlining a rule change that affected clients' capital needs. And he might spend the afternoon and evening putting together a presentation for a client, in which the client's assets were sliced and diced into a panoply of charts, graphs, and tables, all of which combined to explain to a client why they should do business with Goldman Sachs—the only firm that could help them sort it all out.

There was a lot to sort out in the mortgage market in the fall of 2010. The housing market was still clawing its way back from the depths of the crisis, and foreclosures were still happening all over America. Thanks to the Troubled Asset Relief

Program, the so-called backdoor bailout of AIG, and its own risk-management measures, Goldman had emerged from the crisis healthier than many of its competitors, and now it was making money by helping those same competitors get risky assets off their books.

It was a hell of a business model, and Samson liked taking part in what seemed, some days, like solving a giant puzzle — one that involved trillions of dollars in capital and touched on every region and sector of the financial economy. But the banking-type hours and the responsibility, combined with his hard-driving bosses and coworkers, were grinding him down. One night, after a tough day at work, he took his journal out and wrote:

> Work fucking sucks. I can't tell if my job sucks anymore than anyone else's job. I don't think it's just the hours. It's the hours + the people + the work. If I were learning something and around people I liked, I'd be much happier, and the hours wouldn't fucking matter. I'm trying to determine whether or not I learned anything this week. Anything?

That summer and fall, Goldman Sachs continued to struggle with both its public image and its profitability. In July, it settled the Abacus fraud lawsuit by agreeing to pay a $550 million fine to the SEC, without admitting or denying guilt. In September, it began to disband Goldman Sachs Principal Strategies, its profitable prop-trading hub, due to the Volcker Rule and other new regulations. A month later, the firm announced mediocre quarterly earnings that were down 40 percent from the year before, and said it had cut its employee pay pool for the year by 26 percent. And, in a blow that may have hurt more than the others, *Vanity Fair* demoted Lloyd Blankfein—who had been number 1 on its "New Establishment" power ranking in 2009—to number 100 on its 2010 list, from first place to last place in the span of a year. The magazine called Goldman "the Wall Street powerhouse the population at large continues to hate."

Goldman tried to pare some of its image woes by taking out full-page ads in the *New York Times* and the *Wall Street Journal*, touting its green energy investments and featuring images of hard-hat workers and windmills. But it didn't help. The public had identified Goldman as the primary driver behind Wall Street's crisis-era malfeasance, and it wasn't letting go.

Samson and Jeremy both had opinions on all of these issues—from Goldman's compensation to its culpability during the financial crisis. But during their after-work hangouts on Jeremy's roof, they rarely talked about morality, or ethics, or the firm's image on Main Street. Most days, their conversations hewed closely to the daily struggles of their jobs: their bosses, the trades of the moment, their frustrations with the finance lifestyle.

It wasn't that there were no moral questions involved in the work they did every day. Unlike banking analysts, who might be six or seven levels of responsibility away from a finished deal, sales and trading analysts were directly responsible for buying and selling products to clients. Mortgage products and energy derivatives, Samson and Jeremy's respective bailiwicks, were two of the most complex kinds of securities sold on Wall Street, and Goldman's informational advantages in both areas could be huge. Every time a Goldman salesman got rid of an axe, he was unloading it on a client who may or may not have fully understood the risks it held or how it should be priced. That kind of behavior was at the heart of the SEC's lawsuit, and the suspicion that it happened all over Wall Street was part of what had taken the general public's distrust of the financial sector to an all-time high.

Part of what was happening was simple mental compartmentalization. Jeremy and Samson knew that some of what they were doing might have been ethically suspect, and they didn't like many of their coworkers, but much of the time, they found the actual substance of their work intellectually stimulating, and they generally considered Goldman a good place. Moreover, the clients they spoke with every day—large, sophisticated investors—were used to dealing with Goldman and weren't surprised by the bank's cutthroat business model. And so, while they could contemplate their direct, everyday tasks on one hand and the ethics of working at Goldman Sachs on another, the two strains of thought rarely crossed in their minds.

The compartmentalization phenomenon turned out to be bigger than Jeremy and Samson, and bigger even than Goldman Sachs. As I interviewed dozens of young analysts at firms across the financial sector, I heard the same kinds of answers to my questions about morality and ethics:

"I don't know, I never really think about it."

"I'm just trying not to fuck up."

"Dude, I'm so far away from anything like that…"

Entry-level analysts, it seemed, were so routinely exhausted, and so minutely focused on their day-to-day tasks—on pleasing their bosses, nailing every page of their pitch books, and avoiding getting in trouble—that they often avoided thinking about the big picture. It was a sort of cognitive triage, and daily concerns always took priority over long-term, large-scale worries. Still, there was no doubt that these worries existed. (In fact, I often found it much easier to get young analysts to open up about their doubts than senior executives, who had often been in the industry long enough to have built a self-reinforcing moral framework that allowed them to feel no compunction whatsoever about working in finance.)

"There's kind of an inherent conflict between ethical business practice and fiduciary duty," Jeremy once told me, in a moment of moral clarity. "As a person working for a public company, your duty is making money for your shareholders, but what if that means doing wrong?"

So, yes, many of the Wall Street analysts I'd met were thoughtful, robust ethical thinkers in their private lives. But professionally, they were foot soldiers. And at times, asking them to switch modes and reflect on their qualms with Wall Street as a whole was like trying to get a congressional page to pontificate about the constitutionality of gerrymandering. All the page was worried about was getting his boss's lunch order right.

As Wall Street's young analysts got older, and their jobs slowed down, I hoped to get them to reflect about the larger issues framing their work. I wanted to know if they ever stayed up at night worrying about having screwed a client on a deal, whether they thought their pitch books represented honest and forthright analyses, and whether they were ever tempted to turn down an unscrupulous assignment and risk hurting their careers.

For now, though, I had to accept that they were just trying to keep from drowning.

CHAPTER TEN

THE BAND HIT a crescendo into the chorus, and the congregation swayed and sang along.

> *I know Jesus is on that main line*
> *Tell Him what you want*
> *Jesus is on that main line*
> *Tell Him what you want*
> *You can call Him up and tell Him what you want!*

All around the church sanctuary, the sounds of praise reverberated off the walls. Most people were shouting and speaking in tongues, while intermittently singing and clapping along with the music. There were several hundred people in attendance, and all of them—men, women, children, little old ladies—were on their feet, making such a ruckus that the people on the street outside paused next to the door and peered in to see what the fuss was about.

And, way up in the front row, there was J. P. Murray, who was hung over as hell.

J. P.—short for Jean-Paul—was a first-year IBD analyst at Credit Suisse, the Swiss firm whose headquarters was a majestic-looking building at 11 Madison Avenue. During the days, he worked long hours on Excel models and pitch books. He spent most of his Friday and Saturday nights getting drunk in clubs and flirting with women, and on Sundays J. P. liked to repent for his sins at church. His congregation was located in a poor, predominantly black Brooklyn neighborhood all the way at the end of the L subway line, where most people didn't know or care what Credit Suisse was, or what an investment banker did. J. P. found the church's lack of pretense refreshing, and a service often got him out of his own head after a long week at work. Here, in this sanctuary, he didn't have to be Jean-Paul Murray, aspiring Master of the Universe, with a docket full of responsibilities and a career on the move. He could just be J. P., the big black kid with the goofy smile.

J. P., who stands six foot seven in his socks, is the son of a Haitian mother who had emigrated to the United States when she was pregnant with him. Her work as an administrative assistant, and some modest side income from his stepfather, gave them a steady lower-middle-class lifestyle in Philadelphia, where they lived. J. P. had worked hard in high school to get himself into Temple University, where he commuted to class from home and paid for his tuition out of pocket, with money he earned from his part-time job as a bank teller.

J. P.'s mother, a devout Christian who had missed church only a handful of times in her life, wanted him to become a preacher. But J. P. wanted more. He'd always dreamed of working on Wall Street, where a person with drive and ambition could become truly wealthy—the kind of wealth that would buy not only nice things for himself but also provide a plentiful future for his children and grandchildren. During his junior year, J. P. applied for and got an internship at Credit Suisse. That had been before the crisis, and J. P. felt lucky that in 2009, after the crash had taken a hammer to Credit Suisse's profits and a machete to its head count, he'd been able to talk the bank into hiring him back full-time.

He'd gotten placed in health-care investment banking, a group that met the financial needs of pharmaceutical companies, hospitals, and medical equipment makers. He wasn't in love with the work, but he consoled himself with the fact that he had beaten the odds and made it to Credit Suisse, which recruited from all of the Ivy League schools, and had only a few spots reserved for nontarget graduates like him.

"I've come this far, and I'm not going to fuck it up," he told me.

On his first day, J. P. arrived at Credit Suisse for an orientation program in the firm's auditorium. He looked around the room and did what he often did upon entering unfamiliar territory—counted black people. Out of roughly two hundred incoming first-years, he found exactly eight.

I am the biggest, blackest dude in this room, he thought.

Ever since he was only one of a handful of minorities in some of his Temple business classes, J. P. had done his fair share of thinking about how being black would affect his career as an investment banker.

To hear some people on Wall Street tell it, race and ethnicity didn't matter in finance. As long as you were making money for your firm, the sector's long-held mythology went, it didn't matter whether you were white, black, or purple. That, of course, is too easy a gloss, and obscures the obvious fact that today's financial sector, like the financial sector of old, is still dominated by white men. There are no black or Hispanic CEOs of any major Wall Street firms, and the executive committees of many financial institutions are still porcelain-white.

To their credit, all Wall Street banks acknowledge the problem. Many firms recruit at historically black colleges and universities, and most have affiliations with groups like Sponsors for Educational Opportunity that groom minority students for high-powered corporate jobs. J.P. Morgan has an entire internship program, called "Launching Leaders," dedicated to finding spots for promising students of color within the bank. There are conferences, workshops, and affinity groups for ethnic minorities at every major firm.

Those programs have helped diversify the entry-level ranks of Wall Street as a whole. A study by CUNY professors Richard Alba and Joseph Pereira found that the percentage of white men among "core" Wall Street workers under age thirty (defined as workers in securities-industry companies who were not janitorial, cafeteria, or other nonbusiness staff) fell from 48.8 percent to 45.8 percent between 2000 and 2009. The percentage of white women thirty and under also fell during the same time period, from 22.7 percent to 18.9 percent.

But gains at the junior ranks don't necessarily mean that Wall Street is an equal-opportunity industry. A 2010 report by the U.S. Government Accountability Office found that financial services firms still suffered from a major lack of diversity among top managers and executives. As late as 2008, the GAO reported, white males held 64 percent of all senior jobs on Wall Street. Moreover, the diversity hiring efforts at Wall Street firms tend to be narrower than they appear. Most of the progress has been concentrated in a few ethnic minorities—namely, South Asians and East Asians—and students from privileged backgrounds still dominate.

"My bank is a very diverse place, but not in a typical way," one Morgan Stanley analyst told me. "There's ethnic diversity, but it's not very socioeconomically diverse. You've got a lot of kids who grew up in some Asian country and went to a prestigious prep school, then an Ivy League university."

By that metric, J. P. Murray was a double minority at Credit Suisse. He was one of only a handful of new black analysts, and he was one of the only people at the firm who hadn't had at least a middle-class upbringing.

Since joining the bank, J. P. had become close with the other black analysts in his first-year class, and while all of them seemed to be hitting their strides, he had noticed a certain caution in the way they seemed to approach their jobs. Being a black investment banker, J. P. had learned, required certain code-switching abilities. It required being able to talk about the things his white managers cared about, and have a good sense of humor when it came to the more subtle off-color comments and remarks thrown his way. In many ways, it required being able to tone down his blackness for the purpose of negotiating a power structure that still considered him an outsider.

J. P. had learned a lot from watching Denise, another black first-year analyst at Credit Suisse who seemed extremely savvy about how to maintain her identity while climbing the Wall Street ladder. Once, when J. P. and several other Credit Suisse analysts had clustered around her desk to chat during the middle of the day, Denise waved them away.

"Okay, one of you needs to leave," she said. "Too many black people."

Beneath that joke was some truth. Banks *were* largely white enterprises, and too many nonwhite workers cloistering together, even for benign social purposes, *could* seem threatening to white coworkers. J. P. would never have thought about these kinds of subtle, racially tinged social maneuvers before starting his job at Credit Suisse. But now that he had been alerted to their existence, he saw them everywhere.

Foremost in J. P.'s mind, though, was succeeding at his job. He wanted, more than anything, to prove that he could make it on Wall Street, despite the long odds.

"People, in a very cynical way, like to say you're living the dream when you're on Wall Street, but I believe it," he told me. "Look, I'm twenty-two years old, and I'm making more money than both of my parents combined. My earning potential, in a few years, is double, triple, quadruple what they'll make in their lifetime. There is a power structure, and I believe in my ability to impact it and become part of it."

That belief had given him a single-minded focus on doing whatever it took to rise through the ranks. Whenever he found himself wallowing in self-pity after a long night of work, J. P. would don his headphones at his desk and listen to a song called "Live Fast, Die Young" by the rappers Rick Ross and Kanye West, which usually helped put things back in perspective.

They say we can't be livin' like this for the rest of our lives
But we gon' be livin' like this for the rest of tonight

J. P. was living fast, and even though he was probably shaving off years of his life with his frantic days and sleepless nights, he felt sure it would all be worth it in the end, when he had the money and seniority to pull his family into the upper class, with enough left over to finance his lifestyle.

His life wasn't perfect, but standing in church, surrounded by people who were giving thanks to God for much lesser miracles, it was hard for J. P. to feel anything other than truly, inexplicably blessed.

CHAPTER ELEVEN

CHELSEA BALL, the flip-cupping Bank of America Merrill Lynch analyst, slumped down on her bed, pulled the off-white comforter up over her bare feet, and groaned at my question about how things were going.

"Dude, let's talk about your life," she said. "Because mine is shit right now."

It was a Sunday afternoon, halfway through Chelsea's first year in the public finance division, and already her world seemed to be coming apart. Roughly half of her pain was related to her relationship with Anton, the Georgetown sophomore she had been dating. Chelsea's monthly Megabus trips to see Anton had started out as welcome distractions from the bustle of New York, but they had quickly become her biggest burdens. Work proved impossible to escape on the weekends, and logging in remotely from Anton's dorm room, on a tiny laptop with none of her usual tools at her disposal, was an exercise in frustration. And every time she visited him on campus, she found herself feeling contemptuous of her surroundings. *I'm twenty-three years old*, she often thought. *I make six figures, and I have my own apartment. Why am I still eating in a dining hall?*

She and Anton had been fighting almost daily, and Chelsea often thought about breaking up with him. That would certainly make things easier. But she also knew that she didn't have time to pursue a new love interest these days, and wasn't being in a mediocre, occasionally frustrating long-distance relationship better than being alone?

The other half of Chelsea's frustration came from work, where her situation was quickly becoming untenable. Since her group's country-club field day, she had learned a lot about public finance. Most of the group's work consisted of deals involving municipal bonds, or "munis." A muni bond, she learned, is any bond issued by a state or local government, or any 501(c)3 tax-exempt organization, a group that includes school districts, some museums, universities, seaports, and other public spaces. Those organizations issue bonds in order to raise money to build new buildings, repair old ones, and undertake any other kinds of expensive capital projects. In return for providing that money, muni bond investors get tax-free interest and rates anywhere from 2 to 8 percent, depending on the specific bond.

Chelsea actually liked the big-picture substance of her work. She had been staffed on several deals in a row that involved arranging muni bond issuances for nonprofit organizations, and she knew her bank's work would enable these groups to pay to build new facilities, refurbish old ones, and take on other expensive growth projects. That seemed noble enough, and

Chelsea had enjoyed the out-of-town trips she'd gotten to take as a result of her assignments. She had even figured out some of the technical challenges that had tripped her up at first. Recently, she had mastered DBC, a software program that was used to structure municipal bond issuances. You plugged in variables like the duration of the bonds, how much you needed to raise, and what the interest rates were, and DBC would do the rest. By playing around with the software's features in her spare time, Chelsea had gotten to the point where other analysts in her group were asking her for help with it.

Still, despite the progress she was making, Chelsea didn't know whether she'd ever been so unhappy. The reason was simple: her boss, Ralph.

A fortysomething man with frizzy hair and a look of perpetual confusion, Ralph was one of the most perplexing people Chelsea had ever come across. He was so odd, so neurotic and finicky, and with such a tenuous grip on reality, that Chelsea and some of the other analysts in the group had started calling him "the Mad Hatter."

Ralph was Chelsea's primary boss, and he was almost pathologically paranoid about keeping his resources, including her, to himself. Anytime Chelsea went to visit another part of the trading floor, he'd ask why she'd gone, and if another group was trying to steal her away. If another group within the bank was working on a deal that involved his sector, he would accuse them of encroaching on his turf. When it came to managing his analysts and associates, Ralph was prone to unpredictable tantrums, and his face often turned purple when he was worried or upset.

"*Oh my gawwwwwwd,*" he'd say in a nasally whine, four

or five hours before a big project was due. *"Why isn't this dooooooone?"*

Several weeks earlier, Chelsea had gotten her biggest assignment to date. Another boss of hers, a senior banker named Chad Hamilton, had come up with the idea of compiling a weekly newsletter to keep the group's clients apprised of the goings-on in the muni bond market over the previous week. If the spreads between Treasury bond rates and the Thomson Reuters Municipal Market Data index rate (or MMD, a synthetic rate that combined data from lots of different muni bonds) widened by half a percent, the bank's clients would find out from the newsletter. If a group of new bonds from a college in Virginia or a city in Kansas were expected to price in the upcoming week, that information would get to other organizations considering issuing bonds of their own. All told, Chelsea's newsletter would have to contain between two hundred and three hundred pieces of information—every one of which would have to be pulled from her Bloomberg terminal, typed, checked, and put in a clear, organized PDF every Monday morning.

Chelsea threw all her energy into making sure the newsletter was perfect. She formatted data carefully in Excel, ported it over into Word correctly, checked and rechecked her introductory paragraphs for spelling and grammatical errors, and sent it up the chain for a final once-over before it was sent out to clients.

For three weeks, Chelsea heard nothing but praise. Clients, colleagues, and even Ralph had loved the newsletter, and told her so. But in week four, she got called into a meeting with Doug Majors, the head of the entire public finance division.

"I see," Doug said, "that one of our internal metrics has been going out in the weekly newsletter."

Chelsea knew the metric Doug was talking about—it was a component of municipal bond performance that Bank of America Merrill Lynch compiled using client data. Chelsea had thought nothing of including it in the newsletter. But now, Doug was livid. The metric, he said, was used by the bank's own bond traders, and not at all suitable for dissemination to anyone outside the firm's walls.

"That is confidential information!" he told her. "We absolutely cannot put our internal metrics on any client communication. It's a liability to even have this out there!"

"I didn't know," she said. "I thought I was supposed to include it."

"Well, you weren't," Doug snapped.

After being chewed out by Doug, Chelsea reeled, and waited for either of her bosses—Ralph or Chad—to come to her defense. Senior bankers, after all, were the ones who were ultimately responsible for checking the newsletter over before it went out to clients, and they'd never flagged the metric as an issue. But nobody said anything. And eventually, she realized she would have to take the blame herself.

Chelsea was embarrassed and furious. Embarrassed to have made such a rookie mistake, and furious at the higher-ups who had refused to defend her.

"What did these guys think I fucking did?" she later told me, her voice rising with exasperation. "I have no power at all! I'm just doing what everyone else is telling me to do!"

Chelsea's complaints reminded me of a motif I'd heard over the past year. As part of my investigation, I'd been speaking to many of the recruiters and HR executives who are responsible for bringing young people into large banks and keeping them happy once they arrive. And many of these managers expressed genuine puzzlement at the way today's young bankers and traders dealt with being corrected on the job. Young people, they said, were prone to overreacting when their managers called them out on mistakes, and would often get highly emotional when confronted with anything other than unadulterated praise.

"They want feedback, but they don't want just any feedback," one HR executive told me about the new breed of bankers. "They want it to be positive."

Chelsea wasn't getting much positive feedback, at work or elsewhere, and combined with her failing relationship, the knock to her confidence paralyzed her. In the next few days, she checked out completely. She took long lunch breaks, went on long walks around Midtown during work hours, and started using her spare time to open her notebook and sketch logos for imaginary businesses she wanted to start. Chelsea had always been an entrepreneurial spirit—she'd written a half-dozen business plans in college, and was always talking about some side project she was working on—and she couldn't believe she'd locked herself into a job that placed her at the mercy of such inflexible and unforgiving bosses, doing work in which her creativity was severely undervalued.

After hearing Chelsea detail her woes, I began thinking about the kinds of young people I'd seen flourish in finance—the ones who seemed genuinely happy with their careers. It occurred to me that those people tended to fall into three general categories—call them Habituals, Locomotives, and Gunners.

Habituals, generally speaking, are the people who might in the context of college admissions be referred to as "legacies." These are the people who choose to go into finance either because their parents or siblings work in finance, or because they've grown up with financiers in their immediate social circle. Strictly speaking, most Habituals make it to Wall Street on their own, but their upbringings (in wealthy or upper-middle-class communities) and their educational opportunities (at private high schools and top-tier colleges) have made finance a destination that, if not inevitable, is at least a known and respected option for people in their circumstances. For these people, the lifestyle associated with finance is important. They like having beach houses, exotic cars, and the other trappings of the upper-income brackets, and they like spending their time around other moneyed elites. Banking is often a stepping-stone to more lucrative jobs at private equity firms or hedge funds, and the ultimate destination is often the Forbes 400 list.

"I'm not self-loathing at all," one young private equity worker with Habitual tendencies told me. "I could be working in the Peace Corps, and I chose not to, because for natural, selfish reasons I'm maximizing my own utility like any other person does."

Locomotives, on the other hand, come to Wall Street with an underdog's ambition. They tend to come from working-class or middle-class homes, receive financial aid or scholarships during college, and often pull their families behind them as they chug toward success. ("My family calls me 'the meal ticket,'" one Locomotive banker told me.) Many of these young financiers are ethnic minorities or first-generation Americans, and few of them have parents or relatives who have worked in the financial sector before. To these people, making money is *emphatically*

the reason to work on Wall Street. Locomotives can sense that
in a time when economic mobility is shrinking, Wall Street is
one of the last industries that can reliably catapult middle-class
kids into the realm of the wealthy and powerful. And they are
more likely to stay put once they've gotten onto a stable, high-
paying career path.

Gunners, the third group, thrive on the pace and excitement
of the finance world. A Gunner may be a former college athlete
who treats his trading career as a dog-eat-dog competition, or
she may be a female executive for whom succeeding in a male-
dominated industry is a test of endurance and pluck. For these
people, money is only a scoreboard. The real thrill is the perfectly timed trade, the M&A brawl, or the big promotion. These
people can get discouraged when markets are slow or trades
aren't going their way, but they're so addicted to the dopamine
and adrenaline rushes associated with finance that they can't
ever imagine quitting to join a slower, less challenging industry.

Chelsea wasn't a Habitual, a Locomotive, or a Gunner. She
belonged to a fourth group of in-betweeners who hadn't grown
up in poverty, but didn't have the kind of parental safety net
that would allow for more creative and adventurous work. She'd
chosen banking in part because it seemed stable—and because
she hadn't known what else to do after college—but now, she
simply did a very high volume of very boring work, in an environment that made her feel drained and expendable, under the
thumb of finicky and hostile bosses, in an industry that wasn't
doling out the morale-sustaining perks it once did.

These complaints weren't unique to Bank of America Merrill
Lynch—in fact, you could probably walk into any law firm, accounting office, or media company in New York and hear a

similar set from young, dissatisfied workers. But for some reason, Chelsea's work environment felt uniquely horrible. And
whether her situation was representative of a larger clash between a generation raised on praise and the ego-shattering nature of Wall Street's harried and indelicate culture, or just the
result of a bad boss and an unfortunate mistake, it was a loom-
ing disaster all the same.

CHAPTER TWELVE

ARJUN KHAN TOOK the stick, gave it a little chalk, leaned down low on the pool table, squinted, and aimed. With a swift thrust, he connected with the cue ball, which clacked into the striped ball and sent it hurtling toward the corner pocket. The striped ball missed, careening off the wall and into the black eight ball, which slowly traced a path over to the side pocket and dropped in.

"Well, guess that's the game," Arjun said with a sigh.

It was the spring of 2011, and we were at a bar in Lower Manhattan where Arjun, the Lehman Brothers refugee turned Citigroup M&A analyst, was unloading his frustrations about the private equity recruiting process on me over a few rounds of stiff old-fashioneds.

"I heard one guy in my group already has three offers," he said. "I'm kind of freaking out."

Every spring, usually sometime around the first or second

week of March, first-year banking analysts fan out around New York for dozens of imaginary "dentist appointments" and mysterious "family emergencies." What they're actually doing is interviewing for jobs with private equity firms and hedge funds, which grab for Wall Street's most promising first-year analysts in one of the most time-honored rituals of young finance life.

Private equity firms and hedge funds (which are collectively referred to as the "buy side," since they purchase the products and services that "sell side" investment banks offer them) represent the big leagues for many young Wall Street workers. These firms have the most lucrative pay in finance—offers as high as $250,000 a year for a talented private equity analyst are common—and they offer analysts the chance to work on huge deals involving big-name companies. For years, until the crash of 2008 made villains of investment bankers and traders, private equity barons were the most notorious subset of Wall Street financiers. They were thought to be slash-and-burn buyout artists who took over companies and extracted all the profit they could for themselves, then left the limp carcasses behind. These days, though, private equity is perhaps the most prestigious place a young bank analyst can wind up—the equivalent of making the Pro Bowl as a rookie.

Private equity firms used to recruit bank analysts during their second year on the job. But in recent years, as the war for top analysts has heated up, firms have been pushing the process earlier and earlier. Now, analysts are courted during the spring of their first year, just six months after they arrive at their banking jobs, and eighteen months until their private equity jobs actually start. Each of the private equity megafunds (KKR, TPG Capital, the Blackstone Group, the Carlyle Group, and Bain

Capital, to name a few) typically recruits between five and fifty analysts per year—meaning that there are routinely thousands of first-year analysts fighting over as few as a hundred megafirm spots. Bankers whose applications make it through the initial cull are given multihour technical interviews, grilled about their knowledge of the private equity business, and taken to cocktail mixers with the firm's executives in order to be tested for "fit"—industry parlance for how likable they are.

Technically, banks frown on analysts interviewing for outside jobs (hence the dentist appointments), but the buy side recruiting process has become so routine that it is now treated as an open secret at many firms. For the analysts who navigate the recruiting drive successfully and wind up with offers at their top-choice firms, the next year and a half is a relative breeze. For the ones who don't, the search for a postbanking job continues anew. And for everyone, the process can leave a mark on fragile egos.

"The private equity recruiting process is where a lot of really accomplished people deal with failure for the first time," one former bank analyst explained to me. "You take a kid who was summa cum laude at Yale, get him a job at Goldman, then put him through private equity recruiting, and you see what he's made of." The former analyst, who ended up getting an offer at one of his top-choice firms after a lengthy and stressful application process, still seemed scarred by the experience several years later. "I got rejected first round from Bain Capital," he said. "It was the most depressing thing ever. It was like: *How do I deal with this? This is a weird emotion.*"

Arjun, who had already experienced rejection when his Lehman Brothers offer was rescinded in the fall of 2008, was

currently experiencing the worst parts of the private equity recruiting process. His job in Citigroup's M&A division was seen
as one of the best stepping-stones to private equity, since the
skills that made a good M&A analyst—solid ability to value
companies, parse complex financial statements, and look for
regulatory and legal risks hidden in a deal—also made for
sought-after private equity workers. And alumni of Arjun's
group were making millions at KKR, TPG Capital, Blackstone,
and every other megafund, meaning that his quest had plenty of
precedent. But the calls just weren't coming in. Arjun couldn't
understand, for the life of him, why he wasn't attracting more
interest as a private equity candidate.

"I really, really think it's about schools," he said that night,
over a rematch at the pool table. "I just look at people who got
interviews and who didn't get interviews, and it looks like it's focusing on people who went to the top schools."

At Citigroup, Arjun had stood out largely on his merits. He
had been placed on deal teams with analysts from Ivy League
universities and worked alongside people whose parents were
Citigroup executives or major clients of the bank. It hadn't
seemed to bother anyone that he had gone to Fordham and
grown up in less advantageous circumstances. He was talented,
and he was willing to grind, and those two factors mattered
more than a pedigree. But now, faced with a lukewarm recep-
tion from the buy side, he was learning that meritocracy had
limits.

Arjun was deeply unhappy and highly anxious, and yet it was
hard for him to talk to anyone about how he felt. He knew that
outside the finance bubble, it looked like he'd won the lottery.
He had the front-office banking job he'd always wanted, he was

earning what many twenty-three-year-olds would consider an
obscene amount of money, and he had plenty of opportunities
on the horizon. But he was having trouble moving up to the
next, slightly more elite, slightly better-paid level of Wall Street
privilege, and his disappointment was real.

In social psychology, this phenomenon is called the "hedonic treadmill"—the shifting of desires relative to achievements.
And although it applies in every industry, it's baked in to Wall
Street's basic ethos. By virtue of their stations in life, young Wall
Street bankers and traders are rarely unlucky, but they are always *relatively* unlucky—there is always someone, somewhere
close by, making ten times more money or with ten times more
responsibility and status. And after 2008, the element of scarcity
was added to the equation. Now, Wall Street workers were not
just battling for a piece of an infinitely large pie. There was
less to go around—fewer jobs, smaller paychecks, tighter opportunity sets. To borrow David Foster Wallace's description of
literary New York, bankers after the crash became "great white
sharks fighting over a bathtub."

"Everyone's always measuring their dicks," one private equity
analyst explained to me. "If I'm a Goldman banker, I go up
to a McKinsey consultant and I'm like, 'My dick's bigger than
yours.' But then a Blackstone analyst goes to the Goldman
banker and says, 'My dick's bigger than yours.' And a portfolio
manager at Greenlight Capital goes up to the Blackstone analyst and says, 'Well, my dick is still bigger than yours.' It never
ends."

For Arjun, the private equity job hunt was bringing back
the feelings of inadequacy he'd developed during the Lehman
Brothers collapse. He still believed in the Wall Street meritoc-

racy. He still thought that if he kept his head down and worked hard, he could overcome his lack of an Ivy League education and his humble upbringing. But his faith in that ability was being tested.

"I went through all this to build a career, and it's still not working," he told me that night, as we wrapped up our pool game and walked back out into the chilly March night. "I just don't understand."

CHAPTER THIRTEEN

SOMEWHERE AROUND THE one-year mark of my immersion with young Wall Street analysts, an odd thing happened: I started to make friends.

I came to my finance-industry investigation, I must admit, with a fair bit of skepticism. Wall Street, after all, is a place of excess and vice, where time is measured in scandals and convictions, and I still hadn't forgotten that the work young analysts did, no matter how banal it was day to day, served a complicated and problematic agenda. But as I got to know the eight analysts I shadowed on an individual level, I found that they made for good company. They were smart and charming. They had self-deprecating senses of humor about the financial industry and their roles within it. And they were typically thoughtful enough to acknowledge that while being a young banker wasn't always fun, it was a hell of a lot better than being unemployed.

I brought this up with a nonbanker friend of mine. She winced.

"Do you think you're getting the whole picture?" she asked. "Are you sure you're not just talking to the ones you find tolerable and ignoring the douchebags?"

She had a point: I did have a douchebag deficit, and my project had an inherent selection bias. My banker sources were atypical by definition—daring or disillusioned enough to be willing to risk getting fired by talking to me, and kind and introspective enough to spend hours at a time answering probing questions about their lives. They had all bought in to some portion of the financial world's value system, but they all considered themselves outsiders.

To correct for the possibility of missing the whole picture, I decided to try to find the dark heart of young Wall Street—to venture past the likable into the utterly unredeemable. I decided to go to Fashion Meets Finance.

Fashion Meets Finance is a singles mixer series with a simple premise: take several hundred male financiers, put them in a room with several hundred women who work in the fashion industry, and let the magic happen. The series was started in 2007, and it is predicated on the idea that male Wall Streeters and female fashion workers, as the respective alpha ascenders of their tribal clans, deserve to meet and procreate, preserving the dominant line in perpetuity. It's social Darwinism in its purest, most obnoxious form.

"Women in fashion need men who can facilitate their pre-30 marriage/retirement plan," read one early invitation. "And men in finance need women who will allow them to leverage their career in their dating equity."

Fashion Meets Finance hit a snag in 2008, when the financial sector nearly collapsed, taking bankers down a few notches on the Manhattan social ladder and necessitating a brief hiatus. But in 2009, it returned with a vengeance. Its organizers proclaimed proudly:

> 2008 was a confusing time, but we are here to announce the balance is restoring itself to the ecosystem of the New York dating community. We fear that news of shrinking bonuses, banks closing, and the Dow plummeting confused the gorgeous women of the city.…The uncertainty caused panic which caused irrational decisions—there's going to be a two-year blip in the system where a hot fashion girl might commit to a pharmaceutical salesman.…Fashion Meets Finance has returned to let the women of fashion know that the recession is officially over. It might be a year before bonuses start inflating themselves again, but it will happen. Invest in the future; feel confident in your destiny. Hold on. It will only be a couple more years until you can quit your job and become a tennis mom.

I almost admired the candor with which Fashion Meets Finance accepted noxious social premises as fact. (One early advertisement read, "Ladies, you don't need to worry that the cute guy at the bar works in advertising!") But others disagreed. Gawker called one gathering "an event where Manhattan banker-types and fashion slaves meet, consummate, and procreate certain genetics to create lineages of people you'd rather not know." There was no question that if my goal was to find the worst Wall Street had to offer, I emphatically *did* want to know the people who would be commingling inside Bar Basque, the overpriced Vegas-style restaurant and bar where the event was being held.

After signing in with the bouncer, I pushed my way past a few leggy blondes in strapless dresses and heels to the outdoor deck. There, dozens of men with well-tailored suits and good hair were crowding around the open bar, which was sponsored by a midshelf vodka company. Most of the women formed a loose ring around the periphery of the deck, waiting for financiers to approach them. I guessed there were five hundred people in total.

"What does this whole thing stand for, if you think about it?" a Wall Street trader standing near the door asked me. The trader, who had slicked-back hair, a shirt opened to midchest in order to allow his prodigious chest hair to topple out, and a pair of Gucci loafers on his feet, answered his own question: "It's a bunch of gold diggers looking to take advantage of guys who are looking to take advantage of gold diggers." He laughed. "It's sort of perfect, huh?"

This installment of Fashion Meets Finance, held after a year-long break, had undergone a significant rebranding. Now, it was being billed as a charity event (proceeds were going to a nonprofit focused on Africa), and the cringe-worthy marketing slogans had been erased. Now, the financiers and fashionistas were joined by a smattering of young professionals from other industries: law, consulting, insurance, even a few female bankers.

I met up with Beth Newill, a fashion marketer who started Fashion Meets Finance in 2007, and who said that the social and romantic appeal of finance jobs, while better than it was at the depths of the crisis, had still not attained its full pre-crash glory.

"Back in the heyday, you could drop that bomb of, 'I'm in finance,' and women would be like—'Golden ticket!'" she said. "That's changed."

And indeed, the first few men I met at Fashion Meets Finance told me about the fading allure of their line of work.

"I don't even mention what I do for work to girls," a young hedge fund trader told me. "In 2008, with all the stuff happening, I felt bad. When you're associated with a hedge fund, you're seen as taking away people's mothers' retirement money."

"I tell people I drive the 6 train," said the hedge funder's friend, a J.P. Morgan banker, who was standing next to him swirling a Maker's Mark on the rocks.

I believed them, and I could see the appeal of their strategy—in the months following the crisis, if I had been a single banker out on the town, I'm not sure I would have wanted to lead with my job, either. Still, claims of shame and self-consciousness were fairly rich coming from guys who had bought tickets to an event specifically designed to allow them to take advantage of their occupations.

After a few hours of drinking and socializing, I had filled my douchebag quota many times over. I had seen and heard the following things:

- A banker showing off his expensive watch (which he called "my piece") to a gaggle of interested-looking women.
- A former Lehman Brothers banker explaining his strategy

for picking up women. "I use Lehman to break the ice—you know, get their sympathy. Then I tell them I make twice as much as Lehman paid me at my new job. They love my story, and then they end up in my bed."

- A private equity associate using the acronym "P.J." to refer to his firm's private jet.

- A hedge fund trader giving dating advice to his down-and-out friend: "Girls come in many shapes and sizes. But just remember: when you hold them by the ankles and look down, they all look the same!"

As the night wore on, I identified the two primary strains of Fashion Meets Finance attendees. There were the merely curious, the people who had heard about the event from a friend and were intrigued enough about the premise to pay $25 for a ticket. These people mainly stood or sat on the perimeter of the roof deck, where they could observe (and, in some cases, laugh at) the commingling of the other partygoers.

And then there were the true believers. A portion of the attendees at Fashion Meets Finance seemingly had no idea that the event had become a punch line. They were bankers and fashionistas who were determined to find their matches at a superficial singles mixer, and they had no qualms about it.

"I want the real deal!" said one female fashionista, who was sprawled out on a white sofa on Bar Basque's terrace, sipping a vodka soda and watching the men walk by. "I'm really independent," she said, "and I don't want someone who needs to be around me all the time. I want them to work 150 hours a week at Goldman Sachs."

As darkness fell, the music got louder, and most of the

younger-looking bankers filtered out. Left standing were most of the women and a slightly older male crew, whose actions and mannerisms gave off a distinct Old Wall Street glow. Aside from the Rihanna blaring from the speakers, the scene could have been Salomon Brothers, 1987.

I should have been satisfied. After all, I'd come to see the less savory elements of young Wall Street, and I'd seen them in concentrated, potent form. I now knew that in certain corners of the financial sector, the pre-crash culture of self-regard and vacuity was still alive and well.

But as I descended in the elevator well after midnight, I couldn't help but worry. After all, the banker stereotypes who had come to Fashion Meets Finance were as much a part of Wall Street as the thoughtful, reasonable analysts I'd met in my travels. Like every industry, finance contains multitudes, and it's not bizarre to think that an industry whose teleological goal is the pursuit of money will attract more unsavory characters than, say, a charity for orphans. But what if Wall Street doesn't just attract preexisting douchebags, but actively draws normal people into an inescapable vortex of douchebaggery? What if the well-adjusted analysts I was interviewing already had the seeds of Old Wall Street culture inside them and were just months or years away from turning into the kind of craven and shallow people I'd met that night?

As much as I didn't want that to be the case, I had to admit it was a possibility. After all, Wall Street has a long history of exerting a powerful cultural influence on malleable young analysts, who are often taught to succeed by emulating the people above them on the food chain. The fact that any bankers showed up at Fashion Meets Finance at all meant that the financial crisis hadn't flushed all the obnoxiousness out of Wall Street's system. And maybe, if the markets kept recovering, the financial industry's moral awakening would be just a passing moment, a soon-forgotten footnote before the old guard returned.

CHAPTER FOURTEEN

Ricardo Hernandez arrived at the basketball court looking like he'd been on the bad end of a bar brawl. His eyes were swollen and bloodshot. His normal gait had been replaced by a dejected half shuffle. And his shoulders slumped over like an octogenarian's.

"Guys, I gotta go easy today," he told his rec-league team. "I'll die if I run too much."

Ricardo had been going through hell at work. The M&A division at J.P. Morgan was notorious for being hard on first-year analysts, but the division's reputation had failed to capture the full extent of the pain. The director of Ricardo's group, a hypermasculine senior banker named Phil, worked his underlings like dogs in an attempt to give them the same kind of hard-knocks education he'd gotten as a young analyst. He never left work early, and he scoffed at any requests for days off. Once, when a vice president in the group had asked to be allowed to leave the office to attend his daughter's first dance recital, Phil gruffly told him no.

"We're mid-fire-drill here," Phil said. Then, by way of cheering him up, he added: "Don't worry—I haven't been to any of my kid's baseball games."

In the spring of 2011, the M&A market was conspiring to create the most taxing work climate possible for young Wall Street analysts. The number of huge companies doing big, billion-dollar deals fell in the wake of the financial crisis and hadn't yet recovered. Banks, which needed to keep their fees flowing, looked further down the totem pole to small- and medium-sized companies, and decided to pitch enough of those deals to make up for the shortfall at the top. What that meant, in practice, was that M&A analysts like Ricardo were overloaded with deal work, and almost none of it would result in the kinds of ego-fulfilling accomplishments that made it into the *Wall Street Journal*. In fact, because every bank on Wall Street was chasing the same deals, all rummaging for whatever M&A scraps they could pick up, most of the legwork done by people like Ricardo would never result in a finished deal at all.

Ricardo's situation wasn't uncommon. Every year on Wall Street, first-year analysts who were once courted by college recruiters with lines about how they would be given meaningful, creative work and the chance to learn from top executives are shown the harsh truth: they are Excel grunts whose work is often meaningless not just in the cosmic sense, but in the sense of being seen by nobody and utilized for no productive purpose. Some of the hundred-page pitch books analysts spend their late-night hours fact-checking in painstaking detail are simply thrown away after being given a quick skim by a client. In other cases, the client doesn't read the deliverables at all, and the analysts' work is literally garbage.

To help themselves concentrate and work longer hours, some of the analysts in Ricardo's group had procured alertness pills like Adderall and Modafinil. Ricardo had never taken the pills, but he'd often been tempted to. He'd known he was signing up for long hours at the bank, but he'd never imagined anything like this. Most days that winter, he had worked the "banker nine-to-five"—getting to work at 9:00 a.m. and staying until 5:00 a.m. the next morning, at which point he'd trudge back to his Murray Hill apartment, sleep for three or four hours, and do it all over again. Even the money he was making wasn't cheering him up. Ricardo had once made the mistake of calculating what his hourly wage would be, given his salary and a conservative estimate of his year-end bonus. The result—which he estimated was something like $16 an hour, after taxes—was much more than minimum wage, but not nearly enough for Ricardo to be able to justify the punishment he'd been taking.

Ricardo's main task that spring had been making Excel model after Excel model. There were several kinds of models that banks used to value companies they were recommending as merger or acquisition candidates for their clients—including "discounted cash flows," or DCF, a type of widely used model that used a company's projected cash flows to estimate what it was worth on the open market. I'd learned how to make these models in my Training the Street seminar. It's a fragile, delicate process that involves inputting long strings of numbers, linking cells to other cells, and cross-referencing each output so that when one input is updated, the rest of the model updates automatically. If one cell in a model refers to the wrong cell, or contains an extraneous dollar sign or a missing set of parentheses, it can break the entire chain and require hours to fix. Making one model is annoying; doing it twice a day involves getting accustomed to a constant low-level terror that is akin to working at a Christmas light factory, and knowing that one badly installed bulb in a string of ten thousand lights will make all the other ones go dark.

Ricardo's stress wasn't only a function of the fragility of his models. It was also related to his boss Phil's splenetic temper. A few weeks ago, Phil had asked Ricardo to "spread comps," a type of spreadsheet that showed a company's valuation relative to other comparable firms in the same industry. The next day, while looking over the finished comps, Phil barraged him with questions: "How did you calculate EBITDA? Did you adjust for stock-based compensation? Are these consensus estimates?"

Ricardo was a little unsure about his numbers, many of which he'd arrived at during an all-nighter. When he hesitated too long in answering, Phil lit into him.

"You've got to know this!" he yelled. "You have to know everything stone fucking cold!"

Ricardo's treatment was relatively mild compared to what Mary, an associate in his group, had gone through. Mary, a woman in her late twenties with an MBA from Wharton and a piranha's temperament, typically sat through Phil's rants with a poker face. But late one night, when he had railed on her over the phone about the progress of an unfinished project, she broke down crying. Ricardo, who was the only other person left in the office, had the unpleasant task of consoling her.

"I'm naturally an optimistic, positive, happy person," he told me later. "But I feel myself becoming a lot more bitter, a lot more negative."

Ricardo's schedule had also taken a toll on his girlfriend, who lived on the Upper East Side and worked as a TV production assistant. These days, she barely saw him. He cancelled several Saturday night dinner reservations at the last minute due to deals going haywire, and their relationship was becoming increasingly strained.

In the course of my finance-industry immersion, I often found myself asking older bankers about the necessity of the first-year lifestyle. In an era when technology has made working from home much more feasible, why are bankers—whose work comes in fits and spurts—required to be physically present at their desks for upwards of twelve hours a day? Couldn't you hire twice as many recent college grads, pay them half as much, and create a more reasonable sixty-hour week for everyone?

The answers I got came in several flavors, most of which boiled down to "Because it's always been like this." With the same attitude as a fraternity brother who treats the pledges like dirt because he remembers being abused as a pledge, many older managers on Wall Street seem to cherish putting analysts through their paces. And although some bank executives recognize that burnout and exhaustion are common among young analysts, they don't necessarily seem to view it as a treatable issue.

"Is there a way to make this easier on analysts?" one senior Wall Street hiring director asked me, then answered his own question: "Yeah, probably. A lot of it you can't control. But we try to get managers to think about, how do you distribute work evenly to analysts, and do it and sooner in the day? That seems to make a difference."

Some people insist that the masochistic lifestyle adopted by young Wall Street workers was related to the actual needs of their firms (chiefly, the need to demonstrate to clients that they have an army of well-trained junior analysts who can churn out a pitch book at 3:00 a.m. under extreme duress). And others explain it as a self-selection mechanism. When given such unreasonable hours, the logic goes, analysts either bow out under pressure or rise to the challenge. How else are you supposed to find out who is real Wall Street material?

The most reasonable-sounding answers I got to my questions were from people who told me that the hundred-plus-hour weeks of a first-year analyst were one half of a grand, unspoken social contract that had existed on Wall Street for decades. As part of the basic bargain, analysts were asked to demonstrate full loyalty to the firm by becoming a slave to its demands. In order to fully belong, the first-year analyst had to realign his priorities, replacing his own with his bank's. And seen in this light, all the young banker's cancelled dinners and broken relationships aren't just unpleasant externalities—they were central to the process.

Ricardo understood why he had to work hard, and most of the time he didn't mind. He accepted that he had given his life over to J.P. Morgan for two years, and he knew that in exchange he would one day get a shot at a promotion and a raise. But now, he questioned whether even that was true.

In the past few months, Ricardo had begun getting calls from headhunters, who came bearing interview opportunities for jobs at private equity firms and hedge funds, where the workload would be slightly better. He didn't think much of them at first. After all, every first-year got these calls, and most of them were for second-tier shops that would represent a step down, prestige-wise, from his current job. But recently, he'd begun to think seriously about whether any of those jobs might be a better fit.

After all, didn't he like having a life outside of work? And could he make it through one more year in the M&A group, with Phil's temper and a bullpen full of analysts hopped up on pills?

Maybe, Ricardo thought, it was time to start scanning for the exits.

CHAPTER FIFTEEN

MIDWAY THROUGH THEIR second beer, Jeremy Miller-Reed and Samson White started discussing the best ways to kill themselves at work.

"If the goal is, like, how do I inflict maximum psychological damage," Jeremy said, "then I think just going up to your desk and blowing your brains out in the middle of the day would be the best."

"Nah," Samson said. "You know what would happen? All the other analysts would get an e-mail from the associates saying, 'Can you guys clean this up?' And then everyone would go back to work."

It was mid-March 2011, more than halfway through their first year at Goldman Sachs, and Jeremy and Samson were both trying their hands at gallows humor. Their initial excitement about working at the most esteemed bank on Wall Street had quickly evaporated, and devastating depression had taken root.

Sometimes, their misery manifested in humor—calling Goldman's 200 West Street headquarters "Azkaban," for example,
after the prison in the Harry Potter series where inmates' souls
are sucked from their bodies. Other times, it took on a more serious tone. More than once, while walking to work through the
streets of Battery Park City before dawn, Jeremy had pondered
how much time he'd get off from work if he was hit by a car, and
whether the trade-off of a few broken limbs would be worth it.
Samson, who had once been among the huge throng of Goldman workers who gathered at the corner of Murray Street and
West Street every morning while waiting to cross the West Side
Highway, now crossed the highway by himself, a block further
north. The detour cost him five minutes, but it made him feel
less like part of a platoon of soulless banker automatons, and
more like his own man.

All of Goldman's first-year analysts had gotten their first
bonuses several weeks earlier—a $30,000 stub bonus that rep-
resented half of their total bonus for the twelve-month period.
It was an uncharacteristically large number on Wall Street that
year, and it would mean that all of them would be making
$130,000, all told, for a first year of postcollege work. That was
serious money, well above the median national income, but
Jeremy and Samson didn't particularly care. They were barely
getting by, and it had nothing to do with money and everything
to do with the ways in which Goldman Sachs had taken over
their lives.

They had started smoking weed together on Jeremy's roof
deck—first occasionally, then nearly every day as their outlooks
on life worsened. And, during some of these smoking sessions,
they had started plotting a mass exodus of first-year analysts out

of Goldman, in which everyone would announce their departure on the same day, then take to the Internet and tell their
horror stories of working at the bank. They called this fantasy
"Wall Street Drop Day," and had even taken the liberty of reserving the domain name wallstdropday.com, just in case it ever
came to fruition.

For Jeremy, who had started out on such a promising note on
the Goldman commodities desk, most of the change could be
encapsulated in a single word: Penelope.

Penelope was a managing director in Jeremy's group. A tall
brunette with mesmerizing blue eyes and a lean physique
toned by a decade's worth of yoga and spin classes, she had
been feared and despised by her junior analysts for years. Some
of them had taken note of her strong resemblance to the actress
Julia Roberts and given her the nickname "Pretty Woman." And
stories about her wrath were legion.

Jeremy had come into the commodities group working
mostly with Graham Campbell, the executive who was nicknamed "the Senator." But after a few months at Graham's
hip, he'd been staffed in quick succession on a number of
projects with Penelope, who had all of Graham's intensity
with none of his charm. Penelope had spent the last fifteen
years at Goldman amassing political capital inside the firm
and building up an impressive book of clients, and her temper
had grown along with her seniority. She spent much of the
day yelling at support staff and colleagues for a never-ending
string of offenses. She would yell about missing lines of
credit, errors in trade bookings, and restaurant maître d's who
couldn't get her a reservation at the last minute. (Jeremy
knew, from overhearing her phone calls, that she had a par-

ticularly chilly relationship with the mechanics at Land Rover of Manhattan.)

Jeremy had been unhappy enough observing Penelope's belligerence from a few desks away, but in December, she'd turned her wrath on him. She assigned him a twenty-page memo for one of the group's clients, outlining the potential terms of a revolving credit facility that would give the bank more competitive pricing on future commodity deals. Then she went on vacation, leaving him to figure out the project on his own.

When Penelope returned a week later, she told Jeremy that while he'd done good work, she needed a few tiny changes before the client presentation. Over the next four days, those "few tiny changes" expanded to thirty or forty revisions, many of them contradicting earlier revisions, and some as minor as changing double quotation marks to single quotes. And with each revision, her tone would harshen, and her temper would flare.

On Friday, Penelope went to present Jeremy's memo to the client. And during her presentation, she discovered that a chart she'd expected to be nestled neatly on a specific page wasn't there. She was furious. She came back from the meeting, went straight to Jeremy's desk, and proceeded to upbraid him in front of his entire group.

"You had all week to get this right!" she screamed.

That night, after going out to a bar with some friends, Jeremy went back to his usual spot on the roof of his apartment building, lit up a joint, and broke down. It was raining outside, and the tears streaming down Jeremy's face merged with the water droplets running down from his hair.

I can't do this anymore, he thought. *No one deserves to be treated like this.*

He flashed back to a conversation he'd had with his then-girlfriend in August 2009, when he went to visit her at her family's beach house during his summer internship, before his commodities rotation began.

Back then, he'd told her about what had happened that summer—how he'd gotten two bad desk scramble assignments, busted his ass anyway, and ended up charming one of the senior executives in commodities and landing a third rotation with his group. If he got a full-time offer from the commodities desk, he told her, he'd essentially be setting himself up for life.

"I mean, Lloyd Blankfein started in this exact seat," he said. "I'd be getting the same job that made Lloyd Blankfein."

His girlfriend, who didn't fully understand what was at stake but sensed it was important, paused and thought for a moment.

"You know," she said. "If you get this job, it's going to change your life."

Her line stuck with Jeremy, and buoyed him all over the last and most difficult weeks of the summer analyst program. He'd gotten a high from the knowledge that Goldman would, in fact, change his life. He imagined himself using his Goldman gravitas to launch himself to a position, in whatever field he chose, that would afford him real power and influence.

But now, as he found himself in an industry in decline, surrounded by Penelope, the Senator, and dozens of other people whose aspirations extended only as far as their GC counts, he wondered if those words had been more omen than encouragement.

Several days after his encounter with Penelope, Jeremy opened a blank document on his computer, and began listing all the places he'd rather work. He listed things like working at the genome institute run by the famed biologist Craig Venter, Google Ventures, and a sustainable energy start-up. He gave the document a name: "Escape Routes." And then he returned to work, knowing that his days were probably numbered.

*   *   *

Samson, too, had been made a target of his boss's wrath over a mistake.

That spring, Samson had been assigned a huge project—an exchange rate model he'd had to build for a client who was looking to invest in the Brazilian real estate market. He'd worked on it for weeks, pulling many nearly-all-nighters, fueled by dozens of 5-hour Energy canisters, to finish.

After he finally turned it in, he realized that he'd slipped up on page 27 of 40, and accidentally duplicated a previous page's formulas. He thought the mistake might slip by unnoticed, but at breakfast the next day, he got an e-mail from his associate.

"Hey, grab me when you're around," the e-mail read.

When he got in, he plodded into the associate's office, and saw that she wasn't smiling.

"Do you see a problem with these two pages?" she said.

Samson played dumb. "Uh, no?"

"Are you serious?" she said. "They're exactly the same."

"Oh."

The associate glared at him.

"Listen. Do you want to make it here?"

"Um, yes," Samson said.

"Well then, you need to pay attention. You're not there yet.

And you're not going to get there unless you stop making stupid mistakes. Okay?"

"Okay."

Samson was crushed. He'd been entrusted with more and more important projects every week since arriving as a full-time analyst. He'd had a few moments of mediocrity, but overall, he thought he was at least treading water. But now, he was realizing that his performance was below average, and the confidence blow was staggering. It occurred to him that in his entire life, from his early childhood up through his time at Princeton, he'd never truly been bad at anything.

That winter, Samson had seen his work problems manifest physically. He'd been gaining weight, drinking to excess, and getting far too little sleep. And he was sinking into what he feared was an acute case of depression. In an attempt to turn himself around, he began taking improv comedy classes at a theater in Midtown. He went to Vegas with his roommates for a weekend-long bender. He'd started working out at the Goldman gym, and took pains to reconnect with some old friends from college. But nothing was helping.

When he started at Goldman, Samson had begun a daily routine of going up the elevators with a friend at the bank—an analyst named Greg—to Goldman's Sky Lobby. The Sky Lobby was Goldman's name for its spacious eleventh floor, where the firm cafeteria, coffee bar, gym, and lounging area were located. Samson and Greg would escape there for ten or fifteen minutes, get a pastry at the coffee bar, and catch each other up on the gossip of the day. But that winter, Greg noticed that Samson wasn't saying a word during their catch-ups. He would just sit there, looking vacant and exhausted, often so nervous that he would forget to eat his pastry. Greg tried to coax Samson out of his slump by cracking jokes and sharing funny gossip about their coworkers. But it was no use.

"I just don't feel like being here," Samson told Greg one morning.

That winter, Jeremy and Samson bonded over their common misery. They hung out together outside of work nearly every day, and would often end a tough day of work by smoking on Jeremy's roof. On weekends, they'd talk until sunrise, after which Samson would leave and go back to his apartment to sleep. (These all-nighters happened frequently enough that the apartment building's doorman began to suspect that Jeremy and Samson were dating.)

In early March, Samson went out to a bar with Jeremy and a group of his friends. He could always rely on his friends, even the ones who didn't work on Wall Street, to understand him. And, as the drinks flowed, he'd poured forth his woes, letting everyone close to him know how unhappy he was. Several days later, Samson's roommate Mark walked into his room, bearing a gift-wrapped box about the size and shape of a skateboard.

"Dude, I have the perfect present for you."

Samson opened the box. Inside was a large, electric clock with illuminated red letters and four sets of numbers marked, "Days, Hours, Minutes, Seconds."

"It's a countdown clock," Mark explained. "You can set it for the day you want to leave Goldman, and start counting down."

Samson smiled. A countdown clock was perfect. Even if he didn't end up quitting right away, having a device to remind himself that his Goldman tenure was a finite experience would help him immensely. With Mark's help, Samson mounted the clock onto the wall above his bedroom door. He set it for 336 days—the amount of time between that day and when he estimated the following year's bonuses would be paid.

Three hundred thirty-six days, he thought, looking up at the glowing sign from his bed that night. *I may not be able to handle an entire career at Goldman, but three hundred thirty-six days I can do.*

CHAPTER SIXTEEN

PASSPORT, CHECK. TOILETRIES, *check. Shoes, socks, pants, belts, shirts, umbrella, power adapter—check, check, check, check, check, check, check.*

Arjun Khan was going through some last-minute preparations for his big trip to Italy. It would be his first vacation since joining Citigroup's M&A division, and he and two of his college friends, who were accompanying him on the trip, had already devised a rough agenda. Together, they would visit St. Peter's Basilica, marvel at the Sistine Chapel, explore the Colosseum, wander the markets at Campo de' Fiori, and eat every pizza and pasta dish they could get their hands on.

At his desk that afternoon, while looking up tourist attractions online, Arjun got a call from a 212 number he didn't recognize.

"Arjun, this is Dr. Friedman," the voice said. "Do you have a minute to speak?"

Arjun tensed. Dr. Friedman was the general practitioner he'd seen a few days earlier for some medical issues that had been bothering him. For weeks, he'd been coughing a lot, losing weight, and generally feeling more tired than usual. At first, he'd attributed the symptoms to a chest cold, and to the long hours and sleepless nights he'd accumulated while closing several big deals. But when his symptoms worsened, and he began coughing up blood, he called for an appointment.

He expected a minor diagnosis, something treatable with a few pills and a day or two of bed rest. But what came out of Dr. Friedman's mouth was much more serious.

"Arjun, your lab work came back," the doctor said. "There appears to be something quite abnormal going on."

Arjun's heart dropped. "What is it?"

"Well, I'm not entirely sure, but I'd like to have you tested for Goodpasture's syndrome."

Arjun wrote those words on a Post-it note at his desk, and circled them over and over with his pen as Dr. Friedman explained that Goodpasture's syndrome was a very rare autoimmune disease, in which the body's immune system mistakenly begins attacking proteins in the lungs and kidneys, causing internal bleeding and inflammation. Its exact causes are unknown, but the disease can cause permanent lung and kidney damage, and require dialysis and other serious measures if left untreated. In some cases, it can even be fatal.

For the next fifteen minutes, after asking for a referral to a specialist and hanging up with Dr. Friedman, Arjun sat at his desk, paralyzed. It was cloudy outside, and the Citigroup staffer was roaming up and down the bullpen aisles, assigning projects to various analysts. Arjun had no idea what to do. Should he call his parents? Was he supposed to ignore the call and keep working? Eventually, he took his coat, went for a walk around the block, came back, went to the bathroom, washed his face, and returned to his desk. He felt overwhelmed with both pain and panic, and more than that, he felt confused. Rare diseases weren't something that happened to people like him. He had never been a smoker, never done hard drugs, never so much as broken a bone. Sure, he probably slept far too little during the week and drank far too much on the weekends. But overall, he was a healthy, productive twenty-four-year-old. *What the hell was going on?*

A few hours later, while folding laundry for his trip, Arjun got another call from Dr. Friedman, who gave him some referrals to specialists and suggested he see one of them as soon as possible.

"Well, I'm going on vacation tomorrow," Arjun said. "I'll be back in a week, so I'll go see one then."

"If I were you," Dr. Friedman said, "I wouldn't wait. I would want to know for sure what's going on. I think you should go in for a biopsy."

That word—*biopsy*—burned in Arjun's chest. And he decided not to take his chances.

"Okay," he said. "I'll stay here and get it checked out."

Two days later, while Arjun had planned to be eating *pasta alla norma* on a cobblestone street, he was instead in a hospital, where a specialist tested a piece of his kidney and found that the ailment afflicting him was, in fact, Goodpasture's syndrome. He would need immediate treatment to keep it from worsening, the doctor said, including heavy doses of corticosteroids and a one-month regimen of plasma exchange, a dialysis-like procedure that would filter the rogue antibodies out of his blood before returning it to his body. Arjun's disease was in a fairly advanced stage, he said, but if they attacked it aggressively, he'd have a decent chance of making a full recovery.

Arjun panicked, his mind filling with worst-case scenarios. He thought about how his friends would react, how his treatment would feel, how he'd explain his sickness to people, and how fully he'd bought into the myth that youth and health go hand in hand. He kicked himself for not getting his symptoms checked out sooner, and had flashes of lying in a hospital bed, being fed through a tube while a group of worried-looking doctors gathered around him, trying desperately to save his life.

Eventually, his thoughts turned to work. How would it look on his year-end reviews if he had to take time off for treatment? Who would pick up the slack on his deals? Would being sick hurt his chances of getting a private equity job, or a big second-year bonus?

In the following days, Arjun thought a lot about work. He didn't think it was possible, medically speaking, to get an autoimmune disease from working too much. But he wondered if the sacrifices of his body and mind he'd been making for the sake of the bank had exacerbated his condition, or made it harder for him to notice that something was wrong. The more he thought about the antibodies attacking his organs, the more offensive it seemed that he had skipped so many gym visits, done so many rounds of shots at the bar with his colleagues, or pulled so many all-nighters while making tiny edits to pitch books and trying to figure out whether a corporation was worth 8 or 8.5 times pretax earnings.

"This has reinforced to me that my job is not the most impor-

tant thing," he told me, around that time. "The be-all end-all is
the other stuff that happens in the next sixty or seventy years, if
I live that long."

Two weeks later, after he'd undergone his first round of treatment, Arjun decided to try going back to work. He'd been given
a paid leave of absence shortly after he got his diagnosis, but he
missed the energy of the bullpen, which he hoped would dis-
tract him from the dread and anxiety of being sick. And so, for
the next few weeks, Arjun shuffled off to Citigroup every morning. Getting back in his old routine helped ease his nerves,
even though he still couldn't completely ignore his pain. His
boss made sure his workload was light while he was being
treated, and he got get-well cards and gifts from what seemed
like half the bank.

It all felt infantilizing, being coddled and sympathized with.
Arjun knew it came from a good place, but he also feared
that, somehow, he would be penalized for his weakness. This
was Wall Street, after all, where mind over matter was the
law of the land. He had heard about traders who had worked
through blinding migraines, bankers who had come to work
with 104-degree fevers, and men who had missed the births of
their children because they'd been working on a deal. He'd told
himself early on in his banking career that he would never miss
a day of work, for any reason, and he hated having to break his
own rule.

What Arjun feared most was sticking out. He had always
prided himself on propriety and decorum. When he was walking with an older banker, he always let the senior employee
walk a step ahead of him, so as to preserve the pecking order.
He made liberal use of "ma'am" and "sir" at work, and always

took care to give up his seat to senior bankers when they came late to meetings in packed rooms.

It frustrated Arjun to no end that he had spent a year clawing his way onto the linear, upward path at Citigroup after his Lehman disaster, only to fall off a year later. How unlucky could one guy get? But as his mother reminded him constantly, his health came first. Whenever his mind drifted to work-related stress, he thought back to something she had often told him: "Nothing is as important as living."

If he survived this, Arjun told himself, he would change his lifestyle. He would take the same never-say-never attitude that had gotten him in the door at Citigroup and apply it to his physical well-being. Worrying about his health wasn't optimal, but it was the only choice he had.

CHAPTER SEVENTEEN

AFTER TRUDGING BACK to her apartment from work, Deutsche Bank risk management analyst Soo-jin Park slumped down on her sofa, kicked her heels off, and grabbed for the remote. Watching TV was one of the only distractions that worked for Soo-jin, who often needed to unkink her nerves to allow herself to relax after work. In the past several weeks, she had gotten through the first two seasons of *Mad Men*, and was now finishing up the third. When she did, she planned to move on to *How I Met Your Mother*.

Since I met Soo-jin at the Women on Wall Street Conference a year earlier, her concerns about gender equality at Deutsche Bank had given way to a more quotidian set of concerns: namely, she was stuck in a dead-end job.

Risk managers, Soo-jin had been told, were crucial to the functioning of any large financial institution. They were the lifeguards of Wall Street. Before every rate swap, every big bond trade, every structured credit sale, a risk analyst would be called in to assess the bank's vulnerability to losses and unexpected consequences—essentially, how likely the deal was to fall into the pool. The risk analyst would then give an assessment of these considerations to the actual deal makers, who were supposed to take their recommendations into account before doing anything.

But to Soo-jin's frustration, they were often reluctant to pay attention. Three years after a financial crisis had resulted—in large part from a laissez-faire attention to risk management— front-office bankers and traders still tended to treat the life-guards of capital with no more respect than they treated the IT workers who fixed their computers. To them, being told that a given deal was too risky to execute felt like being a kid on the playground whose overprotective parents won't let him go on the big slide. Risk managers, at Deutsche Bank and elsewhere, were still viewed as professional killjoys. And if they nixed a deal they considered too risky, they often put their own bonuses at risk.

"When you're in the front office, you're trying to make money," Soo-jin explained to me. "You're not thinking much about limiting losses."

The past months should have been exciting times in Soo-jin's corner of the industry. A European debt crisis had been raging—one that started with a Greek sovereign debt scare and had grown into a Spanish and an Italian banking panic—and part of Soo-jin's job was figuring out how much of the debt of European countries and companies the bank and its clients held. She had spent days plugging CUSIP codes, which identified individual bonds, into her Bloomberg terminal—looking

up which countries the bonds were from and plugging that data
into a massive spreadsheet that held all of her division's positions. Further up the chain, that spreadsheet would be used by
senior risk management executives to determine if the bank had
too much exposure to Spanish banks, Italian car makers, or Por-
tuguese mining conglomerates, and how much money it stood
to lose if any of these companies defaulted on their debt.

But Soo-jin had been unable to shake the feeling that her
work was just one more spreadsheet on a report that might be
given a cursory glance before being forgotten entirely. She had
often wandered through the trading floors at Deutsche Bank's
headquarters, where powerful men (and a few women) sat at
trading turrets flanked by huge arrays of monitors. There was so
much energy on the floor, she thought. And the noise! It was
a cacophony of shouts, ringing phones, and announcements
over the hoot-and-holler that sounded, to her, like the grinding gears of capitalism. And, in those moments, she understood
the chilly relationship between risk management and everybody else. When faced with such exciting and lucrative work,
who wanted to think about the possibility of a disaster?

All over Wall Street in 2011, financial firms were showing
that although the crisis had changed some lines of business and
consolidated the industry, the basic culture of risk taking and
reward seeking was still very much intact. Banks were still taking on huge, leveraged positions in opaque and little-regulated
markets. The junk bond market, which deals in high-yield corporate debt that is often issued by volatile and risky companies,
was having its strongest year since the crisis. And although the
Dodd-Frank act had effectively shut down the most obvious
forms of proprietary trading at Wall Street firms, that work lived

on under the guise of "market-making" trading desks, which were often functionally similar to their predecessors. Three years after Lehman Brothers, it was still far better to be the guy pushing the button on a billion-dollar trade than the guy hovering just behind him, warning about what could go wrong.

Soo-jin had been trying to get out of risk management and into the front office since her early days on the job. At one meeting, Soo-jin had asked the COO of her division if it would be possible.

"What would it take to move to a different part of the bank, if you don't find what you're doing challenging or comfortable?" she asked.

The COO wavered.

"Well, it's a good question. The bank isn't really set up for people to move, because we recruit you into this division."

He continued to say that on a case-by-case basis, bank employees could, theoretically, move between divisions. But she got the sense he was just being polite. Unless there was an extraordinary exception made, once you were a middle-office employee, you were always a middle-office employee.

Banks had ostensible reasons for their elitism. Foremost among these was that traders who had worked in the back and middle offices tended to have deep knowledge of their firm's technical systems, and could exploit them if given the chance to trade on their own. In January 2008, Jérôme Kerviel, a trader at the French bank Société Générale who had started out in the bank's compliance department, was arrested after losing more than $6 billion in a series of unauthorized trades. In the trial that followed, Société Générale claimed that Kerviel's knowledge of the back-end trading operations had allowed him to amass huge positions by intentionally bypassing internal risk controls. (Later, another rogue trader with back-office experience, Kweku Adoboli of UBS, would be arrested after causing $2.3 billion in losses using a similar scheme.)

Soo-jin knew that the reasons she was trapped in the middle office were somewhat legitimate, but they still didn't satisfy her. With her route out of risk management narrowing, Soo-jin had started applying to other jobs. She'd gone for informational interviews at Google and Charles Schwab, and had done a lot of hard thinking about industries other than finance that appealed to her.

At her college reunion that spring, she'd caught up with a number of her Wellesley friends, many of whom were working in politics, education, or the nonprofit sector. When she told them about her Deutsche Bank role, they nodded their vague approval but hadn't been able to say much else. They had no idea what a risk management analyst was, or how it differed from being a front-office trader with a big portfolio and a massive P&L. All they knew was that it was a Wall Street job, and that it was probably paying a lot more than their work.

But Soo-jin wasn't satisfied with making money or seeming important. She wanted to prove herself in a job that would allow her to interact with clients and do real, meaningful work. She wanted to show Deutsche Bank that she wasn't just content defending against risk and leverage. She wanted to play offense, too.

CHAPTER EIGHTEEN

THE LANKY, BROWN-HAIRED young man got off the plane at LaGuardia, heaved his bags into a yellow cab, cued up "Empire State of Mind" on his iPhone, and directed the driver into Manhattan. It was June 11, 2011, and small-town Wisconsinite Derrick Havens was New York City's newest resident.

Several weeks earlier, Derrick had left his job at Wells Fargo in Chicago, and accepted a job offer with a Manhattan-based private equity firm. The new firm, an arm of a larger investment management company that was headquartered in a lush sky-scraper on Park Avenue, had made him what seemed like a generous offer: a base salary of $80,000, with a bonus estimated at another $80,000, plus every cent of his moving costs to New York and his own expense account.

The offer came at the end of a rocky year for Derrick. He'd spent much of it trying to patch things up with Erica, his long-term girlfriend. They'd recovered from their massive fight during his first year of banking, after Derrick promised her he would do better at prioritizing their relationship over work, and after her college graduation, she'd moved into his Chicago apartment with him. But during Derrick's second year, the fights kept coming, and pretty soon Erica had seen enough. That spring, she dumped him, and moved out of the apartment they shared. Derrick was wrecked.

As a coping mechanism, Derrick worked himself like an ox. He used Adderall and Red Bull—his preferred office nourishments—to stay up all night doing deal work, sometimes multiple nights in a row. One week, he stayed at Wells Fargo's office from Sunday afternoon until late Thursday night—working 110 hours in a row, without setting foot outside the building. His stress boiled over late one night that year, when an associate came to his desk at 2:00 a.m. and tossed a pitch book at him.

"Fix this," he growled, then began walking away.

Derrick—who bristled at being condescended to, especially by an associate who was no more than five years older than him—freaked out. He stood up, picked up the pitch book, and threw it at the associate's feet.

"Jesus!" the associate said. "What the hell is wrong with you?"

Derrick leaned in, until their noses were almost touching, and said slowly and deliberately: "If you ever talk to me like that again, I'm going to break your fucking nose."

After returning triumphantly to his cubicle, Derrick's pride gave way to remorse. Threatening to punch an associate over a small mishap seemed completely absurd in hindsight. Who the hell was he pretending to be? How had he let two years of a stressful job turn him into Scarface?

In May, when the private equity offer came, Derrick realized that it was his chance to escape the Midwest and leave the job that seemed to be changing him for the worse. He didn't know anyone in New York, knew nothing of the city's neighborhoods or culture, and felt anxious about moving hundreds of miles away from his friends and family. But he needed a change, so he signed on the dotted line. He gave notice at Wells Fargo in late May, went home to Wisconsin to see his parents, and slept for thirty-six hours straight to make up some of the sleep deficit he had accumulated. Then he packed his bags and flew east.

Derrick took solace in the fact that his new job would be much less hierarchical than his old one. The private equity firm had only fifty total employees, and only eight other people at Derrick's level. That gave it a flat, intimate structure—and it meant fewer people who were able to boss him around.

For an analyst, the substance of the work in private equity is largely the same as in investment banking—making pitch books, building models, and valuing companies. But the goal is different. Derrick's firm used the money it managed for clients to buy not individual stocks and bonds, but entire companies. The classic private equity deal was a leveraged buyout, in which a firm borrowed millions or billions of dollars in order to acquire an entire company. Once it had acquired the company, the private equity firm's job was to make it more efficient and profitable, and either bring it public again or sell it to another company. The basic process was akin to trying to take the least popular girl in your high school class, give her a makeover and a new wardrobe, introduce her to the varsity quarterback, and get her voted prom queen. Sometimes it worked, and the private equity firms made a killing. Other times, it didn't work, and the private equity firms still generally made out fine, thanks to the up-front fees they took from clients whose money they managed. As business models go, it was one of the most ingenious ones on earth.

Derrick was unsure at times about whether private equity came by its fortunes honestly. He was often reminded of his mom's advice, years earlier, that money wasn't everything.

"I grew up in a small town where people work hard," he once said to me. "Sitting in an office in New York, pulling strings that affect so many people, it's just…I don't know, man. It just feels fundamentally unfair."

For the first three weeks of his New York life, Derrick spent most of his time trying to get settled in. He leased a walk-up apartment near Union Square, where his roommate, another recent college grad who was working as a paralegal, had a divider wall installed in their eighth-floor apartment, turning what had been a roomy one-bedroom into a diminutive two-bedroom. Derrick lived in the bigger of the two rooms, which had a large closet and a view out to Fourteenth Street. He had no furniture yet, except for an air mattress, which he would sleep on for the better part of a month.

But despite his spartan surroundings, he felt good. After years of dreaming about moving to the city, he was a real New Yorker now, and he wanted to experience everything the city had to offer. He wanted to stroll through Central Park, see concerts at Madison Square Garden, eat at Nobu and Per Se and get bottles at exclusive clubs like 1Oak. I saw a lot of Derrick that summer, and each time, he would relate another breathless story about one of his paradigm-shaking "only in New York" experiences.

"All the things I heard about this place are true," he told me. "Every time you walk down the street, you have the choice between looking at the most beautiful girl you've ever seen and the craziest thing you've ever seen."

Derrick knew that to many people, working on Wall Street looked about as morally defensible as being a drug lord. He knew he wouldn't be able to explain everything he saw in New York's financial industry to his family and friends back home without raising their hackles. And he felt nauseated every time he thought about his dad's grocery store chain back home, and imagined how much help was needed. But he consoled himself with the thought that New York was a stepping-stone. In the big city, Derrick would learn how to operate the levers of power and capital that drive the global markets. He would work hard, get valuable skills, and save up money. And then, when he was ready—after he had amassed the tools of the trade and a sizable nest egg, but before he had become a total creature of Wall Street—he would move back home to start the rest of his life.

A week before coming to New York, Derrick had taken several pieces of cheap furniture from his Chicago apartment—most of which were leftover futons and chairs from his college dorm—and burned them in the open field next to his house. At the time, it had seemed like innocuous trash disposal—he knew the furniture wouldn't survive the trip east, and nobody in Waupaca wanted it.

But now, Derrick let the obvious metaphor roll around in his head. Here he was, in New York City, at the center of the world, making more money than his parents, his college friends, and anyone he knew in his hometown. He was young, healthy, and gainfully employed at a reputable firm in a lucrative, prestigious industry. It was almost, he thought, like his past had gone up in smoke.

CHAPTER NINETEEN

IT BEGINS IN June—the lunch-line gossip, the frantic refreshing of message boards and tap-tapping of Bloomberg instant messages with friends across the Street, the amphetaminic all-nighters in a last-minute attempt to suck up to the boss. Every June, young Wall Street loads up like a spring, pregnant with anxiety and hope. And then, when the time is right, it simply happens—the annual earthquake known in the corporatized language of HR as the "compensation communication period," but referred to by everyone in finance by its real name: bonus day.

Every summer, young analysts at Wall Street firms are notified about the amount of their annual bonuses, and placed in top, middle, and bottom "buckets," according to their performances over the previous year. (The exception is Goldman Sachs, which gives its analyst bonuses in January.) Bonuses for analysts are nothing like the eight-figure executive bonuses you read about in newspapers, but they are still hefty sums for twenty-three-year-olds. A top-bucket first-year analyst at a profitable firm might make a $75,000 bonus on top of a $70,000 base salary, for total comp of $145,000. A bottom-bucket analyst at a struggling firm might get $10,000 on top of that same $70,000 salary, for a haul of only $80,000. Because bonuses often make up more than half of an analyst's yearly pay, and because in the process of getting these bonuses, analysts are ranked in relation to their peers, bonus season amounts to a combination of Christmas and Judgment Day. Analysts who land in the top bucket are often assured of a third-year offer; analysts who land near the bottom are often given a subtle hint to start looking for new work.

J. P. Murray, the churchgoing Haitian-American analyst from Philadelphia, was expecting a pretty good number. In the year since J. P. had joined Credit Suisse's health-care banking division, he had grown immensely as an analyst. Complex modeling skills were now second nature to him, and his industry knowledge ran deeply enough that other analysts and associates often came to him for help. Like everyone else in his position, J. P. spent between eighty and a hundred hours a week at his desk. But he'd made a conscious decision to fill the other, non-working hours of his weeks with the kind of lifestyle he'd never imagined getting to live—the kind of over-the-top, hyperactive life his favorite rappers talked about in their songs.

"On Wall Street, you can have two out of the three: a job, a social life, and sleep," he'd explained to me. "I'm picking the first two."

So on the rare nights he wasn't working, he hit the town. He went to birthday parties, house parties, clubs, nonprofit fund-raisers, networking events, gallery openings, and any other event with an open bar and a high likelihood of finding attractive women. J. P. felt, at times, like he was mastering both facets of young Wall Street life—working hard and playing hard. He wasn't getting much sleep, and he had been forced to deal with the same last-minute cancellations and late-night pitch book sessions as the other members of his group. But that was all part of being a Wall Street analyst, and J. P. was starting to consider himself a good one.

But on bonus day, when J. P. was called in to his managing director's office for his first year-end review, he got a shock.

"I'd like to talk to you about some things your colleagues and I have noticed about your work this year," the director said.

J. P. was used to criticism—he'd gotten plenty from senior bankers that year—but what spilled forth from the MD's mouth felt more like a pile-on than a constructive feedback session.

"You've done some excellent work this year, but I have some concerns. Some of your colleagues are very impressed with your work, but others have noticed that you can be inattentive to detail. Some praised you as thoughtful and diligent, but others are unsure whether you're committed to putting in the time necessary to make sure everything is right. One colleague wrote, 'J. P.'s pitch books are sometimes so messy that I often have to redo entire sections myself.' Others have talked about your attitude during stressful deals, which they say is often too unfocused."

J. P. was stunned. Why had nobody told him about these things earlier? And moreover, how were his colleagues' opinions of him so binary? How did some of them think he was a star, and others a schmuck? He didn't have any enemies at the bank, and he thought he'd done a fairly good job of ingratiating himself with the members of his group. Had he been fooled the entire time?

Then came the hammer.

"Your total comp is $90,000," the MD said.

J. P. knew that things had been rough at Credit Suisse. He'd read in the papers that profits were down, and that as a result bonuses probably would be, too. He'd heard through the grapevine that top first-years were being given roughly $50,000 bonuses, and most analysts were preparing themselves mentally for $35,000 or $40,000. But J. P.'s base salary was $70,000, meaning that his bonus was a mere $20,000. It could only mean one thing: he was in the bottom bucket.

The MD continued: "Based on this review, *obviously* we will not be in a position to offer you a third year with the group." She sat back in her chair, somehow affectless despite having just delivered a knockout punch to J. P.'s banking career. She gestured his way and asked, "So, what are your thoughts?" J. P. knew he was being tested on his positive attitude—which was, after all, one of the strongest points in his review, and an asset he could hang his hat on. But at the time, maintaining a poker face was proving to be a challenge. The only thing he could come up with was, "Well, it's not nothing."

After walking out of the MD's office, J. P.'s hard shell disintegrated, and he felt himself getting misty-eyed with rage. Had it meant nothing to Credit Suisse that he'd clawed his way to Wall Street from an underprivileged background as a Haitian immigrant's kid with no connections? Had it mattered that when he'd gotten to Credit Suisse, he'd done everything he could to promote the bank, up to and including volunteering to recruit college students? For fuck's sake, had it meant nothing that he'd missed his parents' anniversary, Mother's Day, the Fourth of July, and two months' worth of church Sundays, all for the sake of work that would probably never see the light of day? J. P. knew he wouldn't find much sympathy on Main Street, where being paid $90,000 as a twenty-four-year-old was still a tremendous accomplishment. But in the cloistered, rich-is-relative world of Wall Street, he'd just been dealt a cruel hand.

J. P. had no idea what he would do, now that Credit Suisse was saying it wouldn't hire him back for a third year. He hadn't planned on hunting for a job so soon after arriving, and he was unsure what his best options would be. He had chosen not to take part in the private equity recruiting process that spring, both because he considered it disloyal to Credit Suisse and because, deep down, he was counting on getting a third-year offer.

The fact that he would likely be unemployed in a year, no matter how hard he worked over the next 365 days, scared and confused him. After working so hard to get to Wall Street in the first place, he could barely believe his high-flying life was spiraling back to Earth.

CHAPTER TWENTY

At 8:00 A.M., Ricardo Hernandez and one of his fellow analysts got called into the corner office. There, their boss, a senior J.P. Morgan banker named William Bishop, sat waiting for them, stone-faced.

"I have a new project for you," Bishop told the pair.

The analysts looked at each other in fear. They had both stayed up most of the previous night, finishing a massive pitch book that had been given to them at the last minute. Both dreaded what they thought was about to be given to them: a new, equally draining project, right on the heels of the last.

Instead, Bishop pulled an envelope out of his jacket pocket and handed it to Ricardo. He looked down and saw what it was: two VIP tickets to that night's Jay Z concert.

"I appreciate what you guys did this week," Bishop said, a

smile spreading across his face. "Take the day off. Go have fun."

Ricardo laughed. He hadn't expected any perks out of J.P. Morgan, and these acts of random kindness still caught him off guard.

Things were going much better for Ricardo since his first year, when he'd worked endlessly in an M&A division that relied on pharmaceutical assistance to handle its massive deal load. As a second-year analyst, he had become better and more efficient at his job, and a new class of first-year analysts had come in to handle the worst of the grunt work. He no longer worked every weekend, and he often got out at a reasonable hour when he did. He moved out of Windsor Court, the "banker dorm" complex where he'd lived since the start of his analyst days, and into a one-bedroom apartment with his girlfriend. And he used his newfound free time to catch up with friends, play more rec-league basketball, and watch Spurs and Cowboys games at a bar in Murray Hill where Texas transplants gathered.

"I feel like I've gotten my life back," he told me.

The other part of his newfound happiness was that he'd been transferred out of the M&A group and into a small group of bankers who worked with the bank's clients in Latin American countries.

"Lat-Am," as the group was called, didn't sit quite as high on the investment banking totem pole as M&A. But it was a better fit for Ricardo. In Lat-Am, the hours were more relaxed, the pay was roughly comparable, and the travel opportunities were much better. Every few weeks, he and a higher-up would fly south to visit one of the bank's clients, and once in a while, he would be given a chance to make presentations by himself.

Ricardo had once insisted that he would leave J.P. Morgan after two years to go to business school, jump to a hedge fund, or quit the industry altogether. But now, with an assignment that was both more exciting and less strenuous than his old one, he could see himself building a career at the bank. There was nowhere better for him to go, at the moment, and he cringed at the thought of risking his stable, well-paid existence just for a slightly bigger paycheck at another firm.

Ricardo's satisfaction with his job provided a striking contrast to the depressed, disgruntled analysts I'd met in the course of my investigation. And watching him progress had given me a sense of how young financiers can eventually settle into stable, comfortable careers.

I'd spoken to a number of older financiers in the course of my fact-finding, and asked them how their lives had morphed as they'd made their way up the ladder. Some of them had kept their noses to the grindstone, worked hundred-hour weeks well into their thirties, and eschewed the pleasures of a normal life for a chance at rapid, lucrative career advancement. They jumped to the buy side when the time was right, or remained on the management track at their firms, and saw their income increase rapidly year after year. Others had stepped off the hedonic tread-mill, accepted the fact that they were likely never going to make it to the CEO's chair, and did the best they could to provide value to their firms in whatever roles they inhabited. This was a less sexy version of the finance path, but one that was becoming in-creasingly appealing as the financial sector struggled, and people attempted to mitigate their personal risks by staying put.

"It's not *Liar's Poker* anymore," one private equity worker told me. "Most people on Wall Street work hard, have a nice family, and are trying to put their kids through private school."

Ricardo didn't love the surges of adrenaline that coursed through the bullpen around the time of a big deal (in fact, they gave him stomachaches) but he liked the other things his job gave him: financial security, a prestigious résumé line, intellectual stimulation, smart young colleagues who shared his interests and were fun to be around. The monetary perks—a comfortable apartment, the ability to take a cab instead of the subway without guilt—were nice, too, but the crux of the finance sector's attraction was what would come in the future. He knew that the pressures of being young and servile would eventually ease up, and he'd be left with a secure career that would give him the time and disposable income to do the things he really cared about.

The mystique and hyperbole that surrounds Wall Street often clouds the fact that many people who work there aren't chasing after ever-bigger bonuses and piling leverage upon leverage. For a sizable number of people, working at an investment bank is a means to other, more boring personal ends. These people aren't (and shouldn't be) immune from criticism when banks screw up, since their willing participation enables a structure that can be mobilized in harmful ways. But they're rarely engaged with top-level strategy, and they hardly consider themselves fighters for a cause. For them, finance is a job, not a calling.

Banking hadn't been Ricardo's first career choice, nor did it represent his truest passions. And at times, he sometimes felt guilty about leaving medicine behind. But after seeing how much his job had given him, and how much he'd grown as a result of it, he knew he'd made the right call.

"A career is such a big, loaded word," he said one day, when I asked him how much longer he planned to stay at J.P. Morgan. "Ideally, you don't want to spend thirty or forty years doing the same thing. But…yeah, I'm happy here."

CHAPTER TWENTY-ONE

AFTER TALKING TO Ricardo about his satisfaction with his banking job, I started to worry again that my sources, aside from him, represented an overconflicted sample.

I knew there were hardcore, remorseless young financiers in the world—I'd met some of them at Wharton, and others at investment conferences and industry events. They were the kind of die-hards who had known their whole lives that Wall Street was their destination—who slept with a copy of Benjamin Graham's *The Intelligent Investor* under their pillows, tacked posters of Warren Buffett and George Soros on their walls, and spent their middle school days practicing their Excel shortcuts. These kids had no compunction about being on Wall Street, even in the post-crash era, and would defend the moral goodness of the financial industry to anyone who would listen.

I wanted to find these people. So I boarded an Acela train

and headed up to Cambridge, Massachusetts, to meet the members of Black Diamond Capital Investors.

Black Diamond is Harvard's most exclusive student-run hedge fund. Its thirty members, who are all Harvard undergraduates, each kick in at least $1,000 (and as much as $25,000) for the privilege of getting to invest alongside other committed finance nerds. This limits membership to students who can afford to part with a thousand dollars, of course, but it also means that, in the patois of investing, the students all have "skin in the game." Each member shares in the gains and losses of the fund, and their buy-in money (or what's left of it, anyway) is distributed back to them after graduation.

Black Diamond's founder, a Harvard junior named Patrick Colangelo, invited me to see the group's weekly Sunday afternoon meeting, where they talk about the global markets and come up with new investment ideas.

I found Patrick in a private dining room off the main cafeteria in Quincy House, sitting around a large table in front of a projection screen. He's a fresh-faced Canadian who plays on Harvard's club hockey team, helps run Harvard's undergraduate private equity club, sports a short haircut with a little ski-ramp flip in front, and was wearing a white Burberry shirt with slacks. Roughly twenty guys were gathered around a table with him—most in collared shirts, a few in blazers. There were no women. (One came in a few minutes into the meeting, looking for a water bottle she'd left there earlier in the day, realized she'd interrupted an all-boys meeting, blushed, and scurried back out.)

Patrick began the Black Diamond meeting with a discussion about what was going on in the news—a nascent recovery in the housing market, Congress's most recent budget talks, and the goings-on in Europe. Lots of people chimed in with observations about how these phenomena might affect the financial markets, and the unmistakable impression given off was that this is a serious group. These guys had opinions about austerity in Greece, the effects of expansionary monetary policy, and the Federal Reserve's forward guidance. They weren't the most brilliant market insights I've ever heard, but for guys who should by virtue of their stations in life be saying "bro" a lot and doing keg stands, they weren't half bad.

Despite their ages, most of the members of Black Diamond are somewhat experienced investors. There's Bryce, a sophomore from Southern California who ordered his first annual report at age thirteen, began investing shortly thereafter, and at sixteen was the youngest-ever person to apply for a job at PIMCO, the giant California-based investment manager. (PIMCO's recruiter was impressed at his ambition, but told him to come back when he had a college degree.) There's Arash, a senior who interned at a hedge fund the previous summer, and is slated to work at another large fund after he graduates. And there's Christian, a freshman who managed a six-figure chunk of his family's money while still in high school.

After some more macroeconomic pondering, Patrick pulled up a chart on the screen and asked the group, "So, what should our market exposure be?"

The group decided it wanted to identify some good shorts—stocks it could bet against. Patrick proposed shorting the stock of a large oil company, pulling up a chart that shows, according to him, that the price of oil has been propped up by a relatively weak dollar and is overdue for a fall. Bryce disagreed.

He's the group's de facto risk management expert, and he spent a good chunk of the meeting pouring water on other members' overly aggressive ideas.

No actual trades are made at these meetings. Black Diamond's members have a secure e-mail listserv to hold their trading ideas, and each member who wants to propose a trade has to write up a short summary explaining the size of the trade, what risks it represents, and how much money he thinks should be put into it. Then, if a majority votes for the trade, Patrick plugs the details into an online brokerage account that holds the group's money and executes. Patrick wouldn't say how much money this strategy has made the group, but he did tell me that they haven't lost money—which is more than many professionally run hedge funds can say.

Despite some minor disagreements, there was no yelling or table pounding at the Black Diamond meeting. In fact, the whole thing felt more like an international relations seminar than a hedge fund meeting.

"Why would we run to metals if the economy is improving?" Bryce said at one point, after Patrick suggested investing in platinum to take advantage of low prices. "Does anyone think the economy isn't improving?"

Later in the meeting, the group video-chatted with a hedge fund trader from San Francisco, a Harvard Business School graduate who serves as an informal advisor to the group. The trader dispensed a few nuggets of wisdom about how to assess risk—figuring out, for example, which assumptions are already factored into the price of a given company's stock, and what you expect to behave differently about the company than the market does. It was solid advice, but the students around the table were bored and browsing Facebook on their laptops the entire time. They'd heard it all before.

People perked back up when the regular investment meeting resumed. The guys began discussing ways to invest in graphene—a new-ish industrial material that is made of a single layer of carbon atoms and is supposed to be three hundred times stronger than steel. They ran through a few more stock ideas— Microsoft, Apple, Nokia, and a clean energy company—before letting out for the day.

Later that night, I went with Patrick, Bryce, Arash, and several other Black Diamond members to dinner at a restaurant down the block. We munched on a hummus plate, and they sipped on wine and whiskey drinks, as I asked them why they were spending their college days staring at stock charts and discussing macroeconomics.

"This isn't something you do as a club," Patrick said. "It's a serious endeavor."

The members of Black Diamond—who are mostly economics concentrators, with a smattering of classics and history students—are eager to distance themselves from the other finance clubs on campus, all of which they believe are more focused on educating neophytes than actually getting down and dirty with real-money trades.

"There are other clubs," Arash said, "and you go there and you just stay for maybe forty minutes, and usually you don't even grasp the material because it goes by so fast. But here, you have guys with commonality; everyone is going into finance, everyone has a background in finance, everyone is interested in making profits. And more importantly, everyone has a personal investment in it."

Nor do they concern themselves with the softer side of finance. Most of them want to work in private equity or at a hedge fund right away after graduation, and when I asked why they'd prefer skipping over the typical stepping-stone bank job at a place like Goldman Sachs or J.P. Morgan, Bryce said, "I was reading something the other day about how in the eighties, Goldman Sachs was very much an aggressive place to work, but now Goldman is becoming this, like, social investing place that gives money to small business and nonprofits and stuff, and it takes me away from wanting to go there."

"Why?" I asked.

"Because Wall Street is about making money," he said.

"Yeah," Arash concurred. "Nobody goes into finance to do charity."

So, if you want to know what kind of overachiever goes to Harvard and joins a student-run hedge fund, there's your answer: a person who is turned off by Goldman Sachs because it's *too charitable.*

It's tempting to accuse Patrick and his fellow hedgies-in-training of being crafted from the same mold as the financiers who plunged the financial system into chaos in 2008. They are, after all, utterly unconcerned with the social vectors involved in working on Wall Street. They don't spend much time thinking about who's on the other side of a profitable trade, or who loses when a Wall Street bank makes money from a complex mortgage-backed security that goes sour.

Still, one observed fact keeps me from total cynicism: namely, investing seems to be these guys' honest-to-God passion. These are young people who obsess over 10-K financial statements like most teenagers obsess over video games, who spend their free time studying the Japanese "lost decade" of the 1990s instead of playing intramural soccer. They're not interested in finance as a culture or a social institution, and money is only important insofar as it serves as a rough proxy for success. At one point during dinner, I took a straw poll to find out who would still want to work on Wall Street if it paid the same as being a lawyer or an accountant. All of them raised their hands.

"I would do it if it paid $100 a week," Bryce said. "This is my social life—I sit in front of a computer and look up stocks."

"My buddies spend time on Facebook when they're wasting time in their rooms," Christian added. "I'll take out my mobile *Barron's* instead."

Maybe none of Black Diamond's genuine enthusiasm redeems the snobbishness of their endeavor, their $1,000 buy-in and their boys'-club elitism. Maybe the desire to make money trading stocks and other financial products, even if it's come by honestly, can't help but metamorphose into something more dangerous later on.

But I find something oddly endearing, and slightly exculpatory, about their dorkishness. They get the same rush from a well-executed trade that a writer finds in a well-turned paragraph—not because there's money in it, necessarily, but because it takes technical skill and some measure of creative thinking to pull off.

So maybe there's a fourth cohort of people to add to those who tend to enjoy being young on Wall Street: the Habituals, the Locomotives, the Gunners, and the Geeks, who are honestly fascinated by the machinations of the global markets, who delight in bond prospectuses and get lost daydreaming about collar trades. And if that's true—if the members of Black

Diamond are genuinely interested in finance qua finance—it would seem to make their Wall Street trajectories a bit more honest than the one taken by many of their classmates, the path that starts with private nursery schools and ends at Goldman Sachs because they're addicted to status and structure.

I asked the guys at Black Diamond about the difference between them and their Johnny-come-lately classmates, who enter the industry with a completely different set of priorities, often planning to stay only for two years before departing for industries that better represent their values and ambitions. They agreed that many of the Harvard seniors who go into the financial industry aren't motivated by the right things. Given the way Harvard's student body loves to sneer at the financial sector, they added, it was amusing to watch the ideological evolution of Harvard students as graduation approached.

Patrick chuckled. "Yeah," he said. "Everyone here hates Wall Street until spring of their junior year."

CHAPTER TWENTY-TWO

"A SIX-INCH TURKEY on wheat, please, and could you cut it in half?" Samson White asked the Subway sandwich artist.

Samson, who had just started his second year as a Goldman Sachs mortgage analyst, was watching his calories, and he planned to eat only three of the six inches now, and save the rest for his next meal. He'd been forced to adopt a hardcore diet by a bet he'd made with two of his Goldman colleagues back in June about who could lose the most weight before Labor Day. Samson, who had started the contest at 226 pounds, was supposed to get down to 200; if he didn't, and the others reached their goal weights, he would have to buy each of the winners a round-trip plane ticket to any destination in the world. To avoid having to pay up, Samson had been working out like a fiend, logging five or six miles a day on the treadmills in Goldman's gym. He'd already lost about fifteen pounds, and was on pace to reach his goal and win the bet.

It helped that Goldman, like many Wall Street firms, gets relatively sleepy in the summer, as executives escape to their homes in the Hamptons and the capital markets slow to a crawl. That summer, there was some economic activity—mainly, a brewing calamity in Europe, where the European Union was threatening to fall apart and bailout talks for struggling countries were in a perpetual state of flux. But unless you were an interest rate trader or dealt with European clients, there wasn't a ton of work to go around.

When not doing cardio workouts, Samson spent much of his summer thinking about his next move. He was still disenchanted with Goldman, and still not sure he would stay on for a third year after his second was up. The countdown clock on his bedroom wall had dipped into the two-hundred-day range, and Samson often considered whether, when it struck zero, he might actually pull the trigger and quit, even if he didn't have a backup plan. He hated most of his colleagues—found them dull, petty, and frustrating to be around—and he'd long ago lost the desire for becoming a Goldman lifer. But the thought of leaving the well-paying womb of "Mama Goldman," as some employees called it, still made him queasy.

Recently, another second-year analyst named Colin had begun asking Samson if he'd ever want to launch a tech start-up together. Colin was an incurable hustler, and he often came by Samson's desk to pitch him on his latest half-baked business idea. But Colin's latest idea had become an obsession. It was a mobile app that would do secondary-market ticket sales for concerts, sports games, festivals, and other events. He had done some research into the ticket industry and thought that there was a lot of money to be made by undercutting giants like

StubHub on fees and offering a better mobile purchasing experience.

Samson laughed at most of Colin's business plans, but the more he thought about the ticketing app, the more he thought it sounded brilliant. He often read tech blogs, and he was curious about what it would be like to try starting a company. He liked the idea of taking a chance on an unproven idea and the romanticism of betting the farm. Building a start-up would allow him to put his financial skills to a use that didn't involve padding Goldman's bottom line. It would get him away from his bosses and colleagues, who were making life increasingly unbearable. And maybe, for once, it would let him feel good about his work.

*   *   *

While Samson was contemplating a career switch, Jeremy was sunning himself in the Hamptons.

Jeremy had gone in with more than a dozen other first- and second-year Goldman analysts on a house share in Westhampton, a tony beachside enclave roughly two hours from the city. Every Friday, the young Goldmanites and their friends and significant others would pile onto the Long Island Railroad or the Hampton Jitney and head to the beach, where they would swim and drink by day and head to clubs by night, before coming back to sleep on floors, couches, and air mattresses sprinkled throughout the four-bedroom house. Packing dozens of people into a relatively modest house wasn't the over-the-top experience many older and richer Hamptons summer home owners had, but it kept their costs down to just over $1,500 a person for the whole summer, and it allowed them to invite their friends to "my Hamptons house," which was half the fun.

Jeremy loved his weekends in Westhampton. He could drink on the deck, overlooking the bay, or play pickup basketball in the driveway, all while surrounded by his favorite classmates. And to top it all off, he'd met someone. She was a Morgan Stanley analyst who had come out to the Hamptons with a Goldman friend one weekend, and the two of them had hit it off. They'd gone to a venue called the Southampton Social Club together, listened to an eighties cover band, hooked up afterward, and spent the entire weekend by each other's sides. (Eventually, they began dating, and stayed together for the next year and a half.)

Jeremy welcomed the distraction from work. He'd never truly forgiven his most antagonistic boss, Penelope—the one who resembled Julia Roberts in looks and Genghis Khan in personality—for making his life miserable that spring. But he'd spent more time working for her on several subsequent assignments, and as he saw her work, he came to a realization that made him feel less hostile toward her: she was deeply insecure.

Sure, Penelope was a great self-promoter, and she'd assembled an all-star book of clients that included some of the biggest hedge funds and pension funds in the world. Some high-ranking people at Goldman thought she was indispensable. But Jeremy saw something poking through her resilient exterior: fear. He saw that after the financial crisis, Penelope, just like him, just like Samson, just like everyone at Goldman Sachs, was concerned first and foremost about protecting herself.

At the height of his anger that spring, Jeremy's behavior toward Penelope had bordered on sabotage. He would shuffle his feet on projects to create more work for her, and speak to clients he knew she was fiercely protective over. Once, after she ordered him to go to the lobby to pick up a pizza she'd ordered for the group, Jeremy gave the delivery guy a $30 tip on a bill of $20, and charged the entire $50 to Penelope's personal credit card. But the realization that she was being cruel because she herself was scared of failure had softened Jeremy's antipathy.

Jeremy and I saw each other several times that summer, and each time, Penelope was the primary topic of conversation.

"Do I really want to be sitting around for three or four more years doing Penelope's bitch work?" he asked me during one chat.

Jeremy had by that point begun thinking about what to do the following January, when his second bonus hit. He knew he would have options—coming from Goldman, you always did—but he didn't want to take just any other job. He wanted something that would be entrepreneurial, that would allow him to take the things he loved about his Goldman job—selling, solving problems, working with large companies—and transport them to a new, more humane endeavor.

In late summer, Jeremy and Samson came up with a plan to try to piece together some of the fragments that had shattered during their individual existential crises, and get some guidance on what to do next. The plan involved hallucinogenic mushrooms.

Jeremy had done shrooms once in college, but Samson had never touched any drug harder than marijuana. Jeremy assured him that it was a gentle experience, and Samson agreed to give it a try. So, on a Saturday morning, they convened at

Jeremy's apartment, made two peanut-butter-and-mushroom sandwiches, and went to Central Park to spend the day tripping.

For the next six or seven hours, Jeremy and Samson lay in the grass, contemplating their lives and the world around them. Samson, who was having his first-ever hallucination, spent much of the morning watching ants move on the ground and thinking about the complexities of life as an insect. What were bug societies like? Did they feel happiness and sadness? How did they pick their leaders?

After Samson's bug-watching session was over, he and Jeremy returned to more familiar topics: money and capitalism. Their conversation wandered to the observation that money was a unit of account for your labor, and nothing else. It had no inherent value apart from the work that you did, and it meant nothing more than that you had performed some kind of work in order to get it. (They later assured me that these points sound more incisive if you're on shrooms.) They also discussed the limits of capitalistic thought, and the need for mindfulness in a busy and transactional world.

"I feel like people in New York don't know how to relax and just *be*," Jeremy said.

"Yeah," Samson concurred. "People here always have to be doing something or going somewhere. Like, just *be*."

Near the end of their day, while still lying in the grass, and periodically marveling at the shapes of the clouds overhead, Samson and Jeremy began discussing work.

"Dude," Jeremy said abruptly. "Are we crazy to think there are better things we can be doing with our lives than Goldman?"

Samson laughed. "Yeah, we're crazy, but *everybody's* crazy. We're all just hiding it."

The trip wasn't exactly *Easy Rider*, and it didn't soothe anybody's nerves. Even in the fog of hallucination, it seemed, neither Samson nor Jeremy had been able to escape Wall Street and the obsessions it wrought.

CHAPTER TWENTY-THREE

CHELSEA BALL, the freckle-faced Bank of America Merrill Lynch analyst, looked down at her hands, which had been taped by her coach an hour earlier. She glanced out at the dingy floor of the boxing gym, where several of her friends were drunkenly cheering her on. She looked at her opponent, a tall brunette in the red corner. She felt her head spin.

Chelsea had never boxed in a real match before. But recently, as her job had slowed down, a colleague had convinced her to take up the sport. She joined a gym, signed up for her first fight, and started training with an old legend of the New York amateur boxing scene. Her coach gave her a nickname—"Wrecking Ball," a play on her last name—and began getting her ready for the fight.

The regimen had been brutal. She'd had to lose about ten pounds to make weight, and spent the days leading up to her debut running in her sweatsuit and consuming nothing but pop-corn and water. As a result, she was beyond tired when it came time for her match, and she didn't know if she could stay standing through all four of the allotted two-minute rounds. But she was determined to put up a good fight, if only to notch one small victory in a year that was shaping up to be the worst of her life.

In March, she'd broken up with Anton, her long-term boyfriend from Georgetown. She'd decided she could no longer swing the monthly trips to D.C. to see him, and as she spent more time in New York, she began to yearn for singledom again. The breaking point had come during a night at the Patriot Saloon, when Chelsea began flirting with a guy in a blue button-down shirt. He bought her drinks, they danced together all night, and she felt, for the first time in many months, real attraction. Nothing physical ended up happening, but the sensation was enough to signify to Chelsea that her relationship with Anton was no longer working. She'd called him the next day to deliver the bad news.

With the burden of a long-distance relationship off her shoulders, Chelsea poured herself into her work on the muni bond desk at Bank of America Merrill Lynch. But that, too, was largely a disaster.

Ralph, her boss, who was known by Chelsea and her fellow analysts as "the Mad Hatter," was still an odd, tumultuous manager. He had overseen several recent projects of Chelsea's, and each time, he made it clear that he was more interested in protecting his job and his turf than producing actual results. He also had a bad habit of assigning Chelsea multiple small projects, then demanding that she take care of them all immediately.

"Ralph, I can't do all three of these things at once," she'd told

him once, after he'd assigned her yet another stack of tasks at
8:00 p.m., on his way out the door. "You can yell at me if you
want to, but if you realistically want me to accomplish one of
these three things, I can't do it like this."

That was the most confrontational Chelsea ever got at work.
Most times, she simply let out her aggression after work at the
boxing gym, imagining that the speed bag she was punching
was Ralph's head.

Chelsea got her first bonus that summer. She knew it would
be bad, since Bank of America Merrill Lynch had struggled
that year (and every year since the crisis), and since Ralph
had conducted her review. And while she considered herself a
decent analyst, she knew there were many analysts who were
smarter than she was, for whom Excel models and swaps cal-
culations came more easily. So she wasn't totally surprised
when she landed in the bottom bucket, with a bonus of
$25,000—bringing her yearly compensation to $95,000.

A disappointing bonus wasn't unexpected, but it was annoying. She knew Ralph considered her a sloppy worker, but she
also knew that he was no stickler for details himself. She had
hoped that someone further up the chain would recognize
the impossible situation she was in and decide to give her a
break. But with no such break forthcoming, Chelsea had simply shrugged it off and put her head back down on her projects.

She had been thinking, even before her bonus hit, about
leaving the bank after her second year. She hated working under Ralph, and her lofty idealism about the work she was doing
had dissipated into a mass of frustrations with the minutiae of
individual projects. The slow municipal bond markets meant
that she had gone to fewer client meetings recently, and with-

out the regular reminders of who was on the other side of the bank's transactions, she found it hard to conceive of these deals as ones involving real people, with real-world consequences.

Chelsea's dilemma was common among the Wall Street analysts I spoke to. Despite Wall Street's reputation for craven profit seeking, many of them had come into finance with high-minded aspirations of making the world a better place. Much of their eagerness was a product of the recruiting pitches of Wall Street banks, which often played up their philanthropic and community service work in an effort to assuage the consciences of college students with moral reservations. But once they got to Wall Street and began working, that do-gooder façade often melted away, revealing the moral vacuum underneath.

It wasn't that working on Wall Street was inherently immoral. For most analysts, it was exceedingly rare to be asked to rip off a client, or concoct a bald-faced lie about a deal. What Wall Street was, I heard over and over again, was completely amoral. It had no regard for whether a given deal represented a net good or a net loss for humanity. All that mattered was the revenue. If a bank could make ten billion dollars by spreading malaria vaccines throughout Africa, it would do it in a heartbeat. And if a bank could make ten billion dollars by spreading malaria itself? Well, the idea might at least be floated.

Chelsea had gotten jaded about the morality of finance early in her career, when Bank of America took a number of its summer interns to a community service day at a local school. The group was tasked with doing some basic landscaping—pulling weeds, planting trees, arranging soil beds. It was an easy enough assignment, but Chelsea found, to her amazement, that no other interns were willing to lift a finger to help.

"I have never seen more people disgusted to get their hands dirty in my entire life," she told me. "There were like two hundred kids just standing there, looking at their BlackBerrys and being like, 'I really want to get back to the office.' I was like, 'Are you guys kidding me? Is this a joke? You're out in the sun, doing something good for the community, and all you guys want to do is go back and sit at your desks?'"

That narrow-mindedness turned Chelsea off most of the people she knew at her bank, and made her hesitate before recommending investment banking to people a year or two below her in school. To her, the great tragedy of Wall Street wasn't that it was evil and greedy, but that it was fundamentally boring, a place populated by the kinds of uncurious corporate drones who had no lives outside of work, who watched CNBC out of personal interest and considered Berkshire Hathaway's annual investor letter the ne plus ultra of high literature. It was those people—and not insider-trading felons, book-cooking CEOs, or sneering plutocrats—who made her want to run screaming from the finance world.

Whenever Chelsea contemplated building a career at Bank of America Merrill Lynch, she thought about Wendy, a vice president in her group. Wendy was a notorious workhorse, and she routinely pulled hundred-hour weeks, which was typical for a first-year analyst but unheard-of for someone who, like her, was in her mid-thirties, with a husband and a toddler, and who commuted from the New Jersey suburbs every day. Wendy's work ethic had become a concern during her pregnancy, when she insisted on staying at the office past midnight even during her third trimester. At one point, Ralph had even stepped in, ordering her to leave at 7:00 p.m. every night. Wendy had grudgingly complied, and had her baby several weeks later. But after a three-week maternity leave, she came back and hadn't let her foot off the gas since.

Chelsea admired Wendy's work ethic, and her refusal to be put on the "mommy track" after her pregnancy. But every time she thought about following in her footsteps, she recoiled. A life spent in constant go mode, and a career that consisted of subordinating her every worldly desire to other people—to *these people*, no less—was not what she wanted.

Later that summer, I met Chelsea and several other analysts in her group at a bar in Murray Hill. It was pub quiz night, but none of them wanted to play. They were all more interested in gossiping about their third-year plans. Chelsea's best friend at work, who worked in a related fixed-income group, said she'd be making at least $150,000, including her bonus, if she stayed for a third year. Another fixed-income analyst said he was going to try and re-up for a third year as well. But Chelsea, who rested her chin in her hand on the bar, couldn't muster any enthusiasm at all.

"I don't mean to act like a rebel," she said, "but I don't want to stay."

The other analysts looked at her curiously.

"I know I sound like an asshole," she continued. "I just really don't want to be here."

That disenchantment stayed with Chelsea as she got her subpar bonus, and—in an attempt to find some other sources of happiness—took up boxing. She'd poured every emotion she had into her training, and more than once left a workout in tears, having spent the previous two hours channeling her deepest frustrations and feelings of inadequacy into punching as hard as she could.

Now, in the ring for her first match, she was trying to drown out her work-related anxiety and focus only on the brunette in the opposite corner. The bell sounded, the referee signaled the start of the match, and Chelsea felt herself snap into focus.

During the first two rounds, the brunette got in some good blows. Chelsea was nervous, and it showed—she danced around, avoiding her opponent's jabs and not landing many of her own. But in rounds three and four, she finally gained her footing and began to let loose. She got in some solid body shots, avoided the brunette's big swings, and, in the fourth round, landed an uppercut that nearly broke the opponent's nose. At the end of the fourth round, the fight went to a decision, and the referee decided in Chelsea's favor by a handy margin.

Chelsea's friends in the crowd roared. They chanted her nickname—"Wreck-ing Ball! Wreck-ing Ball!"—over and over again, as the referee raised her hand in victory. After the match, they took her to a local bar, where they bought her tequila shots and toasted her success.

The next day, after eating a huge meal and sleeping off her hangover, Chelsea looked for a place to put her first-ever boxing trophy. It was roughly three feet tall, and it would dominate her sparsely decorated bedroom. But Chelsea didn't care. She hoisted it up, placed it on her bedside table, and smiled. *I still have value*, she thought. *I'm still good at something.*

CHAPTER TWENTY-FOUR

IN THE FALL, the e-mails began arriving in young bank analysts' inboxes. Most read something like this:

> Hi, my name is John. I work on Facebook's finance team, and I'll be in town next week to host an informal get-together for banking analysts who might be interested in coming to work with us. I'll be at the Ace Hotel from 7 to 10 p.m., and you're welcome to stop by if you're curious to hear more about what we're doing. No reservation required.

In 2011, as Wall Street banks were still struggling to turn profits in the post-crisis era, they had a new stealth threat passing right under their noses: Silicon Valley tech companies, who were staging a massive land grab for their junior analysts. Typically, tech firms compiled lists of analysts at Goldman Sachs, Morgan

Stanley, and other top firms and blasted out messages to large
groups of analysts at once, inviting them for a drink and a sales
pitch. Those pitches proved to be catnip to disgruntled spreadsheet jockeys.

"I just e-mailed a bunch of people at Wall Street firms and
said, 'I'll have a table at such-and-such restaurant, come out,'"
one surprised tech executive told me. "And I got like fifty people."

The timing of Silicon Valley's siren song to Wall Street's
young workers couldn't have been better for the tech industry,
or worse for the banks. In late 2011, the technology sector
was the hottest thing going. Facebook was preparing to go
public the following year, at a valuation that many people expected could reach $100 billion. Apple had become the biggest
consumer-facing company in the world, and venture capitalists
were throwing money wantonly at brand-new tech start-ups, in
a manner reminiscent of the dot-com boom of 1999 and 2000.
The tech industry was also riding a wave of popular interest
that had climaxed the year before with the release of *The Social
Network*, the Aaron Sorkin–written film about the creation of
Facebook.

"I've heard people say *The Social Network* is the *Wall Street*
of this generation," Evan Korth, an NYU computer science professor, told the *Wall Street Journal*.

Meanwhile, Wall Street banks were the opposite of sexy.
They were laying off thousands of people, cutting back on
salaries and bonuses, and nixing recruiting events for college
students. And they were still unpopular as a result of the crisis.
A 2011 survey conducted by the consulting firm Universum
ranked Google, Apple, and Facebook as the most coveted work-

places in America among young professionals; JPMorgan Chase, the highest-ranking Wall Street bank on the survey, was forty-first.

Given the choice between crunching Excel spreadsheets at a bank in a shrinking and reviled industry and working at a beloved tech company where they could wear jeans to work, get perks like free catered lunch and massages at work, and live on a much less demanding schedule while still making lucrative wages, many bank analysts were finding the balance tipping in Silicon Valley's favor.

"The new status jobs aren't at Goldman Sachs," one bank analyst, who was himself considering making the jump to tech, told me.

For Wall Street analysts, the tech world seemed to represent everything finance wasn't. Tech companies appeared democratic, nonhierarchical, and unconcerned with appearances. Many of them brought new concepts and companies into existence, rather than simply serving as financial intermediaries. They were places where a talented twenty-three-year-old could make a real impact, rather than just doing rote repetition of the same ten financial exercises. And, more important, they were growing rapidly, even in New York, meaning that some finance refugees wouldn't even have to move to the West Coast. Between 2007 and 2012, the number of jobs in New York City's tech industry grew by 29 percent, according to the state's Department of Labor, whereas the number of city jobs in the securities industry fell by 6 percent.

Finance workers have a lot to offer tech companies—bankers and traders can provide sorely needed financial skills, and quants are generally highly advanced technical engineers. Hav-

ing been trained in a hard-driving, details-obsessed bank culture doesn't hurt, either.

"They're insecure, they're risk averse, and they're afraid," the
tech executive said of young people on Wall Street. "But they
have the work ethic, and they're smart as hell. If you can peel
them away, they can be rock stars."

Several months earlier, I'd gone up to Cambridge to visit
Harvard Business School. I'd gone because historically, business school has been one of the typical next steps for bright
young investment banking analysts who have successfully made
the jump to the buy side. And among MBA programs, Harvard
is a financier's paradise. For decades, it has trained the very best
of Wall Street's elite, giving them a two-year respite from their
work and teaching them the skills they need to reenter the finance world on the management track.

I arrived at HBS expecting to find a tableau straight out of
a late-capitalist dystopian novel—a bunch of corporate drones
in suits, all preparing for their interviews at Blackstone and
KKR. Instead, I found a campus that had been bitten by the
tech bug. Many of the students I spoke to pitched me on their
start-ups, or told me that I should come back for the annual
HBS business plan contest, in which students compete every
spring for $50,000 in start-up cash by devising models for new
businesses.

Their excitement over tech's rise extended into the classroom. One class I visited, a course on entrepreneurship geared
toward second-year students, was so packed that students were
sitting in the aisles of the lecture hall.

"There was probably a time when the smartest people here
all went into finance or consulting," one HBS student who had

formerly worked in private equity told me. "It's pretty scattered now, and most folks appreciate and respect people who take risk."

Partly, the shift away from finance on campus was a reflection of a deliberate policy change. Nitin Nohria, who was named HBS's dean in 2010, made a conscious effort to make the school more than a pass-through for Wall Streeters. He oversaw the growth of a voluntary pledge called the "MBA Oath," signed by more than half of HBS's students in its first year, that asked students to aver that they would "serve the greater good" after graduation. Dean Nohria's efforts to unhook HBS from the financial sector were visible in admissions, too. In 2009, 20 percent of the incoming class had come directly from the financial services industry. By 2011, that number had slipped to 12 percent.

There was also a psychological sea change among young business students who increasingly saw growth and possibility when they looked at Silicon Valley, and regulation-choked stagnation when they looked at Wall Street. Noam Wasserman, an HBS professor who taught the entrepreneurship class I visited, sat down with me in his office and told me how massive the recent shift in interest into tech and entrepreneurship had been.

"When I was a student here fifteen years ago, there was no entrepreneurship unit. Now, there is one, and it has thirty-five professors," he said. "This whole building is devoted to entrepreneurship, in fact. It's the second largest unit on campus after the finance unit."

Wasserman, a smiley, excitable guy with a neat side part in his hair, explained that much of his work now involves convincing gung-ho HBS students that starting a company isn't as easy as it sounds, and warning them of the pitfalls they might face along the way. He said that while many of his students are already convinced of entrepreneurship's merits, others—especially those who have come from the financial services sector and have the choice to go back after school—need to be reassured that they can become entrepreneurs without giving up all hope of financial stability.

"If they're still thinking about going to a big company after school," Wasserman says, "they have to ask themselves, 'How can I avoid the golden handcuffs that working for a consulting firm or an investment bank is going to impose?'"

Going into tech isn't charity work, of course, and it's possible that certain pockets of the tech world are every bit as materialistic as Wall Street firms. Midlevel workers at large technology companies often earn six-figure salaries, and people who start their own companies or join early-stage start-ups can become phenomenally wealthy—a possibility that surely hadn't escaped HBS students or restless analysts on Wall Street. At large tech companies, like Google and Facebook, there is also the added stability of being part of a corporation with a clearly defined culture, which can ease the transition from finance.

But when the young bankers I knew spoke about their desire to work in a different industry, money and stability weren't usually their focal points. They expressed the very concerns Wasserman talked about—the fear that staying in banking would make them lifers, and entrap them financially in jobs that weren't fulfilling. And they wanted to do something involving real risk—not the indirect risk that most people on Wall Street take by betting with other people's money.

"The people who do shit in the world," Derrick Havens, the Wisconsin-born private equity analyst, once told me over a drink, "those people—Zuckerberg, Steve Jobs, the guy who built Instagram—they're not sitting there taking orders from someone who's incrementally more experienced than them, at a company where they won't have any actual power until they're thirty-five or forty. They're doing their own thing."

I often wondered if Wall Street analysts looking enviously at the tech world knew how unrealistic the popular imagery of Silicon Valley's happy-go-lucky start-ups was. It's an old Valley truism that three-quarters of technology start-ups fail, and even the ones that manage to be successful require an enormous amount of very intense and largely self-directed work. Working at a Google or a Facebook, while safer, isn't necessarily a ticket to freewheeling happiness, either, given the extent to which large tech companies have become corporatized and highly structured. And many of the traits that made a good banking analyst had little correlation with the skills required to succeed in tech.

Still, the rise of the tech industry and concurrent decline of the financial sector had given young people trapped in finance jobs an alternative path to visualize—one that also held the potential of vast riches, and was also filled with bright young people with fancy degrees, yet had an aura of novelty and innovation to it. For the first time since the initial dot-com boom, another industry was Wall Street's equal in the imaginations of talented young people.

Of course, if the financial sector recovers fully, and the second tech bubble ends the way the first did—with the corpses of failed and bankrupt companies littered all over Silicon

Valley—Wall Street may look appealing once again. But if tech companies can keep up their recruiting efforts and their stock prices, the youth of Wall Street will keep finding themselves tempted to leave an industry whose best days may be behind it for one whose greatest hopes lie in the future.

CHAPTER TWENTY-FIVE

IN LATE SEPTEMBER, while on his way to a dinner downtown, Ricardo Hernandez saw something that startled him: several hundred protesters gathered in a public park, chanting about Wall Street greed.

Ricardo, the Cornell grad from Texas who worked in J.P. Morgan's Lat-Am banking group, had heard rumblings of an antibank demonstration, called Occupy Wall Street, for several days. It had made the national news the day before, when there had been a large march through the streets of Lower Manhattan that resulted in the arrest of at least eighty protesters. But Ricardo had been too busy at work to pay close attention, and he assumed it was one of those quick-to-fizzle protests that periodically happened after the crash—the ones where burned-out hippies and libertarian types marched down Wall Street, toting "End the Fed" and "Where's Our Bailout?" signs and shouting incoherencies. He'd seen several of those scuffles, and they usually lasted a few hours, tops, before everyone dispersed and the ruckus died down.

But Occupy Wall Street was shaping up to be bigger and more permanent than anything he'd seen before. In the park, Ricardo saw tents, sleeping bags, and structures for specific communal use, including dedicated spaces marked as a kitchen and library. A drum circle played on the north side of the park, and signs littered the park benches, with messages like "Power to the People!" and "Banks got bailed out—we got sold out!" It looked more like a miniature civilization than a protest.

Over the next few months, of course, Occupy Wall Street would grow from a park gathering into a global protest movement whose reach extended far beyond New York. Within a month, the Zuccotti Park protest had spawned satellite protests in every major American metropolis, and international cities as far-flung as Sydney, Tokyo, and Davos, Switzerland. Occupy's galvanizing slogan—"We are the 99 percent"—became an international cultural meme, and for weeks, the movement garnered front-page news coverage and made Wall Street bankers very nervous.

"I just hope they don't bomb us," one Goldman Sachs analyst told me, half-seriously. "We're the easiest target, if you think about it."

Many of the older, senior-level financiers I spoke to in the following weeks either ignored Occupy, pooh-poohed its aims as too unspecific and vague, or dismissed it as a group of drug-addled dropouts and vagrants who had nothing better to do with their time. They saw that Occupy was gaining steam and attention, but they generally dismissed the idea that it would result in any actual change. How could it? It didn't even have a mission or a concrete list of demands. To most of the logical, action-oriented people I came across who had spent years or decades on the inside of the financial sector, a leaderless, consensus-governed protest with a vague and disparate anticorporate mission sounded like vitriolic gobbledygook. (The exceptions were people like Vikram Pandit, the then-CEO of Citigroup, who called the movement's anger "completely understandable." Later, JPMorgan Chase CEO Jamie Dimon would say that the movement had "legitimate complaints.")

For young Wall Streeters, Occupy was slightly closer to home. Financiers in their early and mid-twenties tended to be around the same age as many of the protesters, and several young Wall Streeters I spoke to had friends or relatives who had been down to Zuccotti Park as part of the protest. Unlike earlier efforts, Occupy was a movement that had drawn in their peers—the people who had been in their college classes and in their dorms just a year or two earlier. Young bankers and traders could log on to Facebook and see their friends posting messages of support for Occupy. And for some young financiers, the protests forced them to choose sides.

"It was weird," Jeremy Miller-Reed told me, after Occupy protesters held a march outside Goldman's headquarters. "They were at our building yesterday, so I'm, like, standing in front of this glass window looking down at these protesters, and they're looking up at me pointing signs. It was so crazy to be on that side of things."

Not all young financiers took Occupy seriously. Several days after he glimpsed the protests for the first time, Ricardo told me that he felt "sort of neutral" about the merits of Occupy's message, which he interpreted as being mainly about lingering anger over the bank bailouts. He understood that anger, but he didn't see how else the financial crisis could have been resolved. What did Occupy want? For millions more people to lose their jobs and savings as a result of bank failures? "I don't have anything against them," he said. "But I doubt they're doing anything productive." Another young bank employee I met just outside the Occupy protests laughed when I asked him if he was doing a lot of deep thinking as a result of what was happening in Zuccotti Park. "I work for UBS," he said, referring to the beleaguered Swiss bank that had just announced a $2 billion loss stemming from the actions of a rogue trader. "We have bigger problems right now."

One dissenting note several young financiers brought up with respect to the Occupy movement was that it made no distinction between the executives whose decisions had brought about the financial crisis and the tens of thousands of back-office, middle-office, and junior front-office employees who made much less money than C-suite executives and had no decision-making capabilities at all.

"There's sixty thousand–odd employees at my bank," a different J.P. Morgan analyst told me. "It doesn't make sense to brand us all with the same stroke. Like, if a person in the NHL got charged with rape tomorrow, would ESPN say that all hockey players are rapists?"

There was some logic in this defense. After all, many back-office and support workers at Wall Street banks earn $40,000 or $50,000 a year, have no idea what a credit default swap is or how to construct a collateralized loan obligation, and can't truly be lumped in with the foolhardy executives who ran their firms into the ground during the crisis. The analysts I was following were well within the 99 percent statistically, even if their colleagues weren't. (The cutoff for the top 1 percent of American tax filers in 2010 was about $370,000 in adjusted gross income—well above what any first-year analyst makes.) In that way, blaming Wall Street underlings for the crisis seemed like blaming George W. Bush's personal chef for the war in Iraq.

Still, by virtue of taking part in a financial system that Occupy found oppressive, young analysts had opened themselves up for criticism.

Jeremy Miller-Reed had always been discreet about telling people that he worked at Goldman Sachs. But now that the Occupy movement was increasing the heat on banks, with Goldman often bearing the brunt of the criticism, he found himself cloaking it even more often.

"I lie whenever I go out now," he told me. "I tell people I'm a consultant, a lawyer, whatever—anything but a Wall Street guy."

Jeremy's paranoia had been boosted during the third week of the protests, during a routine doctor's visit. While getting his checkup, he mentioned to the nurse that he'd recently visited a physician on staff at his office.

"You have a physician at your office?" the nurse asked. "Where do you work?"

He responded truthfully, and watched her face contort into a grimace, as if he'd just emitted a racist slur. It stayed plastered to her face for the remainder of the appointment, and Jeremy left feeling depressed. If a nurse in downtown Manhattan was judging him for working at Goldman Sachs, what did the rest of the world think?

Aside from periodic embarrassment, the biggest change Occupy Wall Street created in the lives of young bank analysts was that it forced them to think about the morality of their work, daily, and in holistic terms. For the first time since the financial crisis, big investment banks were the focus of the world's attention, and Wall Street workers were forced to consider the net social effects of their chosen profession every time they turned on the TV, read a news site, or walked past a protest. The compartmentalization process that allowed them to put off the touchy-feely ethical considerations and simply do their jobs no longer worked. And while not everyone was caught up in self-doubt, those whose consciences were piqued by the sight of a global protest movement rising up against them were seeing their misgivings about finance rise to the surface.

"I hate having to lie about what I do," Jeremy told me, the day after his doctor's appointment. "It doesn't completely ruin the experience of working at Goldman. But I won't lie—it makes me think about what else I could be doing with my life."

CHAPTER TWENTY-SIX

I spent several weeks covering Occupy Wall Street, and in the process of interviewing participants and observers about what was happening in Zuccotti Park, I got a fairly clear sense of what the protests were about, and where it fit into the historical continuum of populist economic movements. But the impact of the movement, and its implications for the future of Wall Street, didn't really sink in for me until I met Marina Keegan.

Marina was a twenty-one-year-old senior at Yale, where she studied English and was training to be a writer. She wrote poetry, plays, and columns for various student publications, and had apprenticed under Harold Bloom, the famous literary critic and Yale professor. She had done a junior-year summer internship at the *New Yorker*, and had gotten an offer to return there full-time after graduation. But in the fall of her senior year, she turned her attention to what she saw as one of the most problematic elements of Yale's student culture: the Wall Street recruiting process.

As target schools go, Yale is no Princeton or Wharton, but it is still home to one of the most highly sought-after student populations for Wall Street. Roughly 20 percent of the Yale graduating class typically goes into business and finance, and among Yale alumni in the industry are such heavyweights as Steve Schwarzman, the billionaire cofounder of the Blackstone Group. All the major banks, as well as many large private equity firms and hedge funds, recruit on campus, with a flurry of information sessions, résumé drops, and group interviews.

To Marina, the fact that 20 percent of her classmates might become investment bankers seemed like cause for mourning. That fall, she saw dozens of her friends head to the on-campus information sessions for big banks and consulting firms, dressed in suits and fake smiles, and every time it saddened her. What, aside from the money, was so great about Wall Street that students with such diverse interests and talents—budding artists, architects, literary critics, filmmakers, education reformers, scientists, and computer programmers—were all willing to drop their ambitions and follow a path of mundane corporate climbing?

That fall, Marina asked dozens of her friends, acquaintances, and professors about their thoughts on the finance and consulting recruiting process, then folded the results into an essay for Yale's weekly news magazine, in which she elucidated her concerns. She wrote:

> What bothers me is this idea of validation, of rationalization. The notion that some of us (regardless of what we tell ourselves) are doing this because we're not sure what

else to do and it's easy to apply to and it will pay us decently and it will make us feel like we're still successful. I just haven't met that many people who sound genuinely excited about these jobs. That's super depressing! I don't understand why no one is talking about it.

Oftentimes at Yale, I'll be sitting around studying or drinking or hanging out when I'll hear one of my friends talk about a project they're doing for a class or a rally they're organizing or a play they're putting on. And I'll just think, really, honestly, how remarkably privileged we are to hang around with such a talented group of people around here. I am constantly reminded of the immense passion and creativity of those with whom I get to spend time every day.

Maybe I'm overreacting. Maybe it really is a fantastic way to gain valuable, real-world skills. And maybe everyone will quit these jobs in a few years and do something else.

But it worries me.

Marina's essay blew me away. I wrote to her and asked her if she could adapt it into a short article for DealBook, the financial news site at the *Times*. She agreed. Then she invited me to see the recruiting phenomenon for myself.

I arrived in New Haven on a stormy Wednesday in late October and met Marina, along with a group of her friends, many of whom had gotten involved in the Occupy New Haven movement. As the rain poured down outside, eight of us sat in an empty classroom and talked about the effects the Wall Street recruiting process had on campus culture.

"I get the appeal of i-banking," said Alexandra, a senior and one of Marina's friends. "It's comfortable for people who are used to succeeding within the system, at a string of prestigious institutions. There's a path laid out, and finance is the next step on that path."

"It's like living at Yale for two more years," Marina added. "You're working with a bunch of smart kids in a highly structured environment. It's like you never left campus."

Marina's friends agreed that financial institutions should be allowed to set up booths at career fairs and hold information sessions on campus, just like any other employer. But they also wanted to remove the stigma associated with questioning the career choices of their classmates. They wanted to make "banking," if not a dirty word, then at least a career field that was subject to ethical scrutiny like any other.

"It needs to be reframed by our campus as a moral question," Alexandra said. "It's weird that we're not allowed to call someone out on the fact that they're brilliant and passionate, that they love working with preschool children or whatever, and that they're going to a bank instead."

"I've been saying to people who are planning to go into finance, 'I'm disappointed in you,'" Marina said.

In the two months since Marina's original essay ran, students at many other top-flight colleges had begun raising questions about the dominance of financial recruiting on their campuses. Offshoots of the Occupy movement had organized several student protests, including one at Princeton, in which a group of students interrupted a J.P. Morgan information session. The protesters rose from their seats midsession and shouted in unison: "Your predatory lending practices helped crash our economy, we've bailed out your executives' bonuses, you've evicted struggling homeowners while taking their tax money....In light of these actions, we protest the campus culture that white-washes the crooked dealings of Wall Street as a prestigious career path."

At a Goldman Sachs information session the following night, the Princeton protesters repeated their grievances, and added a message to their fellow students:

"Dear Fellow Princeton Students, we are here to ask you for a moment of reflection. Deciding on a future career path is difficult. It deserves serious introspection. When you came to Princeton as a wide-eyed freshman, you probably didn't dream of working at Goldman Sachs. What happened? We are all privileged to have made it to Princeton. However, our talents will be wasted if we send all our best and brightest to Wall Street."

Marina and some of her friends had gotten into the protesting spirit, too, and had organized a group to stand outside a Morgan Stanley information session, with signs that read "Morgan Stanley is boring" and chants that included "Take a chance, don't go into finance!"

All over the Ivy League, the Wall Street recruiting process, which had once been as anodyne and accepted a part of the academic calendar as midterms and finals, had taken on the tenor of a student-on-student battle.

"I teach financial markets, and it's a little like teaching ROTC during the Vietnam War," Robert J. Shiller, a professor of economics at Yale, told me that fall. "You have this sense that something's amiss."

There have been industry-centric and company-specific protests on college campuses before. In 1967, students at Harvard and other schools protested the recruiting efforts of Dow Chemical, the company that made much of the napalm that was being used in the Vietnam War. In the early 1970s, Stanford University banned Goldman Sachs from recruiting on campus for five years, after a black Stanford Graduate School of Business student named James E. Cofield Jr. filed a lawsuit against the firm, claiming that it had racially discriminatory hiring practices that kept him from getting a job there. And after the Iraq War in 2003, students at many top-tier schools protested Lockheed Martin, Halliburton, and other military and weapons companies.

But the Wall Street protests of 2011 were different from other corporate recruiting tiffs, in that they were equally addressed to the companies that were doing the objectionable things and the students who were considering working for those companies. At Harvard, a young alumnus named David Weinfeld wrote an op-ed titled, "Boycott Wall Street," in which he urged Harvard students not to occupy Wall Street, but to "simply give up pursuing an occupation on Wall Street."

Weinfeld wrote:

> [Harvard students] can work for nonprofits, for government, and think tanks. They can be engineers and entrepreneurs and educators and environmentalists and journalists and artists and activists. They can work in the private sector for companies that actually make products and create jobs. They can go to graduate school or professional school and become doctors and lawyers and professors and scientists and politicians. Some of them can even win Oscars or play in the NFL.

Many of these careers may not be as financially rewarding as investment banking. But I assure you, they will almost certainly make you less insipid than your profiteering peers.

At Stanford, two student columnists called for the school to "prepare more students for socially productive careers in public service, entrepreneurship, and scientific research," rather than "serving as the vocational training center for reckless banks and hedge funds." And at Duke, another finance feeder school, a majority opinion of the student editorial board added its voice to the growing chorus:

> If more smart people pursue jobs oriented toward creating socially valuable products and services or commit themselves to developing solutions to educational or environmental problems, society will improve in ways that trading in mortgage-backed securities will never achieve. We encourage students headed for Wall Street to stray from that tired road, but recognize the institutional, parental, and social pressures that compel many to pursue careers in finance and consulting. Although these careers promise security, wealth, and status, we believe that Duke students can do better.

Some finance executives, asked about the effects of the Occupy movement on their firms' recruiting abilities, shrugged the entire thing off, implying that the anti-recruiting backlash had extended only as far as the op-ed pages of the student newspapers and radical campus groups. Morgan Stanley CEO James

Gorman emphatically denied that the financial industry's massive unpopularity made an impression on incoming recruits.

"That is not a constraint, it's not going to be a constraint," he said. "There will always be somebody who says, 'Well, I always wanted to be an investment banker, but I've had this sort of moral epiphany, and now I'm not.' I mean, it's ridiculous."

But I'd heard differently from some top industry hiring managers, who said that the Occupy protests and the campus banking backlash they inspired had forced them to change their pitch to college students.

"The way you speak to the audience now is different," one top hiring manager said. "It isn't the audience of five years ago, where they're, like, 'It's Wall Street, it's a job, great—I'll get on the merry-go-round.' They've now heard other things. So we've had to take a step back and say, 'Are we speaking to them in a way they care about?'"

Statistically, Wall Street banks were, in fact, losing their sway on top college campuses. At Harvard, the percentage of seniors with jobs at graduation who went directly into financial services fell from 28 percent in the class of 2008 to 17 percent in the class of 2011. At Princeton, where 46 percent of seniors with jobs at graduation were once Wall Street–bound, that number shrunk to 35.9 percent in 2010. Those numbers fell, in part, because crisis-stricken banks had shrunk their workforces. But the moral and reputational fallout of the crisis had also had an impact.

I decided to find out for myself exactly what was going through the heads of new Wall Street recruits by going to an event that would be filled with them—the annual Goldman Sachs fall recruiting session at Yale.

I arrived at the Omni Hotel in downtown New Haven to

find several dozen nervous-looking Yalies picking at lukewarm sesame chicken strips, cheese puff pastries, and beef skewers. The room was decked out in Goldman blue, and a four-foot-tall vertical sign stood in the corner, with a message that read: "How will you make an impact?" In my wrinkled suit, I must have looked enough like a nervous analyst-in-the-making so as not to stick out. (Goldman's recruiting sessions, like those of all other major banks, are typically not made available to the media—I was counting on being able to pass undetected.)

After more students filed in, the lights dimmed, and a video began playing.

"We...are...Goldman...Sachs," it began.

After the video finished, a group of Goldmanites—many of whom were Yale alums—took the stage to speak about their jobs in greater detail. What followed was a half-hour of corporate agitprop, stuffed to the brim with bromides and b-school jargon.

"We play an important part in moving the economy forward by linking investors and capital with businesses and governments," one employee raved.

"We are a global company, which literally puts a world of opportunity at my fingertips," another employee said.

"There are not a lot of places where junior professionals' opinions really matter," a third added.

Much of what was said mirrored what I'd heard at Morgan Stanley's Wharton session a year earlier. There were promises of real-world responsibility, vague hints of the immense workload that was expected of first-year analysts, and talk of "exit opps" after the two years were up. As usual, there was no mention of the money a first-year analyst stood to make—only generalities about the "generous" compensation package and "eat what you kill" pay philosophy.

But there was something new, too—a set of questions about morality and ethics that hung in the air, just out of reach. No students asked the Goldman recruiters, flat-out, if working on Wall Street was immoral. (To do so would be the quickest way to talk yourself out of a job.) But over and over again, the recruiters made reference to Goldman's "corporate integrity," as if they were shadow-boxing with an imaginary Occupier in the room. By addressing concerns about its morality, even obliquely, Goldman was showing that the events of the past few months had caused it to sweat.

After the panel's pep talk, some students left right away. (Credit Suisse was having an event down the street.) But others stayed behind to talk to the recruiters about the specifics of the jobs. A worried-looking junior named James, who was milling around the drink table while working up the nerve to approach a recruiter, told me that he had spent several weeks attending information sessions for various banks and financial firms, trying to figure out what to do after graduation. An economics and applied math concentrator, James told me that the recruiting backlash, and the larger Occupy movement, had raised some questions for him, but not steered him clear of the financial sector altogether.

"I dunno," he said. "I mean, I think bankers should get some flak for the crap that happened. But a lot of it is misguided. It should be pointed toward Washington."

He said that recently, one of his friends had asked him if he felt like he was giving up his chance to "make a difference" by going to work at Goldman or another big bank.

"I guess I feel like I am making a difference," he said. "It might not be, you know, the best difference, but it's a difference."

Out in the hallway, I met Nicholas, a Yale student who was wearing a skinny plaid tie and a slim-fit suit. He told me that much of the appeal of finance among his friends was attributable to fear.

"A lot of kids don't know what they want to do, and they don't want to get left behind," he said.

Nicholas acknowledged, without my bringing it up, that the protests of the last few weeks had made him think about whether he wanted to go through with his plans to work on Wall Street after graduation or do something more altruistic.

"In an ideal world, everyone would go save the world," he said. "But I realized that you can't just graduate, be the head of an NGO, go to China, and solve the AIDS problem. You need to learn those skills somewhere."

I had doubts about this familiar justification for entry-level Wall Street work. (Do Excel skills really help solve global health crises?) But Nicholas didn't. And so, here he was, unbowed in his attempt to land a spot at Goldman Sachs.

"My friends and I joke about, 'Oh, it's the dark side,'" he said. "But it still seems like the smart thing to do."

As I was talking with Nicholas (before a Goldman recruiter spotted me and asked me to leave the hotel), I realized that although many college students were still interested in Wall Street, something major had changed. Now, in 2011, students like Nicholas were conceiving of a career on Wall Street as something they needed to actively choose, rather than something that just happened to them naturally, by virtue of living on an Ivy League campus. The unbridled enthusiasm I'd seen at Penn a year earlier was now tempered by caution and inquiry. To borrow the language of direct marketing, the Occupy protests, and the popular uprising against the recruiting complex, had turned investment banking from an opt-out campaign to an opt-in campaign.

And while it remained to be seen what larger effects the Occupy protests would have on the financial sector, that subtle shift alone meant that young Wall Street was becoming a far different place.

CHAPTER TWENTY-SEVEN

"GOOD EVENING, Exalted High Council, former Grand Swipes, Grand Swipes-in-waiting, fellow Wall Street Kappas, Kappas from the Spring Street and Montgomery Street chapters, and worthless neophytes!"

The speaker, private equity billionaire Wilbur Ross, was standing at the dais of the St. Regis Hotel ballroom, welcoming a crowd of two hundred wealthy and famous Wall Street figures to the annual black-tie induction dinner of Kappa Beta Phi, Wall Street's most secretive fraternity. Ross, the leader (or "Grand Swipe") of the fraternity, was preparing to invite twenty-one new members—"neophytes," as the group called them—to join its exclusive ranks.

"This is our eightieth dinner," Ross continued, "but a time capsule unearthed in 1929 by the first Wall Street Grand Swipe, W. S. Gregory, shows that we actually date from December 5, 1776, when four C+ William and Mary students designated themselves an honorary society. They wanted to name it Kappa Beta Phi, but their severe dyslexia muddled it into Phi Beta Kappa. When the first set of keys came, they then recognized the problem, but being college students, the gold keys were too expensive to replace. So they stuck with the wrong sequence of letters. This is the most astonishing discovery since Joseph Smith found the Book of Mormon in an abandoned mine in Elmira, New York."

Looking up at Ross from an elegant dinner of rack of lamb and fois gras were many of the most famous investors in the world, including executives from nearly every too-big-to-fail bank, private equity megafirm, and major hedge fund. AIG CEO Bob Benmosche was there, as were Wall Street superlawyer Marty Lipton and Alan "Ace" Greenberg, the former chairman of Bear Stearns. And those were just the returning members. Among the neophytes were hedge fund billionaire and major Obama donor Marc Lasry and Joe Reece, a high-ranking dealmaker at Credit Suisse. All told, enough wealth and power was concentrated in the St. Regis that night that if you had dropped a bomb on the roof, global finance as we know it might have ceased to exist.

Ross continued:

"But Grand Swipe Gregory did not notify the press, because he feared that would cause left-wing students to Occupy Wall Street. Instead, he created a fraternity with the corrected name, but whose members were not pseudointellectuals. In fact, they were not intellectuals at all. He put in place a prohibition, which we have totally honored, prohibiting any Phi Beta Kappa from ever joining Kappa Beta Phi...

"The Wall Street chapter also redesigned the key itself. Instead of a linked left hand in a ruffled sleeve—Phi Beta Kappa's tacit confession of homosexuality—ours depicted a macho right hand in a proper Savile Row suit and a Turnbull and Asser shirtsleeve. In addition, the Phi Beta Kappa key had only three stars, as that was apparently as high as their members could count. Our five stars reflect our greater facility with numbers and our affection for Hennessy five-star cognac. More importantly, our key added a champagne tumbler and a beer mug to symbolize the importance of continuous drinking, both in bull markets and bear markets. After all, our motto is '*Dum vivamus edimus et biberimus.*' For the illiterate neophytes, I will translate it: 'While we live, we eat and drink.' This contrasts with Phi Beta Kappa's wimpy motto, 'Love of learning is the guide of life.'"

More laughter from the audience, and a smattering of applause.

"The capsule also revealed the etymology of the letters *Kappa*, *Beta*, and *Phi*. *Kappa* comes from the early Etruscan word *Kapitalas*, meaning regulatory capital. But during one of Greece's many defaults, the word shrank to Kappa, because the banks ran out of capital, a process then known as 'decapitation.' *Beta* is derived from *Beta Bauhaus*, first used by the Greeks to describe temple replicas, which they booby-trapped to kill barbarians trying to destroy the original ones....*Phi* was the anguished cry of Greeks about to be slain by Roman gladiators. To this day, Athenian protesters scream *Phi* at the riot police. Combining these three letters constitutes a warning that regulatory capital is a booby trap, which can cause sudden death, just like MF Global, Lehman Brothers, and Bear Stearns, all of whose leaders were Kappas. In fact, we have members from every firm that has failed, and we also have members from those that will fail in the future."

Now the crowd was roaring.

"Our chapter has always been egalitarian. We took in women some years ago, even have had women as Grand Swipes, and we no longer call them 'Swipettes.'…"

Ross invited all the former Grand Swipes in the room to the podium to receive their copies of a special Grand Swipe key. He then asked the rest of the Kappas to put on their Kappa Beta Phi hats and recite the group's motto over and over: "*Dum vivamus edimus et biberimus.*"

The financiers shouted out in a thundering bellow: "*DUM VIVAMUS EDIMUS ET BIBERIMUS.*"

The only person not saying the chant along with Ross was me—an undercover journalist who had snuck into the event, and who was hiding out at a table in the back corner in a rented tuxedo.

I'd heard lots about the existence of Kappa Beta Phi, whose members included both incredibly successful financiers (New York City mayor Michael Bloomberg, former Goldman Sachs chairman John Whitehead, hedge fund billionaire Paul Tudor Jones) and incredibly unsuccessful ones (Lehman Brothers CEO Dick Fuld, Bear Stearns CEO Jimmy Cayne, former New Jersey governor and MF Global flameout Jon Corzine). It was a secret fraternity, founded at the beginning of the Great Depression in 1929, that functioned as a sort of 1 percenter's Friars Club. Each year, the group came together for a black-tie dinner to induct a new class of inductees, who were forced to perform comedy skits and musical acts in drag, and suffer mockery at the hands of existing members. The group's induction dinners are filled with X-rated humor and off-color jokes, and its group's privacy mantra is "What happens at the St. Regis stays at the St. Regis." For eight decades, it worked. No outsider, in living memory, had witnessed the entire proceedings first-hand.

I decided to try to break that streak for two reasons. The first was obvious—sneaking in would get me a one-of-a-kind story and shed light on one of the best-kept secrets of Wall Street. The second and arguably more important motive was related to my young finance investigation.

For months, I had tried to get a sense of what happened to young Wall Streeters as they worked their way up the ladder— how the experience of a C-suite executive differed from the ex-perience of a first-year analyst, and what personality changes happened along the climb. To do that, I had to be able to peer into the world of Wall Street's most senior and accomplished executives—the people many of my subjects aspired to be like. What did being the CEO of a big bank do to your psychologi-cal outlook? How did running a $30 billion hedge fund change the way you viewed the world?

Unfortunately, whenever I asked these kinds of questions of the CEOs and industry barons I interviewed, I never felt like I was getting real answers. They were serious, emotionally aus-tere people, and they wanted to discuss deals, earnings, and geopolitics, always with their PR people or lawyers in tow. Whenever I asked them about the effects their work had on rais-ing kids, being married, or living in a country that had turned deeply hostile to the financial sector, they often looked at me like I'd asked about their porn preferences.

I knew I needed to see the titans of finance in their natural social environment, with their guards down. So when I learned when and where Kappa Beta Phi's annual dinner was being held, I knew I needed to try to go. It would be the closest thing possible to seeing these people in a filter-free setting, and maybe it would give me some insight into their real personalities.

Getting in was shockingly easy—a brisk walk past the sign-in desk, and I was inside cocktail hour. Immediately, I saw men whose faces I recognized from the papers, and a handful of women, too, including star Wall Street analyst Meredith Whitney, who several years before had made a name for herself predicting that Citigroup would cut its dividend before the financial crisis. I picked up an event program and saw that there were other boldface names on the Kappa Beta Phi membership roll—among them Citigroup CEO Vikram Pandit, BlackRock CEO Larry Fink, Home Depot billionaire Ken Langone, Morgan Stanley bigwig Greg Fleming, and JPMorgan Chase vice chairman Jimmy Lee. Any way you count, this was one of the most powerful groups of business executives in the world.

I hadn't counted on getting in to the Kappa Beta Phi dinner, and now that I had gotten past security, I wasn't sure quite what to do. I wanted to avoid rousing suspicion, and I knew that talking to people would get me outed in short order. So I did the next best thing—slouched against a far wall of the room, and pretended to tap out e-mails on my phone.

After an hour, the neophytes emerged to line up for their class photo. I, and most others in the room, began to chuckle. They were dressed in women's wigs, form-fitting leotards, gold sequined skirts, and piles of stage makeup, their hairy, pale legs sticking out from underneath their skirts. Some were already falling-down drunk, and the ones who weren't were identifiable by their looks of sheer horror. These were people accustomed to humiliating and emasculating others, not having it done to them.

After the class photo, the entire group moved into the ball-room for dinner. I waited until the program had begun, then moved to an empty seat at a table near the back.

All twenty-one of the new Kappa inductees were expected to sing a musical number, do a comedy skit, or present a prepack-aged video as part of their induction rite. While they per-formed, other members booed, hissed, and threw wine-soaked napkins at them onstage. From my perch, I watched the neo-phytes give performances that, if exposed to public view, may have jeopardized some very public and lucrative careers. Among the night's lowlights:

- Rich Tavoso, an executive at RBC Capital Markets, sang an off-key parody song called "Mama, Don't Let Your Babies Grow Up to be Traders," with finance-inflected lyrics, and got booed off the stage.
- Paul Queally, a private equity executive, told off-color jokes about fellow financiers and well-known politicians to Ted Virtue, another private equity bigwig. The jokes ranged from unfunny and sexist (Q: "What's the biggest difference between Hillary Clinton and a catfish?" A: "One has whiskers and stinks, and the other is a fish") to unfunny and homophobic (Q: "What's the biggest difference between Barney Frank and a Fenway Frank?" A: "Barney Frank comes in different size buns").
- David Moore, Marc Lasry, and Keith Meister—respectively, a holding company CEO, a billionaire hedge fund manager,

and an activist investor—sang a few seconds of a finance-themed parody of "YMCA" before getting the hook.

- Bill Mulrow, a top executive at the Blackstone Group, and Emil Henry, a hedge fund manager with Tiger Infrastructure Partners, performed a bizarre two-man comedy skit. Mulrow was dressed in raggedy, tie-dye clothes to play the part of a liberal radical, and Henry was playing the part of a wealthy baron. (Presumably, not a huge stretch.) They exchanged lines as if staging a debate between the 99 percent and the 1 percent. ("Bill, look at you! You're pathetic, you liberal! You need a bath!" Henry shouted. "My God, you callow, insensitive Republican! Don't you know what we need to do? We need to create jobs," Mulrow shot back.)

- Warren Stephens, an investment banking CEO, took the stage in a Confederate flag hat and sang a song about the financial crisis, set to the tune of "Dixie." (*"In Wall Street land we'll take our stand, said Morgan and Goldman. But first we better get some loans, so quick, get to the Fed, man."*)

A few more acts followed, during which the veteran Kappas continued to gorge themselves on racks of lamb and laugh uproariously. Michael Novogratz, a former Army helicopter pilot with a shaved head and a stocky build whose firm, Fortress Investment Group, had made him a billionaire, was sitting next to me, drinking liberally and annotating each performance with jokes and insults.

"Can you fuckin' believe Lasry up there?" Novogratz asked me. I nodded. He added, "He just gave me a ride in his jet a month ago."

Several minutes later, we turned again to face the stage, as the neophytes were taking their places for the grand finale—an ensemble performance of "I Believe," the hit ballad from the Broadway show *The Book of Mormon*, with lyrics rewritten for the occasion:

I believe that the Lord God created Wall Street. I believe he got his only son a job at Goldman Sachs.
I believe that God has a plan for all of us. I believe my plan involves a seven-figure bonus.
I work on Wall Street. And Wall Street just believes.

As the financiers—now clad in Mormon missionary outfits—broke into a kick line, I pulled out my smartphone, and began recording the proceedings on video. Wrong move. Novogratz looked at me, as did several others at my table.

"Who are you?" he said.

"I, um, I'm really sorry," I stammered.

"No," he said. "Tell me. Who the hell are you?"

I felt my pulse spike. I knew that Novogratz, who wrestled at Princeton before going into the military, could probably do considerable bodily harm to me with his bare hands. And I knew that, if I identified myself as a reporter when asked—as I was required to do by the ethics code of the *Times*—I would be putting myself at his mercy. But I had no choice.

"I'm with the *New York Times*," I said. "I'm a reporter."

Novogratz stood up from the table. I, too, stood, and tried to excuse myself, but he grabbed my arm and wouldn't let go.

"Oh no you don't. Give me that," he said, pointing to my phone, which I was trying to put in the inside pocket of my tux jacket. "There are no pictures allowed in here. You're not allowed to *be* here."

A small crowd was now forming around us. I heard the words "*New York Times*" being whispered, and looks of deep concern spreading over faces.

"*Give me that or I'll fucking break it!*" Novogratz yelled, grabbing for the inside of my jacket with one hand. His eyes were bloodshot, and his neck veins were bulging. The song onstage was now over, and a number of prominent Kappas had rushed over to our table, where it was now very clear something was amiss. Before the situation could escalate dangerously, Alexandra Lebenthal—a bond-investing socialite and a former Grand Swipe—stepped in between us. Wilbur Ross quickly followed, and the two of them led me out into the lobby, past a throng of Wall Street tycoons, some of whom seemed to be hyperventilating.

Once we made it to the lobby, Ross—who looks a bit like an ancient Galapagos turtle, and was wearing purple velvet moccasins with the Kappa Beta Phi logo—congratulated me on having gained entry into the dinner.

"I admire your ingenuity," he said, laughing nervously.

For the next fifteen minutes, he and Lebenthal reassured me that what I'd just seen wasn't *really* a group of wealthy and powerful financiers making homophobic jokes, mocking poor people, and bragging about their business conquests at Main Street's expense. No, it was just a group of friends who came together to roast each other in a benign and self-deprecating manner. Nothing to see here.

"Remember that these are some of the most charitable people in America," Ross said. "Just leave out the vulgar stuff, please."

It was fairly clear, from their initial reactions, that they were terrified that I was going to print their exploits in the newspaper. But the extent of their worry wasn't made clear until Ross offered himself up as a source for future stories in exchange for my cooperation.

"I'll pick up the phone anytime, get you any help you need," he said.

"Yeah, the people in this group could be very helpful," Lebenthal chimed in. "If you could just keep their privacy in mind."

I was appalled. Not so much by the blatant favor trading (I'd had financiers try to bribe me off a story before, though never quite as explicitly) but by the implication that there was nothing morally wrong with what Kappa Beta Phi stood for, and what its members did.

Here, after all, was a group that included many of the executives whose firms had collectively wrecked the global economy in 2008 and 2009—the top executives of Morgan Stanley, Citigroup, Bank of America, Lehman Brothers, Bear Stearns, and other firms that had either failed or required billions of dollars in emergency bailout money. These were public, highly visible companies, and their actions had, in no uncertain way, catalyzed a crisis that resulted in the loss of hundreds of thousands of jobs, tore apart lives and families, and made billions of dollars in middle-class savings simply disappear.

And yet, despite their failures and the economic havoc they'd wrought, these people—all of whom had remained extraordinarily wealthy since the crash—were content to laugh off the entire financial crisis in private, as if it were a long-forgotten lark. (Or worse, sing about it—one of the last skits of the night was a self-congratulatory parody of ABBA's "Dancing Queen," called "Bailout King.")

In any year, the Kappa Beta Phi dinner would be tone-deaf; in January 2012, just a few months after a global protest movement had taken root in opposition to the moral and financial offenses of the 1 percent, it amounted to a gargantuan middle finger to Main Street.

After several more minutes spent trying to talk me out of writing about what I'd seen, Ross and Lebenthal escorted me out of the St. Regis. Lebenthal led me past a group of angry Kappa members, who were sobering up considerably at the thought of having the evening's activities made public, into the elevator and out of the hotel.

On my way back to the newsroom to write up my story, I thought about the implications of what I'd just seen for my young finance-world sources.

The first and most obvious conclusion was that the upper ranks of finance are composed of people who have completely divorced themselves from reality. No self-aware and socially conscious Wall Street executive, in the year 2012, would have agreed to be part of a group whose tacit mission is to make light of the financial sector's foibles. Not when those foibles had resulted in real harm to millions of people.

The second thing I realized was that Kappa Beta Phi was, in large part, a fear-based organization. Here were executives who had strong ideas about politics, society, and the work of their colleagues, but who would never have the courage to voice those opinions in a public setting. Their cowardice had reduced them to sniping at their perceived enemies in the form of satirical songs and sketches, among only those people who had been handpicked to share their view of the world. And the idea of a reporter making those views public had caused them to throw a mass temper tantrum.

The third thought I had, as I walked through the streets of Midtown in my ill-fitting tuxedo, was that many of these self-righteous Kappa Beta Phi members had surely been first-year analysts once. Some of them had no doubt been college graduates, unsure of their places in the world, who just happened to land on Wall Street, some at the same firms whose young workers I was now spending time with. And in the twenty, thirty, or forty years since, something fundamental about them had changed. They had internalized the haughty, uncaring world-views of the Wall Street barons who came before them, and begun to perpetuate those views themselves. Their pursuit of money and power had removed them from the larger world to the sad extent that, now, in the primes of their careers, the only people with whom they could be truly themselves were a hand-ful of other prominent financiers.

Perhaps Kappa Beta Phi is a bastardization of the real Wall Street culture. After all, I know of several top executives who have turned down the group, or who are members but choose not to attend the annual dinners, on the grounds that the skits and jokes are too tasteless to be associated with. There are, in fact, members of the financial elite who want nothing to do with mockery and light-heartedness—who take their respon-sibilities as employers and guardians of investor capital quite seriously. And many of the analysts I spoke to about the event afterward simply laughed. To them, the idea of a bunch of out-of-touch plutocrats gathering to carry out the rites of a secret fraternity seemed absurd and antiquated.

"It sounds like something Occupy Wall Street would invent if they wanted people to hate bankers even more," one told me.

But I am continually scared by the idea that some of the thoughtful, socially conscious young analysts I know will end up succeeding beyond their wildest dreams on Wall Street and will in the process be changed, to the point that the idea of belonging to such a powerful, exclusive group of executives becomes seductive rather than funny.

Perhaps, I thought, it was best to think of Kappa Beta Phi as a barometer of Wall Street's aspirational mood. If in two or three decades, the fraternity is still the kind of club that commands respect and envy in the financial world, and if first-year analysts still hanker to become part of it, then it will mean that the culture of Old Wall Street has endured. If, however, it becomes the kind of antiquated, pitiful event that draws grimaces and eye rolls from those inside the sector as well as those outside it—well, maybe there's hope for New Wall Street after all.

CHAPTER TWENTY-EIGHT

"What the fuck is Justin Bieber doing here?"

I rolled over in bed, pawed my eyes open, and saw Derrick Havens stripped to his boxers and splayed out on my couch. He glanced to the corner of my studio apartment, where a life-sized cardboard cutout of the tween-pop sensation leaned up against the wall.

"Well," he said. "I guess we had a good night."

Derrick and I had spent the previous night at a raucous dance party. After arriving, Derrick proceeded to drink shot after shot of Jim Beam, dance until he was covered in sweat, make out with a woman he'd never met before in a dark corner of the club, stumble out at 3:00 a.m., find the only remaining open business—a twenty-four-hour pharmacy—locate a Justin Bieber cutout in the novelty aisle, shriek with joy, break out his credit card to pay for it, drunkenly carry the corrugated pop star all the way back to my apartment, and end the night by vomiting in my bathroom and passing out on my couch. "I feel like death," he now confessed, rubbing his eyes.

Derrick, who had left Wells Fargo in Chicago six months earlier to take a job at a private equity firm in Manhattan, was settling in nicely to a New York lifestyle. He had more free time now that he was out of the banking cycle, and he'd used it to partake in everything the city had to offer a twenty-four-year-old with discretionary income—parties, fine restaurants, and posh downtown clubs where women far too attractive for him went to mingle with men much richer than he.

Most parts of Derrick's city life still felt like playacting to him. He knew that his parents and friends back home in Waupaca would scoff at the amounts of money he was spending on a weekly basis, and that Erica, his ex-girlfriend, would cackle at the notion of him pretending to be a high roller. Derrick's job was the envy of first-year bank analysts everywhere, but he still acted like a Midwesterner in most ways, and he embarrassed himself frequently on account of how little he knew about the city. (I was there when he'd asked a cab driver to take him to "*Hyoo-ston* Street," before being corrected to "*How-ston*.") His colleagues, most of whom had gone to fancy East Coast schools and considered themselves sophisticates, often mocked him by imitating his flat Wisconsin accent, which turned *bag* into *beg* and *sorry* into *sorey*.

A lot of Derrick's day-to-day work at the private equity firm was the same as it had been at Wells Fargo—making presentations and Excel models in order to value companies and prepare client deliverables. But he also had more hands-on responsibility when it came to evaluating deals, and he spent a lot of time flying around the world to the headquarters of companies his firm was in the process of bidding on. He liked this work, known in the industry as "due diligence." He enjoyed rubbing shoulders with the blue-collar workers and the local executives, many of whom reminded him of his friends and family back home in Wisconsin. And he liked that this work felt grounded in reality, unlike at Wells Fargo. He wasn't just pushing numbers around on spreadsheets. He was getting his hands dirty with the work of capitalism.

At the same time, Derrick's due-diligence visits always made him slightly afraid of what would happen to these salt-of-the-earth manufacturing workers once his firm acquired their employer. Often, private equity firms—his included—laid off workers and shipped manufacturing jobs overseas in an effort to make the companies they acquired more profitable.

Derrick knew that layoffs and closures were sometimes unavoidable. He'd seen his dad lay off workers at his grocery stores during down years, and while it was always painful, it was part of the normal life cycle of a business. Derrick's boss had often compared the work of private equity to surgery—if they, the surgeons, needed to amputate a limb to save the life of the patient, then it was better than letting the patient go untreated and die.

What made private equity different than surgery, Derrick was learning, was that his firm usually succeeded even if its surgeries ultimately failed to save the patient. They pulled this off through the use of leverage, and a financial engineering tactic known as a "dividend recap," or recapitalization, which involved loading a company with more debt in order to pay out the private equity firm and its investors. The dividend recap had been invented decades ago, but had only truly been popularized during the buyout boom of the early 2000s. It was, Derrick thought, a useful way to return money to shareholders, but it often accelerated the deaths of failing companies.

He was also bothered by the tone in which his firm's executives spoke about the components of their turnaround plans in depersonalized business-school jargon. Laying off workers and cutting pension plans was often referred to as "right-sizing" or "rationalizing head count," and outsourcing was euphemized as "streamlining" or "leaning out the business." It wasn't wrong to cut jobs or outsource if you needed to save a dying company, he thought, but at least have the decency to call it what it was.

One night, over dinner, I asked Derrick if he felt ethical about working in private equity—an industry that had been attacked as a form of "vulture capitalism" during Mitt Romney's 2008 presidential run (and that would soon taint his 2012 run). He thought for a minute, took a sip of his beer, set it back down.

"Being ethical is kind of on a spectrum, right?" he said. "Like, I really like my firm, I really like the people I work with, and I think that within private equity, we do a good job of actually improving businesses rather than just going for quick money. But what conflicts me is that we don't play by the same set of rules as everyone else. It's a completely rigged system."

I asked him what he meant.

"Well," he said, "we buy these little companies, we put the best lawyers and consultants in the world on it, and if it goes bankrupt, we never lose. We put in stipulations that don't leave us liable, there are seventeen blocker corporations between us and the company." He paused, then chuckled. "How are you going to out-money private equity? Good luck."

But surely, I said, it wasn't easy to identify the right investments, find the right ways to engineer a portfolio company's finances, and time an acquisition with trends in the market. Wasn't there also some skill involved?

"Well, look at it this way," Derrick replied. "My dad's up there, intelligence-wise, with anyone I work with, but the money doesn't flow to him like it does to the guys I work with. It's the system. People in private equity are smarter than your average person, but they're not that much smarter. And as long as the system is structured like this—where, two years after the world's worst financial crisis, you can get four-times-debt on a bankrupt business—it's not going to change."

Derrick let that hang in the air for a moment, then added with a wry chuckle: "Of course, I say all this knowing that the fucked-up system is how I have an apartment that I don't worry about the rent for, how I take cabs everywhere and go out for nice meals and wear clothes that I don't care how much they cost."

Derrick's rant threw me off guard. I knew he was less than convinced about the basic goodness of the financial industry than many of the analysts I knew, and I suspected that the Occupy movement had resonated with his left-of-center political conscience, but it was rare to hear anyone in finance using phrases like "the system," or undercutting the myth that people who engineered complex financial transactions were smarter and more capable than people in other sectors. The supremacy of Wall Street's intellect was, in many ways, the financial sector's founding myth, and it was part of the reason that thousands of high-achieving Ivy League graduates flocked there after college.

But although Derrick's words were surprising, I couldn't say they rang false. My shadowing of first-year analysts—and my interviews with top executives for my day job at the *Times*—had convinced me that many Wall Street workers were, by and large, as smart as top achievers in any other sector. They read the news constantly, they studied foreign affairs and domestic economic trends, and they were conversant on lots of nonfinancial topics. But, on the whole, they weren't *brilliant*. Only four or five of the people I met struck me as actual, bona fide geniuses, the kinds that could foment a groundbreaking, industry-changing insight or invent a revolutionary new product. And many of the rest were essentially escalator riders—people who worked hard to get on a machine with an automatic upward trajectory, and, once they got there, only had to hold on.

Part of this is surely the fault of the stodgy workplace culture of banks, which can stifle creativity and genius if it appears outside the hierarchy they're accustomed to. But another part of it, I suspected, was the kind of people banks tend to attract—confused, insecure college seniors, who are smart and capable in a general, all-purpose way, but aren't phenomenally talented at any one thing.

Derrick knew that if he wanted to be a visionary, or even particularly creative, he would probably have to exit the private equity industry sooner or later. But it was far too early to consider that. He'd just gotten to New York, and he was still enjoying the high life. When it came to balancing ideological comfort with material comfort, the contest still wasn't close.

One night that winter, Derrick met me for drinks at a downtown bar after work. He arrived late, looking every bit the harried private equity associate in a sharp suit, a blue tie, and a watch with a face the size of a golf ball. He ordered his usual

(Tanqueray and tonic) and proceeded to vent about work. What had set him off was a conversation about Occupy Wall Street that had quickly turned into a humorous pile-on.

"Everyone at my job jokes about Occupy Wall Street, but there is a problem in this country," he said.

Derrick maintained that his stance, as a private equity worker, wasn't completely contradictory. ("The people at Zuccotti Park aren't protesting me," he said. "They're protesting the guys who are thirty-five and making $5 million a year.") But the ethical and moral challenges of the past few months had clearly gotten to him and driven a wedge between him and the rest of his colleagues.

That night, we sat at the bar watching the local news, which was primarily composed of Occupy scenes interspersed with Jets highlights. And before we left, Derrick began to switch from criticizing his bosses to criticizing himself.

"Do you know any good charities or nonprofits I could get involved in?" he asked me. "I mean, Jesus, I'm so self-centered, and I spend so much time feeling so sorry for myself and worrying about my shit and my life. I need to give back."

Derrick's crisis of conscience surprised me, but it shouldn't have. After all, he was the young financier I knew who was the most removed from Wall Street culture. He had been in New York for only a few months, and he had yet to fully absorb the private equity industry's values. Most of his heart was still back in Waupaca, with his father's grocery business and his down-to-earth friends. And he was being pulled between that world—where people made tangible things, clocked in and out at work every day, and got paid hourly wages—and the exotic and cutthroat world of Wall Street, where you could make

$200,000 a year as a twenty-five-year-old and still consider your-self below average.

In a way, Derrick was hoping to pull off an expert-level bal-ancing act. He wanted to work in finance, with all the glitz and glamour the Wall Street lifestyle afforded him, but he also wanted to keep himself grounded in the values of Main Street. He wanted to absorb the good parts of the private equity experience—the management experience, the deep knowledge of how businesses work, and the ability to turn around strug-gling companies—without buying into the industry's abiding principle of "shareholder value," which held that a strategy of mass layoffs, pension cuts, and tax avoidance could be good, as long as it made more money for the private equity firm and its investors.

If Derrick could truly thread that needle, and harmonize the cognitive dissonance of working in finance as a nonbeliever, it would be a rare feat, and it would mean that perhaps he'd be able to sustain his New York life after all. But until he figured out how, he was in for a lot more sleepless nights spent listening to the angel perched on his shoulder, yelling in his ear.

CHAPTER TWENTY-NINE

SAMSON WHITE BARELY spoke a word of Spanish, but somehow he'd ended up playing the bongo drums in an Argentinean jam session. He knew none of the songs and understood nothing the band members around him were saying, but he kept the beat loyally, and hit the skins of the drums with the heels of his hands until they were swollen and sore, a wide grin on his face the entire time. After one song, a friend pulled him aside.

"Has anybody at this party asked you what you do, or where you work?"

Samson chuckled. "No."

"Exactly!" the friend said. "Here, it doesn't matter!"

Earlier that day, Samson and his friend had arrived in Buenos Aires for a nine-day vacation. Samson, who was nearing the halfway point of his second year at his Goldman Sachs mortgage job, had been looking forward to the trip for months. The first night, they found themselves at a house party at the home of a local musician, where they drank and played music into the wee hours with the jam band. In the ensuing days, they would eat massive amounts of steak, drink worrisome quantities of wine, and do something called the "Buenos Aires Pub Crawl," an all-night tourist affair that was popular with foreign students, who paid 120 pesos for a ticket that allowed them to hop between different bars in the city, drinking shooters and beer at each one.

Samson needed a vacation badly. There were now just ninety-four days left on his bedroom countdown clock, and he was strongly considering quitting the day after his second-year bonus hit. His overall happiness hadn't improved since the terrible winter of his first year, and he now felt sick every time he got up in the morning for work. Several weeks earlier, in his diary, he'd written:

> I hate my job, hate the people, hate the work. The question is no longer whether I will make it past the two years. That's definitely the cap. Now, the question is: Will I make it that long? Should I leave earlier?

Samson had spent months e-mailing people he knew who had left jobs on Wall Street in an attempt to gather advice for his next move. He browsed job listings on Doostang and other job sites, and looked into opportunities to work for a San Francisco–based technology education organization.

But what he really wanted to do, he decided, was start his own business. He'd been strongly considering the idea pitched to him months before by Colin, his fellow analyst at the bank, who was trying to rope him into doing a two-man

start-up that would sell event and concert tickets through a
mobile app.

Samson loved the ticket-app idea and thought it could succeed, but he couldn't quite get over the fear that leaving Goldman would mean giving up his only chance at stability in a
high-paying job. He worried about not having health insurance, about having to scrounge to pay his rent if his savings
dried up, and about telling his colleagues at the firm that he
was quitting—not to go to a prestigious private equity firm or a
hedge fund, but to live a volatile existence as an entrepreneur.

"They're going to think you're fucking up," an ex-Goldmanite
friend told him.

"I know," Samson said. "I hate that what they think matters
to me, but it does."

What bothered Samson more than the prospect of losing his
Goldman salary and bonus was that leaving banking before his
two years were up would be seen by many of his peers as an ad-
mission of failure. Samson took pride in the fact that he'd made
it to Goldman, even if he hated his actual job once he got there,
and he cringed at the thought of his Princeton friends thinking
that he hadn't been able to hack it on Wall Street. Even though
Samson hated the superiority complex of finance, he had still
bought into it subconsciously. Building a start-up, even a successful one, *did* feel less noteworthy to him than slaving away at
Goldman, even if objectively he knew that wasn't true.

Samson tried to drown out the voices of doubt ringing in his
ears and focus on what was really important. He wrote in his diary:

Real life is incredibly difficult. I hope I figure it out. It's
possible that figuring it out just means living it, making it

as much of a roller coaster as possible. Embracing it, not
settling for the path of least resistance, seeing all there
is to see, having beautiful, loving relationships, dancing, laughing, learning, understanding, enriching your
soul instead of your wallet, realizing that life is a brief
opportunity for joy and that those moments that don't
contribute to that joy immensely, are really wasted moments. That success in and of itself is meaningless if it
doesn't make you happy.

*   *   *

Several thousand miles north of Buenos Aires, Samson's friend
Jeremy was also struggling with his happiness. After spending
much of the summer getting rejuvenated in the Hamptons, he
had settled back into his miserable routine at work. His boss,
Penelope, was still treating him like garbage and subjecting
her underlings to seemingly random freak-outs and blow-ups.
Worse than those, though, was that Penelope's brusque personality seemed to have infected several of the associates and vice
presidents in the group. When Jeremy arrived, his team had
been largely a genial bunch. Now, hardly a day passed without
an analyst being chewed out publicly over a minor offense, or a
support staffer ending up in tears due to the unprovoked rage of
a higher-up.

Part of what scared Jeremy was that he, too, felt his personality changing as a result of his surroundings and the people he
worked with daily. He'd come into Goldman as a soft-spoken,
cerebral kid. But in less than two years, he had developed a
shorter temper and was quicker to point out others' mistakes in

a way that was often unkind. He was still capable of sucking up to his superiors, but he had little patience for people whose intelligence he didn't respect.

At first, Jeremy's sharper, more unsparing personality was subtle. But as time went on, his friends and colleagues began to notice that something about him was different. Even Samson saw it once, during a lunchtime discussion of their weekend plans. Samson asked Jeremy what he was doing on Saturday, then got distracted during Jeremy's answer.

"What?" he said.

"Dude, fucking listen to me when I talk," Jeremy snapped.

Samson looked at Jeremy with raised eyebrows, apologized, then slowly went back to his desk. He and Jeremy had always been two of the most laid-back analysts in their class, and they'd bonded, in part, because they weren't the type to get worked up over small things. But Jeremy, it seemed to Samson, had caught the Goldman bug as well.

To avoid being caught in the circular firing squad in his group, Jeremy had at first retreated to the safety of his desk, where he'd spend hours a day reading the *Economist*, the *Atlantic*, and the *New York Times*, while earnestly hoping that no clients would call.

But the oil market was still fairly active that fall, and Jeremy couldn't separate himself entirely from the rest of his group. So he came up with a new coping strategy: Every time he felt himself growing angry, he would tell himself, "Don't get mad. Leave." And then, instead of letting his emotion spill out, he would spend a few minutes e-mailing a contact outside the finance industry, polishing his résumé, adding a name to his "Escape Routes" list, or doing something else tangible to try to find a new job. This way, he could channel his anger into an effort that would one day help him escape Goldman's hothouse environment altogether.

That fall, Jeremy's whispered phrase became a personal maxim. Every day, when the circumstances of his job or the petulance of his coworkers made his blood boil over, he would put his head down, massage his brow, and think to himself: *Don't get mad. Don't get mad. Don't get mad. Just leave.*

CHAPTER THIRTY

J. P. Murray smiled as the plane touched down in New York.

He'd just come back from the best vacation of his life—a weeklong, all-inclusive island sojourn in Barbados, during which he'd gotten far away from Credit Suisse, far from his church in Brooklyn, and the "live fast, die young" mantra he'd adopted in order to make it on Wall Street. In fact, the trip had been so good that his memory of it was already beginning to take on the hazy, mythic quality of a religious experience.

The trip had been made possible by a rule at Credit Suisse that required all employees to take a mandatory weeklong vacation every year. (Later, it was extended to two weeks.) The policy, known as "block leave," had been instituted not to give burned-out employees a week away from the grind, but to catch traders who were engaged in irresponsible or illegal activity. By making all employees at the bank go off the grid for a week every year, the logic went, supervisors and compliance officers would have time to comb through their trading logs and computer for evidence of suspicious activity. The necessity of block leave had been hammered home by Jérôme Kerviel, the convicted rogue trader who lost more than $6 billion for French bank Société Générale and later told officials that the fact that he hadn't taken any vacation days in 2007 "should have alerted the management" that something was wrong with his books.

Even though J. P. was a banker, not a trader, he was also covered by the mandatory leave, and he scheduled his for the second week of December. A friend of his had invited him to Barbados for an all-inclusive tour and resort stay. The trip coincided with the Barbados Food, Wine, and Rum Festival, which was held at the ultraexclusive Sandy Lane resort, and which drew famous chefs like Marcus Samuelsson and Tom Colicchio for a four-day festival of wine and rum tastings, cooking demonstrations, and live local music. J. P.'s group had spent the week going on charter boat rides, drinking free rum punch, swimming and snorkeling in a crystalline bay, and going on a personalized "jungle island tour." For the first time in a year and a half, J. P. was able to put work out of his mind completely.

On his last night in Barbados, he met Melissa. She was half black, half Puerto Rican, with smooth skin, long hair, and a slim waist, and she worked as a doctor at a New York hospital. She was out of J. P.'s league, he thought, but he couldn't shake the feeling of possibility he got when he looked at her. After a long night of wine tasting, J. P. pulled her aside.

"Hey, you want to take a walk?" he asked. "You can see the stars really nicely from just over there on the beach."

Melissa smiled coyly, knowing what he was really asking, but she was game. They'd gone on a walk, followed by a starlight kiss, followed by a trip back to J. P.'s room, where they had sex—some of the best of his life—for what seemed like three or four hours straight.

J. P. had replayed the night over and over again on the plane ride. He knew work would be tough when he got back, and he would have to hold on to that memory, and the memory of the entire trip, to tide himself over until next year's block leave. But despite the inevitable letdown of coming back to rain-drenched New York from a tropical paradise, J. P. was actually looking forward to getting back to work.

He'd gotten over the disappointment of his meager first-year bonus, and he had consoled himself with the fact that this year's would probably be much better. The year 2011 was shaping up to be a good one in the markets—not nearly as good as the pre-crisis days, but the best J. P. had experienced since he was hired. Already, there was talk of increased deal flow, and of promoting a few of the third-year analysts to associate during the next bonus cycle.

But when he turned on his BlackBerry after a week of inactivity, J. P. got a startle. Among the hundreds of e-mails waiting for him upon his return was a farewell e-mail from an analyst in his class, a kid named Terrance Hawk.

It wasn't unusual to get an e-mail from a departing colleague. The notes were invariably addressed to the entire division, and invariably contained platitudinous expressions of gratitude, along with contact details at a new bank, hedge fund, or private equity firm. But Terrance's note had no new contact details, only a brief expression of thanks along with his personal e-mail address.

Terrance had been fired, J. P. surmised. But why? Terrance

was an analyst in the health-care group, a hardworking Duke grad who kept his head down. J. P. knew him fairly well, and he wasn't the type to make mistakes.

Despite the fact that the financial sector was recovering slowly from its crisis-era lows, it had been a very tough year for Credit Suisse. Regulations, slow capital markets activity, and increased capital requirements had eaten into profits, and like many other banks, the firm had been forced to lay off some employees. But J. P. felt certain that nobody he knew would get the boot. For starters, his division—the investment bank—was the most prestigious one at the entire firm. And even if bankers were laid off, first- and second-year analysts would surely be spared. Their labor was cheap, and the marginal savings to be gained from firing them would barely make a dent in the bank's total payroll cost. For years, it had been an unspoken rule on Wall Street: you don't lay off analysts. To do so was considered the height of cruelty, the closest thing Wall Street had to child abuse.

Later that night, J. P. called Terrance to get the scoop on what happened. Terrance confirmed that he had, in fact, been laid off, and he wasn't sure why. All the HR representative had told him was that it was a tough time for the bank, and that they had to reduce the size of his group. Nothing to indicate that he hadn't been doing a good job, and nothing specific about his performance at all.

J. P. was terrified. If Terrance was getting laid off, it meant that there would be more analysts laid off. And if they were laying off a certain fraction of the class, it wouldn't matter that he'd made great strides since his disaster of a year-end review. All they'd be looking for was numerical data about who was in the bottom 10, 20, 30, or however many percent of the class. And those people would be gone.

J. P. took solace in the fact that his bosses had scheduled him on some long-term projects during his vacation—not something you do if you're about to fire your analyst. And the following Monday, he came to work ready to work on his biggest project, a deal involving a midsized pharmaceutical company.

An associate came to his desk in midmorning, and asked for a walk-through of the model J. P. had built, the one they'd be basing the financials of the proposed deal on. J. P. talked him through step by step, fingers flying adeptly on his keyboard as he told the associate that yes, the multiple was in range, that yes, the bridge financing could—

The phone rang. He saw that it was from an unassigned number in the bank. He picked up.

"Hello?"

"Jean-Paul, it's Elizabeth. Could you meet us in the conference room?"

J. P.'s heart dropped. Elizabeth, the COO of his division, was the woman who had fired Terrance, in just the conference room she was asking to meet J. P. in now. And she said "us," meaning that there would be more than one person there, just as Terrance had said.

"I…uh…yeah," he said. "In a minute."

J. P. stood up from his desk, looked around, and headed to the elevators. He went downstairs and took a walk to calm his nerves. His heart was somersaulting, and his pulse had spiked uncontrollably. After one lap around the building, J. P. went back inside, and rode the elevator back up to the twentieth floor. He put his jacket back on his chair, then walked, terrified, to the conference room.

He knew it was over before he sat down.

"We've been going through some tough times," Elizabeth told him. "And we've had to make some tough decisions. Unfortunately, your job has been impacted."

Impacted, J. P. thought. *What kind of sanitized, corporate HR bullshit is that?*

J. P. left the meeting five minutes later, after having been told about his severance package (three months' pay) and his other exit benefits (the services of an outplacement firm, which he knew he would never use). He went back to his desk and began stuffing his personal belongings into his Credit Suisse duffel bag. He wrote a farewell e-mail to his entire group, delay-timed it so that it would send at 6:00 p.m., and walked to the elevators.

At the elevator bank, J. P. saw Denise, the second-year analyst who had become one of his only real friends at the firm, and who had taught him much of what he knew about playing the corporate game as a black man.

"Where are you going?" Denise asked.

"I'm gone," J. P. replied.

A look of panic crossed her face. "What do you mean, gone?"

He gestured to his duffel bag. "I mean, I'm gone."

Denise began to tear up. Not wanting to make a scene, J. P. hugged her quickly, promised to meet up with her later for a drink, and left the building.

J. P.'s good-bye e-mail went out as scheduled at 6:00 p.m., and by 6:10 his phone was ringing off the hook. He took a nap, then went out with a friend to drink his disappointment away.

J. P. hadn't counted on making it to his third year at Credit

Suisse, but he'd been certain of making it to the end of the second year. He thought there was a rule on Wall Street—you kept your analysts for two years, then gave the ones who weren't rehired for a third year ample time to figure out their next moves. But the basic rules had changed since the crisis. And J. P. had been caught unaware.

He wasn't the only one. Across the financial sector, many analysts were being laid off that year as their firms struggled to cut costs and boost their share prices. One analyst who survived the cuts, a Goldman Sachs third-year, explained to me the effect the layoffs had on the psyches of the sector's youth.

"You're working with this constant fear," he said. "You go to this bulletproof firm, it gives you a ton of options, and it's really self-validating. And then all of the sudden, you have no options, you're not getting paid nearly as much as you thought, and you might get fired. And then you start thinking, *Well, shit, I could be halfway through law school, and instead I'm in New York dicking around doing models and bottles, and at the end of it I won't even have that much to show for it.*"

In the weeks following his abrupt layoff, J. P. had several interviews at other financial firms, but nobody seemed to be hiring. He knew that Wall Street was where he wanted to end up, but he was no longer sure how to make that happen. And with his options running out, he was seriously considering switching fields, or going back to business school and getting out of the workforce temporarily.

J. P. and I had lunch at a Thai restaurant in Midtown shortly after his layoff, and he was unusually calm about his situation. Getting fired seemed to have triggered something deep in his cerebral cortex. The guy who had once adopted Rick Ross's line

"Live fast, die young" as his motto was now thinking seriously about slowing down.

"Yeah, I want a job, but at the same time, I don't think I should let economic ebbs and flows govern what I do with my career," he said. "I don't want my career to be a series of jobs I took just to have a job."

After lunch, J. P. got on a bus to Philadelphia, where he was meeting some of his college friends and spending some much-needed time at home. And as he walked to the Port Authority Bus Terminal, I asked him how he planned to spend the weeks and months until he got back on his feet.

"I'm going to party a lot," he said. "And I'm going to spend the days thinking about what I want to be when I grow up."

CHAPTER THIRTY-ONE

IN THE WINTER of 2011, a joke started circulating among New York's financial crowd:

Q: What's the difference between a pigeon and an investment banker?
A: A pigeon can still make a deposit on a SoHo loft.

As Wall Street banks began handing out their bonus numbers that year, recipients found themselves turning to self-pity and dark humor. At nearly every bank, flagging profits had made for bonuses that, while still massive compared to any reasonable norm, looked minuscule compared to the bounties of years past. Bank of America Merrill Lynch reduced the size of its cash bonuses by 75 percent. Morgan Stanley capped cash bonuses at $125,000 for everyone, even the cigar-chomping executives at the top. And at Goldman Sachs, the amount set

aside to pay compensation and benefits was $12.22 billion, or
$367,000 per employee, down 21 percent from the year before.
("A bloodbath," is how one Goldman analyst put it to me.) The
sector-wide compensation disappointment, combined with the
layoffs that were still occurring, made Wall Street's collective
blood pressure rise.

"Seriously man, sinking ship," Jeremy Miller-Reed wrote me
after one particularly disappointing earnings report at Goldman
Sachs. "I've been thinking more and more these days that I
need to get out after bonuses hit in January. Although that is, of
course, contingent on the world not having blown up by then."

The thing scaring young Wall Streeters wasn't really the
money. That always ebbed and flowed with the markets, and
while many post-crash recruits had never seen that kind of
cyclicality, they had been conditioned to expect it. And in any
other year of subpar pay, whining and complaints would have
been tempered by the realization that the next year would almost certainly be better. What bothered people that winter and
spring was the sense that what was happening to Wall Street
was no longer part of a familiar boom-and-bust cycle—that they
were witnessing the fundamental transformation of the entire
financial industry.

Since the crisis, nearly every week had brought a new structural change to Wall Street's business model. First came the
Dodd-Frank Wall Street Reform and Consumer Protection Act,
the law that was passed by Congress in order to try to prevent
another 2008-style crisis. Dodd-Frank, which was signed into
law by President Obama in July 2010, was the most sweeping
piece of new regulation on the financial industry since the
Great Depression. In addition to cracking down on prop trad-

ing, the law set up new regulatory agencies to manage systemic risk, created a so-called resolution authority that would give government the power to wind down a failing financial institution in an orderly way, and gave private equity firms and hedge funds tougher disclosure standards. Many of the rules in Dodd-Frank had yet to be written and implemented (and would subsequently be watered down by lobbyists) but it was immediately apparent that the law would put a crimp in Wall Street's profitability for the foreseeable future.

Next came Basel III, an international regulatory standard that the United States decided to adopt in 2011. Basel III raised the amount of capital banks had to hold against their assets, which gave them bigger cushions and reduced the likelihood that a big, unexpected loss could wipe an entire firm out. By requiring banks to hold more capital relative to their assets, Basel III made the financial system less risky, but it also reduced the amount of leverage that banks could use to juice their trading returns.

That winter, JPMorgan Chase reported fourth-quarter profits that were 23 percent lower than the previous year's. Goldman Sachs's profits for all of 2011 fell more than 50 percent from the previous year's levels. The net income earned by Bank of America's investment banking division, which includes Merrill Lynch, dropped by 53 percent, and Morgan Stanley's earnings fell by 42 percent for the year. With Dodd-Frank and Basel III kicking in, it wasn't clear when Wall Street would get its mojo back, if ever.

"The new regulatory framework will undoubtedly make Wall Street less valuable than it was before," William A. Sahlman, a professor at Harvard Business School, told me. "Whatever Wall Street used to look like, it looks half as good now. People thought of some of those organizations, like a Morgan Stanley or a Goldman Sachs, as safe career bets. They didn't have a history of laying people off, and they were pretty great places for people to work. But after Lehman Brothers and Bear Stearns got in trouble, everybody got in trouble."

Nearly every older Wall Streeter I spoke to that year was dismissive of Dodd-Frank and Basel III, which they viewed as annoyances at best and a waiting cataclysm at worst. Younger bankers, though, often recognized that tougher regulations were, on the whole, a good thing for society. Their concern was closer to home; they were just nervous about their jobs.

They had reason to worry. The financial crisis had been disproportionately hard on young Wall Street workers, who were getting displaced at a greater frequency than their elders. According to data from the Bureau of Labor Statistics, the number of employees in the securities industry in New York City between ages twenty and thirty-four fell by 25 percent from the third quarter of 2008 to the third quarter of 2011, whereas the overall decline in workers of all ages was only 17 percent. That difference—and the fact that younger Wall Street workers often don't have substantial nest eggs saved up to cushion against the possibility of a job loss—made many twentysomething financiers fret that much harder about their futures.

"I'm interviewing for jobs in Asia," one anxious Goldman Sachs analyst told me that winter. "With all the regulatory things over here, they're the only ones hiring."

What bothered many of Wall Street's youngest workers was that although making it to the top of the financial world had always required elbow grease and dedication, the path itself had always been fairly straightforward. You put in two years of back-breaking work at a bank, then moved over to a hedge fund or a private equity firm for two more years of nonstop number crunching, went to business school, then came back with an MBA and began climbing the buy-side ladder. At each of these steps, your pay grew—from $120,000 to $180,000 to $400,000, perhaps—and one day, you woke up at forty as a managing director, making a few million dollars a year and living the good life.

But that basic formula for success was quickly eroding. That year, I met with dozens of young Wall Street analysts, and almost all of them seemed deeply confused about how to make it in the post-crisis world. Many of the a priori assumptions about how to succeed in finance seemed inadequate and outdated. An analyst could come from the right school, get a job at the right bank, live and breathe investment banking for two years, excel at every task, never complain about late nights or tough assignments, be the shining star of an analyst class, and still be kicked to the curb by a sudden round of layoffs. In the world of Wall Street, the crisis had created an alternate reality, in which performance and outcome weren't always meaningfully correlated.

"Not that I was ever part of the old days," Ricardo Hernandez, the J.P. Morgan analyst, mused to me. "But I think I'm resigned to the fact that the world of 2007 is never coming back."

The clearest sense I got of how the economic realities of the post-crash era had affected the ambitions of young Wall Streeters was when I met with Trevor Nelson. Trevor works for a financial education company called Training the Street (the same firm that conducted my Excel spreadsheet-making seminar), and his specialty is helping young people prepare for their interviews at private equity firms, hedge funds, and investment banks. He's a former Lehman Brothers banker who looks a bit like a young Christian Bale, with gray-flecked scruff on his face and intense eyes, and he charges nearly $500 an hour for his interview-prep services.

I went to Trevor's office on Madison Avenue to ask him a bunch of questions about the private equity recruiting process. But when I sat down across a boardroom table from him, he immediately started telling me how bizarrely his clients had been acting.

"These are excellent kids who have been groomed for success," he said. "They've gone to the best schools, gotten the best grades, worked at the best banks. For a long time, they've been searching for the highest level of attainment. And for a long time, private equity and hedge funds were the next step in that track. Now, it's different."

The way Trevor described it, young people who several years earlier might have happily jumped onto the time-tested track between top investment banks and private equity megafirms were no longer doing so quite so predictably. Instead, after their time in banking was up, they were going to work at small technology start-ups, joining large companies in fields unrelated to finance, and going back to school. It wasn't because they were fed up with working hundred-hour weeks, or because they objected morally to the work of high finance. These financiers simply thought there were better and more enjoyable ways to make money. So they jumped ship.

"Seven years ago," Trevor said, "the only way to succeed was in private equity or hedge funds. The folks I was in i-banking with weren't asking about personal fulfillment. But now with the financial crisis and a tech boom, people are saying, 'I don't need to sacrifice twenty years of my life to get where I want to be.'"

As I walked home from my meeting with Trevor, I reflected on all the things I'd learned about the passions of the young financiers I was getting to know. I recalled Jeremy's love of car mechanics and engineering, Chelsea's business ideas scrawled in her notebook, Ricardo's desire to be a doctor. I thought of how none of them had grown up wanting to be investment bankers, but had at some point been convinced to forgo their truest aspirations in order to work on Wall Street.

I couldn't really begrudge them that choice. It's a rare luxury, reserved mainly for children of privilege, to be able to make a job decision straight out of college based solely on passion, with no regard at all for money or security. Most entry-level jobs, in any field, involve corporate drudgery of some sort. And many of the young people I knew in New York who were pursuing artistic or creative endeavors also had substantial safety nets. In an economic climate where nearly 20 percent of people under twenty-five were unemployed, and far more earned less than they should have, it's no mystery why finance jobs remained a desirable plan B.

Still, I knew people like Jeremy, Samson, and Chelsea well enough to know that banking wasn't what they wanted to be doing, and that finance had been a poor use of their skills.

The British economist Roger Bootle has written about the difference between creative and distributive work. Creative work, Bootle says, involves bringing something new into the world that adds to the total available to everyone — say, as a doctor who treats patients, or an artist whose sculptures decorate

public parks. Whereas distributive work—which could characterize many corporate jobs, but especially those that involve
intermediary functions like banking and law—only carries the
possibility of beating out competitors and winning a bigger
share of a fixed-size market. Bootle explains that although many
jobs in modern society consist of distributive work, there is
something intrinsically happier about a society that skews in favor of the creative. "There are some people who may derive
active delight from the knowledge that their working life is devoted to making sure that someone else loses, but most people
do not function that way," he writes. "They like to have a sense
of worth, and that sense usually comes from the belief that they
are contributing to society."

Not all young financiers would, given their druthers, aban-
don distributive work and become musicians and painters. Nor
should they. Whatever your views on Wall Street banks, their
basic functions (advising on mergers, underwriting bond of-
ferings, lining up buyers and sellers of securities) need to be
done somewhere. Even though regulations and political pressure could eventually shrink those banks to a more reasonable
size, they can never go away completely. As long as we want
to have an economy where companies can merge and acquire
other companies, and where businesses can raise money and
compete in the global markets, we will always need some number of twenty-two-year-olds churning out Excel spreadsheets
night and day in the bowels of investment banks.

After talking to Trevor, though, I began to feel some hope
that in the future, those twenty-two-year-olds won't clamor to
stay on Wall Street simply because it's the prefabricated and
remunerative thing to do. Their restlessness, coupled with a

shrunken financial sector that no longer pays as well as it used to, could mean that some of the brilliant and talented young people who would otherwise have ended up as career investment bankers will instead start great companies, contribute their talents to amazing organizations, and do creative work that rewards them, even if it doesn't come with a five-figure bonus.

If the Wall Street career path continues to break down, in other words, it may lead to a more equitable allocation of resources, in which talented, highly creative young people use their abilities for purposes other than padding an investment bank's bottom line. And if that happens, the financial crisis will have sparked at least one good change.

CHAPTER THIRTY-TWO

"COME IN, JEREMY."

The Senator, rightfully known as Goldman Sachs managing director Graham Campbell, beckoned Jeremy Miller-Reed into his office. Jeremy entered the room, sat down, and crossed his legs.

"How are you doing?" Graham asked.

Jeremy took a breath. "I'm doing really well, Graham, how are you?"

"Well," Graham said.

There was a long, tense pause.

"I'm going to be very straight with you," Graham said finally. "You're one of the best analysts we've ever had. You're killing it. But we all know you don't give a fuck."

Jeremy smiled. Had it become that obvious?

After a summer mostly spent waiting to leave the office for the Hamptons, and a fall during which he simply went through the motions of trading oil and gas derivatives, Jeremy had fully checked out of his Goldman job. He'd continued to perform well, handling big trades and racking up more and more GCs. But his heart wasn't in it.

The biggest factor in Jeremy's disenchantment was still Penelope, the managing director who had made his life difficult that spring. But there were other reasons. As time went on, and people around him began to speak about staying on for a third year, he was also scared of losing his ability to make a clean break from Goldman. He knew that traders and salespeople at Goldman became addicted to the money and ended up valuing their yearly bonuses more than their independence. He saw some of that in Graham, whom he'd long thought could be the CEO of a Fortune 500 company, or an actual senator, if he could only start caring about something other than his bonus.

He also began to question the value he was adding by trading derivatives all day. He remembered that once, during his senior year of college, he'd been visiting a friend who was slated to work as a management consultant at McKinsey, and the two of them had talked about the societal value of their respective professions. To Jeremy, consulting—which involved advising corporate executives on how to improve their businesses—had seemed relatively low-impact compared to finance. But he was changing his mind.

"Ultimately," he told me, "the product Goldman is selling is its balance sheet. At the end of the day, if you have the Goldman balance sheet in your pocket, your job is pretty easy."

That day, in Graham's office, Jeremy had tried to say as much of this as possible while remaining polite. He told Graham that he was being weighed down by "all the interpersonal stuff"—which they both took to mean Penelope's mercurial management style. And then, after discussing some flaps he'd had with her and other managers, he turned the question back to Graham.

"So, what motivates you?" he asked.

Graham leaned back in his chair.

"Making money," he said. "Making as much money for myself and the firm as possible. You know, if money is not your main concern here, you should leave."

What Graham didn't know was that Jeremy had already been angling to leave. A month earlier, at a recruiting event put on by a prominent Silicon Valley tech company, Jeremy met a woman who told him about a growing start-up that was looking for help on its business side. Jeremy followed up on the tip, and several weeks later, went to meet with the company's founder about a potential job.

Jeremy liked the start-up, which had nothing to do with oil, gas, or any of his other areas of expertise. But more than that, he liked what the start-up *represented*—the boldness of breaking out of a stable corporate environment, the relaxed work atmosphere, the colleagues who cared more about improving their company than playing politics and angling for promotions. Working there would put him in the company of a bunch of smart, young, creative people doing interesting things. And although leaving now, instead of in February, would cause him to miss half a year's bonus, who cared? If the start-up became a behemoth, his stock would make him rich.

"Maybe I'll grow out a little stubble," Jeremy told me, dreaming about the freedom his new life in start-up land would bring him. "Maybe I'll get some hoodies."

Several weeks after his meeting with Graham, Jeremy received an offer from the start-up, which said it would match his Goldman base salary, as well as give him some equity in the company. He didn't hesitate. The next morning, he called Graham, who was on a work trip in Texas.

"I'm going to cut to the chase," he said. "Today is my last day at the firm."

Graham went silent. Jeremy heard him chuckling on the other end of the line. He'd seen it coming, clear as day.

"Congratulations," Graham said. "You've done a great job, and I think very highly of you. I'll miss working with you, but I understand why you're leaving."

Jeremy thanked Graham, hung up the phone, and told a few of his friends on the desk that he had just quit. He'd expected a blasé reaction, but they were ecstatic for him. They knew how unhappy he'd become in recent months, and they were excited to see him declare his emancipation. One even joked about reciting Morgan Freeman's monologue from *The Shawshank Redemption* as he left.

Jeremy then began composing his good-bye e-mail. He decided to write two different versions—one for the entire division he worked in, and one tailored to his fellow analysts.

To the larger group, he wrote:

Dear all, today will be my last day at the firm. My new contact details will follow shortly. It has truly been a pleasure working with you all.

To the analysts, he tweaked his message slightly:

Dear all, today will be my last day at the firm. I really enjoyed getting to know you all and hanging out with you. Unfortunately, my sentiment about working at Goldman Sachs is not nearly as positive, which is why I'm quitting. My new e-mail address is below, and please be in touch.

Jeremy sent his e-mails, then turned in his ID card and his corporate AmEx, and went downstairs to the security checkpoint in Goldman's lobby.

"I don't have my ID," he told the security guard. "Can you scan me out?"

"How are you going to get back in?" the guard asked.

Jeremy smiled and replied, "I'm not coming back."

He was gone by 9:30, and he walked through the streets of Lower Manhattan with tears in his eyes. This was, he felt certain, the best day of his life—on par with his college graduation, or winning his first crew race. After a year and a half of what felt like torture, his life was finally back in his own hands.

Jeremy went back to his apartment and logged on to Facebook, so that all his friends could see the momentous step he'd just taken. In the status box, he wrote: "The nightmare is over. As of today, I am no longer a Goldman Sachs employee."

CHAPTER THIRTY-THREE

DERRICK HAVENS'S APARTMENT, a two-bedroom walk-up on Fourteenth Street, was the platonic ideal of a young Wall Street abode. Everything about the place, from undecorated walls to the constant smell of beer and old socks, screamed young, male, and overworked. The living room centered on a big-screen TV, and the fridge was nearly empty, alcohol excepted. On the coffee table sat a few magazines, including *Maxim* and *Men's Health*, and a giant bucket of whey protein powder. Derrick's bedroom, too, was an ode to minimalism, with a queen bed that sat directly on the floor and clothes that were stacked in crooked piles on his dresser.

While working at Wells Fargo in Chicago, Derrick had learned to live with as little as possible. Every extraneous object in the apartment was a potential time-suck. And when you were working a hundred hours a week in private equity, and your roommate was a paralegal who didn't have much free time, either, there was no benefit to be had from interior decorating.

Derrick invited me over on a rare night off to eat Thai take-out and drink canned Bud Lights. I thought he wanted to talk about the buyout business, but it turned out that he wanted to discuss a merger of another sort.

"So, uh, yeah, I fucked a model last night," he said.

A sly smile spreading across his face, he told me how he'd met Kyla, a model with one of the city's premier agencies who had done some runway work for a top fashion line. She was a blonde with legs like stilts and a face that started cold and angular, then warmed into a coquettish smile whenever she was amused. They'd met at a club several weeks before, and had added each other on Facebook. Derrick thought he'd stood no chance with Kyla—who the hell did?—but he tried to charm her anyway. And the next week, when a friend of hers bailed on a concert they were supposed to attend together, she'd offered the extra ticket to Derrick. They went to the concert together, had a few drinks, and eventually found themselves making out. Several hours later, she finished the night wrapped in his sheets.

"I seriously can't believe this is happening to me," Derrick said. "Does she know who I am? Does she know who *she* is?"

Derrick's liaison with Kyla had distracted him from his actual work at the private equity firm, which was far less tantalizing.

He had never fully believed in the moral goodness of private equity. At best, he thought it could produce accidental gains for society when a firm's interests in buying a company happened to coincide with improving that company by adding workers and bettering its products. But recently, he had begun to question even that.

His firm's newest deal—a buyout of a midsized company— had looked uncomplicated at first. The acquired company had many things going for it—competent management, a steady revenue stream, and decent profits. But it had huge liabilities and aging equipment, and it had lost market share steadily to newer competitors in the last decade. In short, it needed a classic private equity turnaround, and the kind of immediate cash infusion and corporate reinvigoration that only deep-pocketed Wall Street investors can supply.

As the deal progressed, though, the kinds of feedback Derrick got from his firm's principals had nothing to do with the kinds of improvements he thought the firm could bring to the business. Their ideas were all about cutting costs quickly to increase short-term profits, and reselling the business for a higher price than they paid without having done anything to improve the company at a fundamental level.

"We can easily grind out 50 mil on rationalizing labor and liquidating assets," one principal said, meaning that he thought the firm could increase the value of the company by $50 million simply by firing workers and selling off equipment. The reaction played right into Derrick's worst fear: that he was working in an industry that paid lip service to turnarounds and corporate improvements but was really practicing a particularly venal kind of fee-seeking finance.

He'd occasionally harbored that fear when he first started, but it had intensified during Occupy Wall Street, when he'd seen protesters levying some of the same accusations against the financial services industry. He still maintained that his firm was better than most, but he couldn't help feeling at times like he was participating in a rich man's caper.

Recently, Derrick had gone home to Waupaca, his hometown in Wisconsin, for a long weekend away from the bustle of the city. He went to a football game at the local high school, devoured his mom's home cooking, and went to sleep in his childhood bed. And he got the distinct sense that he was among his people again.

"I can find myself in a few people on Wall Street, but 90 percent of them I can't," he later told me. "At home, I can find my soul in 90 percent of those people."

After Derrick updated his parents on his New York life, his dad caught him up on the family business. Things had been hard in the grocery business, he said, because of the slow economy and rising food prices. He'd been advised to close a few stores, to save on costs until things got better. But knowing he would have to look laid-off workers in the eyes around town afterward, he hadn't been able to go through with it. Instead, he chose to take out a big, onerous loan in order to keep paying the employees while hoping that things recovered.

Derrick had always planned on moving back to Waupaca to take over the family business someday. His parents had been supportive of his move to New York and his budding career in high finance, but he still felt guilty for not being there through the hard times. His dad was nearing seventy, and his health was getting worse. He wanted to retire soon, but he didn't have enough of a financial cushion to make it feasible.

Derrick had often daydreamed about going back home to Waupaca. He imagined a simple existence—one with a beautiful wife, a large home in the cornfields, and a couple of chubby-cheeked kids roughhousing in the yard. He imagined taking over his dad's business and expanding the grocery chain into a national conglomerate, one with thousands of employees and a name known all over the country.

He wanted that eventually, he thought. But twenty-five still seemed too early to settle down. He loved his life in New York, with his lucrative job and his one-night stands with models. Living in the big city was exciting, and working on Wall Street had given him the confidence he used to lack. He liked knowing that his mom could tell people in the grocery store that her son worked on Wall Street—*the* Wall Street—and that the amount of money he made would drive his high school classmates insane with envy.

Derrick had plenty of problems with Wall Street and private equity, but he couldn't deny that the financial industry had been good to him. At roughly $200,000 in annual pay, he was outearning the adults in Waupaca, many by a factor of five or ten. And that earning power, coupled with the respect he felt as a member of a mythologized industry, made it hard for him to imagine giving it up. Derrick was in danger of getting trapped by both golden handcuffs and status handcuffs—the inability to give up the benefits a Wall Street career afforded a guy who wanted, above all, to feel like he had standing and respect.

"I have this two-sided fear," he told me that night in his apartment. "One fear is that I'll stay in private equity and wake up when I'm thirty-five and find out that I'm not necessarily that much smarter or better than I was when I was twenty-five."

"And the other?" I asked.

"The other is that, here I am on this path, and if I don't fuck it up, I'll be wealthy."

Most times we hung out together, I'd been happy to simply serve as a sounding board for Derrick's angst. He was one of the most thoughtful people I'd encountered in finance, and I was glad that he was being self-critical about his work. But this time, in the comfort of his living room, I felt the need to challenge his sense of hopelessness. He was, after all, the single biggest case of transformation I'd seen among the young financiers I'd interviewed. His was the story that most clearly showed the benefits of working on Wall Street as a young person—the opportunity for social and economic advancement, the intro-duction into a network of powerful and accomplished people, the ability to escape a normal existence for one that can be gen-uinely remarkable. And yet he was unsatisfied—not because he'd been asked to do anything particularly unethical or legally suspect, and not because his employer was worse than any other private equity firm, but simply because he was uneasy about the basic machinations of the financial industry.

"Can I play devil's advocate?" I asked him. "The last four or five times I've sat down across the table from you, there's always something wrong, there's always an existential crisis. If a Mar-tian came down from Mars right now and looked at you, he'd see a guy who's healthy and good-looking, with a job that makes him richer than anyone he grew up with, who has an apartment in Manhattan—stuff that easily puts him ahead of not only vast swaths of America but vast swaths of *New York City*, at the age of twenty-five. If I'm that Martian, I'm saying to myself: *When is this guy ever going to be happy?*"

Derrick thought for a second, picked at his dinner, and

replied: "You know, I think it's a part of our nature, people not ever being satisfied. You're right that I have the luxury of picking my life apart. I'm not on the margin trying to figure out where I'm going to get food tomorrow. It's completely a luxury—like, when I was at Wells Fargo, I didn't have time to think about this existential bullshit. I was just concerned with getting enough sleep to make it through the next day. And I do worry that I find something wrong with everything. When I was in Wisconsin, I wasn't in the right city. When I was working in Chicago, I wasn't making enough money. And then I moved out here, and it's the best city in the world. I really like my job; I'm making a lot of money. But what value am I fulfilling?"

He lowered his eyes to the floor.

"Yes, I think that's a fair question: 'Are you ever going to be happy?' I think it's a hard thing to do to be like, *This is as good as it's going to get.* But at some point, I have to be okay with what I've got, and quit looking to the next thing."

I couldn't fault Derrick for searching for new and better options. After all, most of the young, accomplished people I know—in all industries—do the same thing. People in our generation flit around from job to job, city to city, relationship to relationship, always looking to one-up their last moves. There is a certain anxiety that comes with being twentysomething and facing a wall of opportunities and risks, and Derrick was going through it just as much as all of my friends outside of finance were.

"This is a group of people that are given a lot of money and responsibility at a very young age," he told me of his Wall Street cohort. "From the time you graduate from college until you're thirty or thirty-five, it's a weird metaphysical transition. Our parents did it at twenty or twenty-five. But the schedule in finance doesn't leave a whole lot of time for self-reflection."

As Derrick spoke, it occurred to me that my young Wall Street immersion was revealing just as much about being young as being on Wall Street. The analysts I was interviewing, after all, were not mature, developed titans of industry, with full conceptions of themselves and their values. They were kids, roughly my age, who wanted to build a good life for themselves but were unsure which bricks and beams to use. They were being bombarded with definitions of success and chances to tweak and expand those definitions. And slowly, they were trying to figure out where in the world they stood, and what they wanted their lives to represent.

And I realized that along with investigating their industry, and analyzing the work they performed, I was also watching these young financial hotshots do the grueling, painstaking work of growing up.

CHAPTER THIRTY-FOUR

"CHEERS, MAN!"

Ricardo Hernandez, the J.P. Morgan Lat-Am banking analyst, hoisted a pint of lager in a plastic cup and tapped it against mine. We were at a bar in Midtown, day-drinking on a Sunday afternoon and watching a dense crowd of assorted banker types flit by. Next to us, a waitress carried out a wooden alpine ski with five shot glasses built into it, and helped a quintet of polo-clad frat bros line up and align themselves with the glasses. When they were ready, she lifted the ski high and tipped it over, sending Jack Daniels spilling into their waiting mouths and down their shirts.

"The shot-ski, huh?" Ricardo said, as the bros cleaned themselves up. "Bold move."

Ricardo had invited me out drinking as a celebration of his recent promotion. His manager had informed him that after the end of his third year at J.P. Morgan, he would be made an associate in the Lat-Am investment banking group. The associate level, a designation typically reserved for bankers who had gotten their MBAs, came with a generous raise and added responsibility. As an analyst in the investment bank, you were a grunt whose work consisted of producing Excel models and pitch books. As an associate, you also were in charge of client deliverables, but you had a team of analysts working on projects below you, and you were given slightly more responsibility when interacting with clients. Associate jobs weren't laid-back by any stretch of the imagination. But they lacked the torturous quality of the analyst role.

That year, Wall Street had continued to struggle with profitability and the effects of new government regulation, and the investment bank at J.P. Morgan had been threatened by several targeted rounds of layoffs. The cuts began at the senior levels, but they made their way down to the VP, associate, and analyst ranks. The previous month, the guy that sat near to Ricardo—an amiable VP who kept a photo of his two young daughters on his desk—had been laid off unceremoniously after nearly a decade at the bank. Ricardo knew the same fate could await him if things got worse.

Sometimes, when Ricardo looked around the office, he remarked on how different the J.P. Morgan he joined in 2009 was from the one he now worked for. In 2009, the bank had seemed like it was undergoing a momentary setback. The financial crisis had dealt the entire industry a punch in the gut, but everyone knew Wall Street would regain its full strength in time. Didn't it always?

Now, though, Ricardo wondered whether things might have been changed for good. Pay certainly wasn't coming back to its pre-2007 levels anytime soon, but there were more structural psychological changes that had taken place since the crisis. The people he knew in finance didn't act like cocky, entitled Masters of the Universe. They were shell-shocked survivors, people who lived in perpetual fear of losing their jobs and incomes, who spoke of nest eggs and 401(k)s instead of helicopters and Hamptons houses.

For Ricardo, who had once wanted to become a doctor, making it to the associate level justified his decision to tough it out in banking. Now, like a new mother forgetting the pain of childbirth, he was letting go of the worst parts of his analyst days and focusing instead on what lay ahead. Might he get a promotion to VP? Could he run his division someday? What about becoming CEO?

*   *   *

Arjun Khan, the second-year Citigroup analyst, was also looking to the future. He had undergone four months of intensive treatment since being diagnosed with a rare autoimmune disease called Goodpasture's syndrome, and he had recently been given a provisional all-clear by his doctors. He would have to go back for more preventive treatment in several months, but the worst of it was over, and with it his fear of an early demise or years hooked up to a dialysis machine.

When Arjun got his diagnosis, his job-search efforts fell off the wagon. With his options for traditional buy-side jobs narrowing, Arjun had begun looking for spots in infrastructure private equity—a lesser-known area of finance that invests in roads, bridges, dams, airports, railroads, and other basic assets when governments are either unable or unwilling to fund them entirely with public money. Private equity firms had flooded into the infrastructure business after the financial crisis, and Arjun figured he could identify a growing infrastructure fund and hop aboard. Eventually, he found an open job—at a firm based in São Paulo, Brazil, that was expanding and needed a new junior associate. He applied on a whim, they made him an offer, and several days later he accepted.

Before seeing the job opening in Brazil, Arjun had never seriously thought about moving away from New York. The city was where his friends and family were—and more to the point, it was where Wall Street was. But the more he turned it over in his mind, the more the job seemed like the best of both worlds. Staying in finance would give him the security and stability of a corporate environment and a paycheck that would allow him to maintain the lifestyle he had gotten accustomed to in New York. But being in São Paulo and working in infrastructure investing instead of investment banking would give him better hours, a sunnier climate, and the chance to try something entirely different.

Unlike some of the analysts I'd met, Ricardo's and Arjun's experiences in finance hadn't made them want to flee the industry altogether. Both of them had reservations, sure. They both hated the hundred-hour weeks, the endless revisions of pitch books and Excel models, and the threat of getting called back to work at a moment's notice. But they'd survived. And now, they were advancing up the ladder to positions that would reward them with large pay packages and give them significantly more responsibility.

As I spoke to Ricardo and Arjun that winter, I began to understand why they were intent on remaining in the financial sector for the foreseeable future. And I couldn't necessarily blame them. They were twenty-four and twenty-five years old, respectively. Both had been raised by immigrant parents who stressed the value of earning money and having stable careers. And if they stayed a few more years in finance, they would be able to guarantee themselves a generous standard of living for the rest of their lives. For those who can make it work as a career, Wall Street is still an unparalleled personal economic engine.

"By the time I'm twenty-nine or thirty, I'll never really be worrying about money again," a young Goldman banker once told me, by way of explaining why he was remaining in finance. "I'll have decent control over my life, and by that point, I'll be making decisions that have a real material impact." (Of course, even the rich worry about money, but they do so from the comfort of their mansions.)

Money aside, a career on Wall Street does carry some benefits. One of them is that the finance world is a huge umbrella, with thousands of different jobs that involve varying functions and work environments. If you don't like corporate finance, you can move to prime brokerage. If you hate your job in equity research, you can move to a hedge fund whose specialty suits you better. The analysts' obsession over "hot desks" and stratification within investment banks obscures the fact that these are all high-paying jobs with lots of mobility and opportunity. Even the lowliest back-office manager at a major investment bank earns more than the leading practitioners in many other industries.

The people who do manage to move up the chain of command, of course, have it much better. They not only have the opportunity to become rich beyond belief, but they are given work that is genuinely important, that affects the fates of huge corporations and markets around the world. Their competence (or lack thereof) can have a material impact on our largest cultural, corporate, and governmental institutions, and the clients their firms serve often live or die on their advice. And as long as you're willing to put up with the harried lifestyle, the internal politicking, and the risk of being fired or laid off, Wall Street can still catapult its high achievers into true power.

Even the most disgruntled analysts I spoke to believed that the skills they'd gained in their jobs would prove useful later on, no matter which field they ended up in.

"That's the thing that I can't quite reconcile in my head," Jeremy Miller-Reed told me shortly after quitting his job at Goldman Sachs. "On one hand, to anyone who asks me, 'Should I go work in finance?' I'd say, 'Fuck no.' But, at the same time, having that business experience is hugely valuable."

Of course, the skills an analyst picks up on Wall Street are more narrowly applicable than they appear, and a meaningful percentage of the young people who come to Wall Street for two years after college stay in related fields for the rest of their professional lives. (One headhunter I spoke to estimated that only 10 percent of young Wall Street workers ever leave to work in a completely different industry.) Although a few will make it to the CEO's office, many more ambitious young financiers will get stuck in a middle-management role, or end up being bounced around like a pinball between firms—always landing on their feet, but never achieving the status they once dreamed of.

It saddened me to imagine Ricardo and Arjun spending their lives as the vice presidents of such-and-such obscure finance subdivisions. Both of them had outside passions that, statistically, they were extremely unlikely to ever pursue, now that they'd survived their first two years on Wall Street and decided to press on in the financial industry. And I couldn't help but think that they'd be able to contribute more, on balance, doing things other than serving as well-paid investors and intermediaries.

But they seemed to be happy to remain in finance. And all I could do was hope that they would remain scrupulous and thoughtful as they climbed the ladder, and that a career on Wall Street would leave their basic decency intact.

CHAPTER THIRTY-FIVE

Samson stirred awake. He grabbed in the dark for his iPhone, silenced his alarm, and looked up at the clock on the wall. It read:

0 days, 0 hours, 0 minutes, 0 seconds.

This was it. After nearly a year of staring at that clock every morning — a clock that had come to symbolize every remaining bit of hope in his life — it was finally time to quit his job in the mortgage department at Goldman Sachs. That night, for the first time in nearly two years, he would go to sleep a happy, un-encumbered man.

Samson had decided to quit after talking with Jeremy and several other friends. He was jealous of Jeremy's newfound free-dom and the pep that had seemed to return to his step after he'd left Goldman. And shortly before Christmas, he had ap-proached his friend Colin, who was about to quit the firm to work on his mobile ticketing start-up idea. *I'm in*, he said. *Let's do this.* He told Colin he would quit, and join him, on the day his second-year bonus cleared his bank account.

Samson hadn't known, for months, whether he would actually have the nerve to quit his job when the clock struck zero. He'd hemmed and hawed, at moments feeling quite sure that he would quit, and at others feeling like a third year (and bonus) would be worth another 365 days of unhappiness. But he decided, ultimately, that he liked the idea of being self-employed. He'd hated every minute of his Goldman experience that involved taking directions, and he couldn't bear the thought of spending any more of his career working for people whose intelligence he didn't respect. The start-up would be different. Now, he and Colin would be calling their own shots, lining up their own funding, reaping their own rewards.

Still, he was nervous. That winter, while he was deciding whether or not to follow Colin to his start-up, he wrote in his journal:

> I worry that I'm a lazy piece of shit. It takes me mustering up some serious willpower to get out of bed. How am I going to work on a start-up when I can't motivate myself to do externally assigned tasks? I feel like I'm going to be throwing up a lot in a bit, from the stress, from terror that I might be ruining my life. But it's much better to throw up because of leaps you've made rather than because you're caged.

After deciding to quit, Samson had begun making preparations. The day before, he'd cleaned out his Goldman gym locker, removed some of his personal belongings from his desk, and taken a final walk around the building. And on the day itself, he woke up an hour early, showered, got dressed, and grabbed his bag for the walk to 200 West Street.

As he walked toward the Goldman building for the last time, it began to rain. Samson took out his earphones, plugged them into his phone, and played one of his favorite songs: "The Storm Is Over Now," by R. Kelly. As the ballad's familiar refrain started up (*"The storm is over / And I can see the sunshine / I can feel Heaven, yeah / Come on and set me free"*) Samson started to cry—first softly, then in a visceral outburst that came from the depths of his abdomen, the kind he hadn't experienced since his childhood. His shoulders heaved, and he sobbed as the raindrops slid down his face, not caring if passersby heard or what they might think had happened to him.

Samson got to work at 6:45, dried his eyes, and sent his managing director an e-mail: "Need to speak with you whenever you get in." The MD arrived two hours later, and called Samson into a room off the trading floor.

"Hey, I'm going to get right to the point," Samson said. "I'm leaving the firm."

Samson told the MD that he was going to work at a tech start-up, one he was starting with a fellow Goldman drop-out. The MD said little as Samson spoke, nodding and asking him logistical questions, like when his last day would be.

Samson agreed to stay through the end of the week, handing off a few projects, and helping the other analyst in his group pick up some of his live deals. And on Friday, after a mostly idle week spent saying good-bye to his friends at the firm, Samson left 200 West Street. He wrote a good-bye e-mail to his colleagues, then logged on to Twitter and sent a good-bye tweet to nobody in particular:

I quit. #madeit #peaceoutazkaban

That night around midnight, I went to a swanky downtown dance club, where Samson was throwing a good-bye party for himself. I found him in the back of the club, bottle of champagne in hand while he danced to Katy Perry's "Firework" in the center of a circle formed by his friends. He was very, very drunk, but there was something else in his eyes.

"He's so happy!" one of his friends told me. "I've never seen him like this."

"That's what quitting Goldman does," said Jeremy, who had come to celebrate his best friend's departure from the firm, three months after his own.

A week after the party, Samson took out his notebook one more time. He wrote:

Free at last. Free at last. Thank God Almighty. We are free at last. I write this entry as I'm on a flight to my first conference as a representative of a company I'm cofounding with my good friend. We both quit Goldman Sachs a week and a half ago and are coming off our first week working full-time. The decision to leave GS, I think, will prove to be one of the best of my life. Who knows where it will go, but it's clear to me now that I should be in media, not finance. I don't want to be a Carl Icahn or Bill Gross or Steve Schwarzman. I want to be an L. A. Reid, a Richard Branson, a Michael

Jackson—where the shit I create will impact people for-
ever.

Real life is hard. I'm pretty sure I just made it harder.
But I'm doing what I wanna do, not what "prestige" says
I ought to be doing. GS is firmly a thing of my past, a
memory that I never have to relive. Was it real or imagined? Either way, it's over and excitement lies ahead. I
will say, I'm thankful for the experience, for all it's taught
me about me, for the fact that it was a miserable experience, a quality without which I doubt I would've
ever made the jump, and eventually become stuck. So,
thanks for that chapter. On to the next.

CHAPTER THIRTY-SIX

ON A SUNNY fall Friday in 2012, hundreds of students flocked to the Dillon Gym for the Princeton Career Fair, an annual event that is attended by tech giants, Fortune 500 companies, and large nonprofit organizations. I walked past orange-shirted career services workers, past booths sets up by investment banks and consulting firms that came bearing slick banner displays and free golf balls, and into a phalanx of job-seeking students.

I went to Princeton in order to finish my young Wall Street investigation the way I began it—on the campus of a top-flight university that sends a plurality of its graduates into the financial sector every year. I was curious about how the events of the past two and a half years had changed the way students at target schools saw the financial industry, and whether the same frantic desire to secure banking jobs still existed among them.

In *Liar's Poker*, Michael Lewis wrote that when Wall Street banks began recruiting at Princeton each year in the 1980s, the

campus career center "resembled a ticket booth at a Michael
Jackson concert, with lines of motley students staging all-night
vigils to get ahead." But at this year's career fair, many of the
most prestigious banks were no-shows. There was no Goldman Sachs booth, no eager recruiters from Morgan Stanley or
J.P. Morgan handing out key chains and Frisbees. The biggest
names from Wall Street were Credit Suisse, Barclays Capital,
the hedge fund Bridgewater Associates, and a number of midsized hedge funds and private equity firms. Trumping them
all was the Anheuser-Busch booth near the back of the gym,
where Princeton alumni in red track jackets were giving out
free, Budweiser-branded sunglasses under a sign that read: "Increase your liquid assets!"

The financial firms in attendance were using largely the
same vague pitches I'd heard years earlier at Wharton. One
bank advertised its "global transaction advisory for the new
economy." Another offered students a chance to "bring your
career into focus." Jane Street Capital, a medium-sized hedge
fund, had a banner promising its recruits a "dynamic, challenging environment. Rapid advancement. Idea-driven meritocracy. Informal fun and open atmosphere." (Oh, and last on
the list: "Generous compensation.") I walked around the gym
for an hour, listening to recruiters attempting to reel in students
with time-tested come-ons:

"I love my job, and I love what I do."

"Just because you don't have a finance background doesn't
mean you won't like the job."

"It's a total rush. Wouldn't lie to you, dude. And even if it's
not for you long-term, it's just two years."

But most students didn't seem to be jumping at the bait. Several of the ones I spoke to told me they weren't interested in finance at all. A Princeton senior named Maxwell told me that he had once considered working at a bank, but had instead decided to pursue his dream of working in the sports industry.

"Look, I could work myself to the bone and make a lot of money in finance," he said, "but I've known people who did that, and it's not rewarding. In finance, you're just playing around with numbers. I feel like, for me, it wouldn't really be accomplishing anything besides making money. I would get bored."

Other Princeton students I talked to said that while they were interested in finance, they didn't want to work at just any big bank.

"I'm personally looking for a place that can promote economic development and growth in whatever industry it's working in," a junior named Shawn said. "I mean, everyone wants to make money. But when I'm working in the place, I want to know that I'm doing some good."

I talked to dozens of Princeton students that day and found, to my surprise, that hardly any of them were gung-ho about becoming financiers. Many were applying for programs like Teach for America or AmeriCorps, and a significant number planned to go work for tech companies. I met aspiring accountants, management consultants, and graphic designers. And although I did meet a cadre of students who were planning to do two-year stints at a bank after graduation, they sounded apologetic about it. Many of them swore that they would leave Wall Street after their two years were up to do something "good" or "useful" or, barring that, "more fun."

As I made my way back to the Princeton Junction train station that day, I found myself trying to envision what Wall Street will look like ten years from now, when students like these have had a chance to settle into their careers and the finance industry has fully absorbed the shocks of the 2008 crisis. And I came up with three predictions.

The first and easiest prediction is that Ivy League schools will never again send massive hordes of their graduates to Wall Street, as they did before the crisis of 2008. For one thing, in a financial sector that has been made permanently smaller and less profitable by new regulations, there will never again be room on Wall Street for vast numbers of *any* prestigious school's students. But there will also be more competition during recruiting. Already, nonprofit organizations like Teach for America and companies like Google are cutting deeply into the territory that used to be dominated by Wall Street. One out of every six Ivy League seniors now applies to Teach for America, and in 2011, the program recruited more seniors than Goldman Sachs at schools like Brown and Columbia. These organizations have figured out that they don't have to offer six-figure paychecks to entice students to join their ranks. They just have to recruit early in the school year, equip students with specific on-the-job skills, surround them with other smart young people, and give them prestigious and meaningful roles that will look good on their résumés and not limit their options in the future.

Prediction two is that the Wall Street recruiting process will never again attract the same assortment of college students it once did. The hardcore finance majors, Black Diamond hedge fund members, and Wharton graduates of the world will still beat a path to Wall Street's doors, but there will be many fewer dilettantes—political science majors, say, who wind up on Wall

Street because it's the most popular thing to do at their school. Those students will either have considered the ethical implications of working on Wall Street and decided against it, or they'll apply anyway and be beaten out for prime spots by students from less prestigious schools who already have years of finance experience and technical know-how—in other words, students who actually *want* to be bankers.

The third prediction involves Wall Street firms themselves. In the coming years, most banks will eliminate their "two and out" analyst programs and revert to hiring analysts like they used to—as career-track workers who are given indefinite, at-will jobs. Partly, banks will make this switch in order to preserve their labor advantage. (It does them no good, after all, to lose their best second-year analysts to private equity firms and hedge funds every year.) But they will also recognize that in an era of tighter budgets and greater competition, they can't afford to fill their ranks with analysts who are simply notching a line on their résumés en route to their true passions. They will realize that hiring intelligent, committed A students from nontarget schools does them more good in the long run than hiring B students from Yale who will bolt at the first sign of trouble or disillusionment.

There will still be Ivy League recruits on Wall Street, of course. And those recruits will enter a gauntlet that is largely the same as it ever was. They'll work hundred-hour weeks, alienate their significant others, and get Seamless Bellies from too many in-office meals. The next generation of young financiers won't necessarily be more moral, or more scrupulous in their dealings, than the ones who currently work on Wall Street. There will still be fraudsters, insider traders, and creators of financial products that explode at regular intervals, to the detriment of taxpayers and the economy at large. Barring more and better regulation, nothing about the financial industry will be improved, systemically speaking, from its current state.

But college students will no longer coast onto Wall Street's shores uncritically, and investment banks will stop serving as two-year halfway houses for aimless Ivy League graduates. That will be a healthy change, if you ask me. Because one of the main lessons I've taken away from my finance immersion is that the financial sector is not a neutral pass-through, and people who work there—even for just two years—are often transformed in lasting ways.

Over the past three years, I'd seen surprising changes in all eight of the young financiers I shadowed. A few of those changes were positive—they'd developed professional personas, gotten more mature, and learned skills that were necessary for running and analyzing businesses. But other changes were more worrisome. I'd seen most of them become less happy and optimistic, more cynical and calculating. They were slower to smile and quicker to criticize. Many of them began to talk about the world in a transactional, economized way. Their universes started to look like giant balance sheets, their appetite for adventure waned, and they viewed unfamiliar situations through the cautious lens of cost/benefit analysis. Sure, some of them had decamped to tech firms, but they had all stayed in industries that were highly paid and traditionally prestigious, and none of them had gotten out of the private sector entirely. Many of them, I suspected, would never be able to make art, volunteer for nonprofits, or give their time to nonwork hobbies without keeping a running P&L in their head.

There is, in other words, an enormous cost associated with our nation's long-standing practice of sending huge numbers of our most promising college graduates into finance. These financiers form an elite class that will go on to become influential in the top ranks of government, technology, and culture. And if they all share the experience of having spent their formative years working as entry-level bank analysts, performing and internalizing the ethos of the financial sector, it means that, in a way, we've allowed Wall Street's culture to enter our national bloodstream.

It's the consequences of that cultural contagion—and the genuine misery I saw Wall Street inflict on so many young people—that makes me glad that the financial sector is smaller and less dominant now than it was before the crisis. Wall Street is just one part of a much larger economy, and it should have no monopoly on brilliance. Every company in every industry could benefit from having a few more superbly talented young people knocking on the door looking for work, and I suspect that many of them will, now that finance has been knocked from its pedestal.

Make no mistake: financial firms will never have a problem filling their ranks with smart, capable twenty-two-year-olds. Among the young and ambitious, Wall Street is still a draw. But at the margin, for the first time in decades, the big banks are beginning to lose their grip. And that's good for us all.

EPILOGUE

Even as I wrapped up my investigation of post-crash Wall
Street, the financial industry kept changing in ways that hinted
at just how transformative the crisis had been.

In March 2012, Greg Smith, a vice president at Goldman
Sachs, quit his job at the bank with a highly publicized resignation letter printed in the op-ed pages of the *New York Times*, in
which he claimed the bank's culture was "as toxic and destructive
as I have ever seen it." In the months following Smith's resignation, workers from financial firms continued to depart in droves,
in part because the big money simply wasn't reliably there any
longer. The *Wall Street Journal* reported that the wave of depar-
tures was baffling to financial executives because, in many cases,
the workers were simply "bailing out with no Plan B."

In their recruiting drives, Wall Street firms still had no trouble finding eager young workers. (Goldman Sachs president
Gary Cohn announced in 2013 that the bank received 17,000

applications for 350 summer intern spots—an acceptance rate of 2.1 percent.) But the percentage of Ivy League seniors heading to investment banks remained significantly depressed. At Yale, the career center's 2013 student survey found that "there is no one industry that attracts Yale graduates as a critical mass." A *Harvard Crimson* survey found that the percentage of Harvard seniors with jobs at graduation who were headed to Wall Street fell to 9 percent in 2012, then ticked up to 15 percent in 2013.

The crisis had shrunk Wall Street tremendously; as of 2013, only 30 percent of the more than 28,000 New York City financial sector jobs lost during the crisis had come back. Meanwhile, the growing technology industry kept picking off many of Wall Street's recruits. In early 2013, the *Journal* captured the flood of interest into technology and out of finance, explaining, "Wall Street is no longer the beacon of high pay and innovation it once was." A 2013 study conducted by a recruiting firm found that 89 percent of financial executives were having problems with recruiting, and 83 percent were worried about losing their employees to other opportunities. Harvard Business School saw the share of its graduates going into the tech sector rise from 8 percent in 2010 to 18 percent in 2013, while the number heading into financial services shrank from 34 percent to 27 percent. And Wharton—that fabled training ground for high finance—revealed that applications to its MBA programs had declined 12 percent since 2010.

As they struggled to keep their workers from jumping ship, Wall Street firms began reconfiguring their young analyst programs to make them more attractive. Goldman Sachs formed a task force to examine the working conditions of young analysts, and announced it was ending its "two and out" analyst programs in the investment banking and investment management divisions, meaning that college seniors would be hired like any other employees, with no end date to their tenure. And in late 2013, the firm shocked the rest of Wall Street by announcing that it was encouraging junior banking analysts to take weekends off from work. "The goal is for our analysts to want to be here for a career," David Solomon, Goldman's co-head of investment banking, told Bloomberg News.

As the crisis got smaller in the rearview mirror, corporate profits continued to soar, even though unemployment rates remained high and the average wages earned by workers stagnated. The Dow Jones Industrial Average and the S&P 500 both reached new nominal all-time highs in late 2013, and housing prices across the country continued to rise. Wall Street banks, though smaller, also began to return to their former levels of profitability. U.S. banks made $141.3 billion in net income in 2012, according to the FDIC, their best year since 2006.

Despite efforts to make their lives easier, young financiers continued to struggle with long hours, demanding bosses, and a grueling work environment. In the summer of 2013, a twenty-one-year-old summer intern in Bank of America Merrill Lynch's London office dropped dead after an epileptic seizure. The intern, Moritz Erhardt, had worked until 6:00 a.m. three days in a row, according to some reports, and his fellow interns described him as an intensely focused workaholic who was focused on getting a full-time offer. Following Erhardt's death, Bank of America Merrill Lynch launched a task force of its own, in order to "look at all aspects of our working practices, with a particular focus on our junior populations."

Arjun Khan is an associate at an infrastructure private equity firm in São Paulo, Brazil. He's made a full recovery from his autoimmune disease, and he reports being thrilled with his decision to leave New York.

Chelsea Ball left Bank of America Merrill Lynch after her second year for a job at a small financial services company that paid her $50,000 a year, roughly 60 percent less than her total compensation as a banker. She moved into a smaller apartment with a lower rent, and has only recently been able to afford boxing lessons again, but she's happier than ever. Recently, she left her financial services job to launch her own start-up.

Derrick Havens is still employed at his private equity firm. He remains conflicted about his job and the private equity industry overall, but he loves living in New York City and has not yet seriously considered moving back home to Wisconsin. Despite repeated attempts, he hasn't slept with any more fashion models.

Jeremy Miller-Reed's start-up raised millions of dollars of funding from major venture capital firms shortly after he left Goldman, making his stock extremely valuable. Although his hours are still long, he is excelling at his job and loves the people he works with, even if he no longer gets to yell out trading orders.

Samson White's mobile ticketing start-up secured a sizable round of funding from a group of investors in 2012, and is currently working on raising more money. He and Jeremy still talk frequently, and friends who still work in finance often ask him about when they should leave for another industry. His advice to them is always the same: "The sooner, the better."

Ricardo Hernandez is an investment banking associate at J.P.

Morgan. He works just seventy or eighty hours a week in the bank's Latin American division, and he uses his newfound free time to volunteer with a youth mentoring organization, play more basketball, and drink with his college friends. Recently, while on vacation with his girlfriend, he was able to check his BlackBerry only a few times a day.

Soo-jin Park left her job in Deutsche Bank's risk management division and is now a front-office worker at a commercial bank in New York. She loves her new job, which affords her the chance to deal with actual clients and do business development. And although she's working longer hours than she did at Deutsche Bank, she's enjoying bringing in new clients, keeping existing ones happy, and getting to know the players in her industry. She is strongly considering going to business school or working abroad as her next move.

After being laid off from Credit Suisse's health-care group, J. P. Murray got a job doing corporate finance for a large hospital chain. He still hopes to make it back to New York someday, but he is enjoying his job for what it is, and he has joined the boards of several nonprofit organizations in an attempt to keep himself busy. "It's weird—everyone here is happy," he said of his slower-paced corporate finance job. "My work life is exponentially better. That said, I could stand to make a little more money."

Marina Keegan, the Yale senior who provided me with a glimpse into the campus recruiting culture after Occupy Wall Street, was killed in a car crash in May 2012, a week after her college graduation. This book, which would have been one of the duller cameos in her long and luminous literary career, is dedicated to her memory.

ACKNOWLEDGMENTS

While I was writing this book, people would occasionally ask me, "Why *on earth* did these bankers agree to talk to you?" It's a great question—and one for which I still don't have a satisfactory answer. The eight financiers I shadowed from 2010 until 2013 had no particular reason to spend three years taking my calls, responding to my e-mails, and meeting me in out-of-the-way locations to give me the dirt on their industry, during some of the most demanding and time-crunched years of their lives. And yet, out of the goodness of their hearts and at great personal risk, they kept on talking.

For that, I am grateful beyond measure. This book would not exist without the generosity and patience of the real people behind Arjun, Chelsea, Derrick, Jeremy, Samson, Ricardo, Soojin, and J. P. Their names may never be known, but their contributions won't be forgotten. To them, and the dozens of other financiers who spoke to me for this book: Thank you all, sincerely, for entrusting me with your stories. (And may you never treat your financial transactions half as recklessly.)

Thanks are due, as always, to Ben Greenberg, my star editor, and the rest of the Grand Central Publishing crew: Jamie Raab, Deb Futter, Brian McLendon, Pippa White, Amanda Pritzker, Tracy Brickman, Andrew Duncan, and Kristin Vorce.

Thanks to Kate Lee, my literary agent turned online-publishing mogul, who saw potential in this book from the start, and Sloan Harris and Kari Stuart at ICM, who guided it to completion with steady hands. Also at ICM, I'm grateful to the tenacious Josie Freedman and Liz Farrell.

Many thanks to my colleagues at *New York* and Daily Intelligencer, who inspire me every day: Adam Moss, Ben Williams, Jeb Reed, Genevieve Smith, Jessica Pressler, Dan Amira, Joe Coscarelli, Jonathan Chait, Stefan Becket, and Margaret Hartmann, among many others.

I'm indebted to my ex-colleagues at the *New York Times*, in particular DealBookers Andrew Ross Sorkin, Peter Lattman, Susanne Craig, Jeff Cane, Adrienne Carter, Ben Protess, Azam Ahmed, Evelyn Rusli, and Michael de la Merced, all of whom taught me the ins and outs of high finance. A special debt is owed to Floyd Norris, who kindly wrote to me about my first book, and ignited my interest in Wall Street's inner workings.

I'm thankful for Alex Yablon, who provided invaluable research help and fact-checking; Cynthia Colonna, who turned my garbled tapes into transcripts; Paul Roose and Anne Lawrence, who lent me their home to finish this book and provided crucial feedback when I needed it most; Scott Rostan, Trevor Nelson, and the rest of the Training the Street team for letting me crash their classes; the members of Kappa Beta Phi for not killing me on the spot; Patrick Colangelo and the rest of the Black Diamond hedge fund members for their hospitality; and Rachel Gogel, who designed this book's gorgeous cover (literally) overnight.

I'm also grateful to all those who aided this book in ways big and small: Andrew Marantz, Nick Montoya, Lucas van Praag, Dayna Tortorici, Ariel Werner, Dan MacCombie (whose Runa tea kept me awake for many late nights of writing), Caroline Landau, Matthew Zeitlin, Carolyn Roose, and Janine Cheng.

Special thanks go to A. J. Jacobs, author extraordinaire, who gave me a job when I was far too young and has been a tremendous mentor ever since; and to my entire family, including my parents, Kirk and Diana Roose, who remain the best pro bono publicists in the world.

And most of all, to Tovah Ackerman, who makes everything possible.

NOTES

A NOTE ON SOURCES

I gathered the personal stories contained in this book during hundreds of interviews with people working in and around the financial sector. Where possible, I have tried to fact-check their anecdotes without compromising a source's anonymity. In some cases, I've relied on the interview subject's account of an incident, and my account is only as good as his or her memory.

READING LIST

For general research into Wall Street's culture and history, I enjoyed and learned from the following books:

Anderson, Geraint. *Cityboy: Beer and Loathing in the Square Mile*. London: Headline, 2008.

Bruck, Connie. *The Predators' Ball: The Junk Bond Raiders and the Man who Staked Them*. New York: American Lawyer, 1988.

Burrough, Bryan, and John Helyar. *Barbarians at the Gate: The Fall of RJR Nabisco*. New York: Harper & Row, 1990.

Cohan, William D. *House of Cards: A Tale of Hubris and Wretched Excess on Wall Street*. New York: Doubleday, 2009.

Damn, It Feels Good to Be a Banker: And Other Baller Things You Only Get to Say If You Work on Wall Street. New York: Hyperion, 2008.

Dillian, Jared. *Street Freak: Money and Madness at Lehman Brothers: A Memoir*. New York: Simon & Schuster, 2011.

Fisher, Melissa S. *Wall Street Women*. Durham, NC: Duke University Press, 2012.

Greif, Mark, Dayna Tortorici, Kathleen French, Emma Janaskie, and Nick Werle. *The Trouble is the Banks: Letters to Wall Street*. Brooklyn, N.Y.: n+1, 2012.

Ho, Karen Zouwen. *Liquidated: An Ethnography of Wall Street*. Durham: Duke University Press, 2009.

Lane, Randall. *The Zeroes: My Misadventures in the Decade Wall Street Went Insane*. New York: Portfolio, 2010.

Lewis, Michael. *Liar's Poker: Rising through the Wreckage on Wall Street*. New York: W. W. Norton & Company, 1989.

Lewis, Michael. *The Big Short: Inside the Doomsday Machine*. New York: W. W. Norton & Company, 2010.

Little, Jeffrey B., and Lucien Rhodes. *Understanding Wall Street.* 4th ed. New York: McGraw-Hill, 2004.

Lowenstein, Roger. *The End of Wall Street.* New York: Penguin Press, 2010.

Rolfe, John, and Peter Troob. *Monkey Business: Swinging through the Wall Street Jungle.* New York: Warner Books, 2000.

Smith, Greg. *Why I Left Goldman Sachs: A Wall Street Story.* New York: Grand Central, 2012.

Sorkin, Andrew Ross. *Too Big to Fail: The Inside Story of How Wall Street and Washington Fought to Save the Financial System—And Themselves.* New York: Viking, 2009.

Stewart, James B. *Den of Thieves.* New York: Simon & Schuster, 1991.

Stiles, Paul. *Riding the Bull: My Year inside the Madness at Merrill Lynch.* New York: Times Business, 1998.

Chapter Notes

Introduction

ix.   **"You must be an Excel wizard—a grandmaster of the XLS file format"**: I took Training the Street's five-day "Financial Modeling & Corporate Valuation" course, which is open to the public and is held several dozen times a year at various locations around the world. For more information on these courses, visit trainingthestreet.com.

x.   **"The all-time record for total beautification was thirty-five seconds, set by a freakish junior analyst from an investment bank called Moelis and Company"**: I have since been informed that as of 2013, the new record is twenty-three seconds, set by an analyst from Wells Fargo. I have no idea how this is humanly possible.

x.   **"Armed with Bloomberg terminals and can-do attitudes"**: The Bloomberg terminal is one of the most important tools on Wall Street. Every major investment bank uses them for data analysis, news gathering, and trading, and most analysts are assigned a license to the software—which costs roughly $20,000 a year per user—on their first day on the job.

xi.   **"HBO talk show host Bill Maher quipped about executing Wall Street higher-ups"**: From the February 20, 2009, episode of HBO's *Real Time with Bill Maher.* Maher's actual words were: "I don't think we should put all the bankers to death. Just two. I mean, maybe it's not technically legal, but, let's look at the upside. If we killed two random, rich, greedy pigs. I mean, killed. Like, blew them up at halftime at next year's Super Bowl. Or left them hanging on the big board at the New York Stock Exchange. You know, as a warning, with their balls in their mouth. I think it would really make everyone else sit up and take notice."

xi. "one online clothing vendor sold 'I Hate Investment Banking' T-shirts for $18.99 apiece": Prices have since been raised slightly, but you can still find these T-shirts at http://www.cafepress.com/ramit/807964.

xi. "a new arcade game called 'Whack-a-Banker' was introduced in the United Kingdom": "Bankers 'Whacked' in Arcade Game," BBC News, December 13, 2009.

xii. "You earn significantly more than your peers in other industries": Catherine Rampell, "Outlook Is Bleak Even for Recent College Graduates," New York Times, May 18, 2011. Rampell reports that the average income for graduates of four-year schools in 2009 and 2010 was $27,000, less than half the base salary of those first-year analysts profiled in the book.

xiii. "At Harvard in 2008, 28 percent of seniors who had jobs at graduation were headed into the financial services sector. At Princeton in 2006, it was a staggering 46 percent": Catherine Rampell, "Out of Harvard, and Into Finance," New York Times (Economix), December 21, 2011. Note that Rampell's statistics include only students who had jobs as of graduation. If you count all students, the percentage of graduates working in finance is considerably lower (about 14 percent at Harvard in 2008 and about 16 percent at Princeton in 2006, according to data provided to me by those schools' career centers).

Chapter One

2. "wasn't among Wall Street's so-called target schools" For a more entertaining, less politically correct look at which schools Wall Street considers target and nontarget, see the relevant discussion in *Damn, It Feels Good to Be a Banker*, a book written by a pseudonymous blogger named Leveraged Sell-Out. (Sample passage: "Duke is prime evidence to the fact that merely being affluent and white in America can no longer thrust one into the upper echelons of the finance industry.")

2. "The firm's stock price had tumbled, thousands of workers had gotten laid off, and one well-regarded hedge fund manager jolted Wall Street that summer by proclaiming that Lehman wasn't properly accounting for its real estate investments": The hedge fund manager, David Einhorn, was profiled by Hugo Lindgren in "The Confidence Man," New York, June 15, 2008.

2. "In September 2008, while Arjun was starting his senior year at Fordham, Lehman filed for bankruptcy": The nitty-gritty details of the financial crisis are available in thousands of books, websites, and articles. I found Andrew Ross Sorkin's *Too Big to Fail* the most comprehensive guide to the events of 2008, but others, including Roger Lowenstein's *The End of Wall Street* and Bethany McLean and Joe Nocera's *All the Devils Are Here*, were indispensable as well.

4. "Arjun knew that Wall Street operated on a strict power hierarchy": For more on the employee hierarchy at investment banks, see chapter 2

of Ho's *Liquidated*, in which she discusses the stratification within firms, and writes that "the boundaries between front, middle, and back offices reinscribe social hierarchies."

4.   **"Tiny boutique firms were weathering the changes better than global financial conglomerates"**: Theresa Agovino, "Cleaning Up After Real Estate Debacle," *Crain's New York Business*, December 13, 2009.

5.   **"*Reconsidering Wall Street?*"**: http://www.wallstreetoasis.com/forums/ reconsidering-wall-street.

5.   **"*Will banking recover? How long?*"**: http://www.wallstreetoasis.com/ forums/will-banking-recover-how-long.

5.   **"*Are banks really not hiring for the fall?*"**: http://www.wallstreetoasis. com/forums/are-banks-really-not-hiring-for-the-fall.

5.   **"The most famous example was Sidney Weinberg"**: More on Weinberg's rise to the top of Goldman Sachs can be found in Malcolm Gladwell's *New Yorker* article, "The Uses of Adversity," published November 10, 2008.

6.   **"there had been a Lebanese-American executive who had gone to Pace University"**: After Bear Stearns crumbled, this executive, Fares D. Noujaim, landed at Bank of America Merrill Lynch, where he became executive vice chairman of Global Corporate & Investment Banking. See: Landon Thomas, Jr., "A Bear Stearns Refugee Gets a New Start at Merrill," *New York Times*, June 2, 2008.

6.   **"Even Citigroup's CEO, Vikram Pandit, was an Indian-born outsider"**: For more on Pandit's rise at the bank (which was later interrupted by a management coup in October 2012), see Joe Hagan's "The Most Powerless Powerful Man on Wall Street," *New York*, March 1, 2009.

Chapter Two

9.   **"Bank of America had acquired Merrill Lynch"**: Again, Sorkin, Lowenstein, and McLean/Nocera provide good background on the Bank of America Merrill Lynch merger, including all that went wrong.

9.   **"John Thain was revealed to have spent a Croesus-like $1.2 million renovating his office"**: Peter S. Green, "Merrill's Thain Said to Pay $1.2 Million to Decorator," Bloomberg News, January 23, 2009.

9.   **"$50 billion deal from hell"**: Heidi N. Moore, "Bank of America–Merrill Lynch: A $50 Billion Deal from Hell," *Wall Street Journal* (Deal Journal), January 22, 2009.

10.   **"the country's largest commercial bank"**: As of September 30, 2009, Bank of America had the most domestic assets and local branches of any American bank, according to the Federal Reserve, though JPMorgan Chase had more consolidated assets.

10.   **"Chelsea quickly found she could scan the room and pick out the Merrill kids"**: More on the elite culture of Merrill Lynch before the crash can be found in Paul Stiles's *Riding the Bull*, in which he says that the

firm "dominates almost all major areas of the securities industry." (Bear in mind, his book was published in 1998.)

Chapter Three

15. "a Morgan Stanley recruiter pressed Play to begin a promotional video": This video, called "Futures and Options," can be found online on various video sites, and is really worth the four minutes and forty-three seconds.
16. "Penn sends a chunk of its graduating class into the financial services industry every year": For more information about Penn and Wharton's extremely close ties with Wall Street, I recommend Nicole Ridgway's *The Running of the Bulls*, a 2005 book that traces seven students through Wharton's on-campus recruiting process for finance jobs.
16. "Wharton School, a business program that contains both graduate students and undergrads, is considered America's primo farm team for budding young financiers": Ridgway's book contains an amazing anecdote about the hypercompetitive nature of finance recruiting at Wharton. At the beginning of the 2000 school year, she writes, Wharton gave its students 1,000 "points" each, which could be used to bid on interview slots for companies they wanted to work for. The idea was that students would spread their points out among several firms, but "several students who had hoped to get their foot in the door at Goldman bid all 1,000 of their points to meet with the firm's recruiters."
18. "in the early 1980s, banks began instituting what became the modern Wall Street recruiting program": In *Liquidated*, Ho writes: "In the 1980s, [banks] began to recruit at elite universities on a grand scale, creating the two-year analyst programs for the express purpose of targeting undergraduates directly out of college. This new cadre of workers, no longer handpicked through small-scale networks of family, friends, and close business associates, was legitimated by placing even greater cachet on the universities where they were recruited."
19. "first-year analyst jobs pay a starting salary of around $70,000, with a year-end bonus that can be upwards of $50,000": According to Mergers & Inquisitions, first-year analysts in 2007 could make up to $150,000 in total compensation. After the crash, I never heard of a first-year investment banker pulling in more than $130,000, though it's certainly possible that some standouts were making 2007-style money.
20. "Wall Street banks had made themselves the obvious destinations for students at top-tier colleges who are confused about their careers": The *Washington Post*'s Ezra Klein interviewed one anonymous Harvard graduate, who explained the appeal of Wall Street jobs thusly: "In the midst of anxiety and trying to find a job at the end of college, the recruiters are really in your face, and they make it very easy. One thing is the internship program. It's your junior year, it's January or February, and you interview for

internships. If all goes well, it's sort of a summer-long interview. And if that goes well, you have an offer by September of your senior year, and that's very appealing. It makes your senior year more relaxed, you can focus on your thesis, you can drink more. You just don't have to worry about getting a job." ("Why Do Harvard Kids Head to Wall Street? An Interview with an Ex–Wall Street Recruit," April 23, 2010.)

Chapter Five

34. **"young bankers are 'oriented into a culture of instability and competition where they must hit the ground running.'"** Ho, chapter 2.

35. **"At Goldman Sachs…what used to be the human resources department is now known as 'Human Capital Management'"**: Most other Wall Street firms have stuck with "human resources." If, for some odd reason, you're interested in why corporations like Goldman Sachs call their employees "human capital," and how the term differs from "human resources," there is an entire book on the subject: *Human Capital Management: Achieving Added Value through People*, by Angela Baron and Michael Armstrong (Kogan Page, 2008).

36. **"I reflected on a passage from *The Financiers*"**: This book, by Michael Jensen (Weybright and Talley, 1976) is cited in the introduction to Ho's *Liquidated*.

Chapter Six

39. **"the Series 7"**: In *Why I Left Goldman Sachs*, former Goldman vice president Greg Smith describes the Series 7 as "your first big test on Wall Street, a rite of passage that allows you to start calling clients and being useful. The exam is six hours long, and the material is about the thickness of two large encyclopedias."

39. **"the Series 63"**: Smith describes the Series 63 as being "deceptively shorter but actually harder" than the Series 7.

40. **"Goldman's internships paid around $15,000 for ten weeks of work"**: Kevin Roose, "Fewer Perks and More Work for Wall Street's Summer Interns," *New York Times*, July 21, 2011.

40. **"At Goldman, the hierarchy of prestige was shifting rapidly"**: Matthias Rieker, "Goldman to Close Prop-Trading Unit," *Wall Street Journal*, September 4, 2010.

40. **"an elite team of investors known throughout the bank as SSG—the Special Situations Group"**: Christine Harper, "Goldman Sachs's SSG: Lending or Trading?," *Bloomberg Businessweek*, March 31, 2011.

41. **"a successful trader with several years of experience could easily make $500,000 or $600,000 a year"**: A 2013 *Bloomberg Businessweek* article put the average Goldman Sachs worker's pay for three months at $135,594, which translates to about $542,000 per year (Peter Coy, "At Goldman, the Average Pay for Three Months Is $135,594," April 16, 2013).

42. "The commodities division's prestige could be traced to 1981, the year that Goldman bought J. Aron": Susanne Craig, "The J. Aron Takeover of Goldman Sachs," *New York Times* (DealBook), October 1, 2012.

48. "200 West Street in Battery Park City, was a $2.1 billion monument": Paul Goldberger, the architecture critic at the *New Yorker*, wrote that the Goldman headquarters "appears to have been designed in the hope of rendering the company invisible." ("Shadow Building," May 17, 2010.)

49. "The popular backlash had started in the summer of 2009 with a *Rolling Stone* story": Matt Taibbi, "The Great American Bubble Machine," *Rolling Stone*, July 9, 2009. Taibbi's article was later expanded into part of a book, *Griftopia* (Spiegel & Grau, 2010).

49. "a mortgage-backed CDO called Abacus 2007-AC1": Gregory Zuckerman, Susanne Craig, and Serena Ng, "Goldman Sachs Charged with Fraud," *Wall Street Journal*, April 17, 2010.

50. "Goldman's mortgage trading desk, the same one Samson was slated to work on, was at the center of the scandal": Kate Kelly, "Goldman's Take-No-Prisoners Attitude," *Wall Street Journal*, April 26, 2010.

Chapter Seven

55. "On Wall Street, this is called the 'Seamless Belly,' after the website that is used to order restaurant meals on the company dime": *Fast Company*'s Austin Carr wrote about how Wall Street analysts have discovered how to game Seamless in order to squeeze the maximum possible use out of their meal stipends. ("How Wall Street Bankers Use Seamless to Feast on Free Lobster, Steak, and Beer," March 5, 2012.)

56. "He lived in Windsor Court, a massive apartment complex in Murray Hill": The *New York Times* described Windsor Court as a place where "recent college graduates can find themselves among fellow alumni, meet up for familiar drinking rituals and flock to the frozen-yogurt shops and sushi bars that help them stay fit and find a mate for the next stage of life." (Joseph Berger, "In Murray Hill, the College Life Need Never End," January 18, 2011.)

57. "abbreviations: DCF, CIM, LBO, VIX, and hundreds more": If you're curious: discounted cash flow, confidential information memorandum, leveraged buyout, and CBOE Volatility Index.

58. "bars like Joshua Tree…and the Patriot Saloon are considered first-year watering holes": For more establishments in the same vein, see Business Insider's "The Most Obnoxious Bars on Wall Street" slideshow (Linette Lopez, August 3, 2012.)

58. "Most large investment banks block…social media services in their offices": William Alden, "On Wall St., Keeping a Tight Rein on Twitter," *New York Times* (DealBook), March 21, 2012.

59. "A recent academic study of young bankers": Alexandra Michel, "Tran-

scending Socialization: A Nine-Year Ethnography of the Body's Role in Organizational Control and Knowledge Workers' Transformation," *Administrative Science Quarterly*, September 2011, vol. 56, no. 3.

Chapter Eight

63. "A few minutes earlier, Soo-jin had finished hearing Deutsche Bank's male investment bank chief": Kevin Roose, "The Continuing Trials of Wall Street's Women," *New York Times* (DealBook), October 26, 2010.

64. "he, too, was a veteran": Caroline Copley, "Swiss to Vote on Scrapping Social 'Glue' of Military Draft," Reuters, September 17, 2013.

64. "the uniformed officer, outfitted in military fatigues, who stood outside the bank's 60 Wall Street headquarters every day": From personal experience, I can tell you that these guards look scary, but they are in fact incredibly kind, even to reporters attempting to sneak into the Deutsche Bank atrium.

65. "Zoe Cruz, the number two executive at Morgan Stanley, was fired in late 2007": Joe Hagan, "Only the Men Survive," *New York*, April 27, 2008.

65. "Erin Callan, the CFO of Lehman Brothers, was fired in 2008": Patricia Sellers, "The Fall of a Wall Street Highflier," *Fortune*, March 15, 2010.

65. "Sallie Krawcheck, a high-ranking Citigroup executive, was forced out of her bank": Geraldine Fabrikant, "When Citi Lost Sallie," *New York Times*, November 15, 2008.

65. "Krawcheck, who was later hired (and ousted again) by Bank of America Merrill Lynch": Dan Fitzpatrick and Robin Sidel, "BofA Shakes Up Senior Ranks," *Wall Street Journal*, September 7, 2011.

65. "On a case-by-case-by-case basis": Sallie Krawcheck, "Should We Care About Diversity? (Yes, It's a Serious Question)," LinkedIn, October 18, 2012.

65. "According to Melissa S. Fisher": Fisher's statistics are credited to a *Wall Street Journal* article (Kyle Stock, "Ranks of Women on Wall Street Thin," September 20, 2010).

65. "Fisher blames the loss of female bodies, in part, on the crisis": Melissa S. Fisher, *Wall Street Women*, p. 156.

66. "No longer are job applicants to Wall Street firms asked": Ibid, p. 51.

66. "A 2006 analysis conducted by the *New York Times*": Jenny Anderson, "Wall Street's Women Face a Fork in the Road," *New York Times*, August 6, 2006.

66. "At Deutsche Bank, where Soo-jin worked": Angela Cullen, "Merkel Seeks Women on Boards as Ackermann Draws Howls," *Bloomberg News*, February 28, 2011.

66. "both Goldman Sachs and Citigroup were hit with class-action lawsuits": Bob Van Voris and Christine Harper, "Goldman Sachs Sued Over Alleged Gender Discrimination," *Bloomberg News*, September 15, 2010;

Thomas Kaplan, "6 Women Accuse Citigroup of Gender Bias," *New York Times* (DealBook), October 13, 2010.

67. **"real gender inequality was only given a light gloss":** For more on the experience of being a female on Wall Street, read Nina Godiwalla's *Suits*, a memoir of her time as an analyst at Morgan Stanley. (Atlas, 2011.)

67. **"Several months later, Soo-jin saw something even more troubling":** Tom Bawden and Julia Kollewe, "Pretty and Colourful: What Women Bring to the DB Boardroom, Says Ackermann," *The Telegraph*, February 7, 2011.

Chapter Nine

71. **"Can I get an offer on the 70-by-110 collars in Cal 15 for 50 lots per month?":** If you want to learn more about complex options trading, a good place to start might be Lawrence G. McMillan's *Options as a Strategic Investment* (Prentice Hall Press, 5th ed., 2012), which is considered the bible of options investing. (I say "might" because I cannot actually vouch for the book's quality, having gotten only about a dozen pages into it before getting a headache.)

76. **"Traders who came through on big axes would often get congratulated in the morning meetings, and often found their year-end bonuses increased as a result":** Greg Smith talks about Goldman's "axe" culture as well, describing axes as "something…Goldman wants to clear from its inventory, making a compelling but not always completely accurate case for clients to buy them." Smith also writes that "double GCs were sometimes awarded for axe-filling successes." (*Why I Left Goldman Sachs*, p. 231.)

78. **"In July, it settled the Abacus fraud lawsuit":** Sewell Chan and Louise Story, "Goldman Pays $550 Million to Settle Fraud Case," *New York Times*, July 15, 2010.

78. **"In September, it began to disband Goldman Sachs Principal Strategies":** Christine Harper and Saijel Kishan, "Goldman Sachs Said to Shut Principal Strategies Unit," Bloomberg News, September 3, 2010.

78. **"the firm announced mediocre quarterly earnings that were down 40 percent":** Susanne Craig, "Lower Profit at Goldman Reflects Wall St. Slowdown," *New York Times* (DealBook), October 19, 2010.

79. **"*Vanity Fair* demoted Lloyd Blankfein":** "The Vanity Fair 100," *Vanity Fair*, October 2010.

79. **"Goldman tried to pare some of its image woes":** Shira Ovide, "Goldman's New Ads: Healing the Damage from 'God's Work'?," *Wall Street Journal* (Deal Journal), September 29, 2010.

Chapter Ten

85. **"There are conferences, workshops, and affinity groups":** A few of many examples include Citigroup's "Hispanic Heritage" and "African

Heritage" employee groups, Morgan Stanley's "Jet Career Management Program," and Credit Suisse's "Black Professionals Network."

85. **"A study by CUNY professors Richard Alba and Joseph Pereira"**: "Progress and Pitfalls of Diversity on Wall Street," CUNY Center for Urban Research, December 2011.

85. **"A 2010 report by the U.S. Government Accountability Office"**: Orice Williams Brown, "Overall Trends in Management-Level Diversity and Diversity Initiatives," testimony given before the Subcommittees on Oversight and Investigations and Housing and Community Opportunity, House Committee on Financial Services, May 12, 2010.

Chapter Eleven

94. **"Young people, they said, were prone to overreacting when their managers called them out on mistakes, and would often get highly emotional when confronted with anything other than unadulterated praise"**: Many studies have been done about the challenges of managing millennials—the dumb name given to people in Chelsea's and my generation—in the workplace. One, by University of California Santa Barbara professors Karen K. Myers and Kamyab Sadaghiani ("Millennials in the Workplace: A Communication Perspective on Millennials' Organizational Relationships and Performance," *Journal of Business and Psychology*, June 2010) suggests that "Millennials thrive on recognition and promotions, but they also expect to become involved in projects that have a major impact on the organization." Clearly, first-year investment banking doesn't fit the bill.

Chapter Twelve

99. **"offers as high as $250,000 a year for a talented private equity analyst are common"**: Kyle Stock, "Private Equity Paying More for Less Experienced Analysts," FINS Finance, June 6, 2011.

99. **"They were thought to be slash-and-burn buyout artists who took over companies and extracted all the profit they could for themselves, then left the limp carcasses behind"**: This reputation was not entirely undeserved. See Bryan Burrough and John Helyar's *Barbarians at the Gate*, the classic book about the 1980s leveraged buyout business.

99. **"firms have been pushing the process earlier and earlier"**: Kevin Roose, "A Grab for Wall Street's Rising Stars Before They've Risen, *New York Times* (DealBook), March 9, 2011.

102. **"In social psychology, this phenomenon is called the 'hedonic treadmill'"**: Shane Frederick, "Hedonic Treadmill," entry in *Encyclopedia of Social Psychology*, eds. R. F. Baumeister and Kathleen D. Vohs, Sage Publications, 2007.

102. **"There was less to go around…tighter opportunity sets"**: Max Abelson

and Ambereen Choudhury, "After Massive Job Cuts, Wall Street's a Different Place," *Bloomberg Businessweek*, December 1, 2011.

Chapter Thirteen

105. "I decided to go to Fashion Meets Finance": Kevin Roose, "Fashion Meets Finance, After the Crisis," *New York Times* (DealBook), May 6, 2011.

105. "Women in fashion need men who can facilitate their pre-30 marriage/retirement plan": Brian Niemietz, "Dough Job," *New York Post*, June 10, 2008.

106. "But in 2009, it returned with a vengeance": Amy Odell, "Thank God for Goldman Profits—Fashion Meets Finance Is BACK," *New York* (The Cut), July 29, 2009.

110. "who are often taught to succeed by emulating the people above them on the food chain": See Ho's *Liquidated*, p. 52.

Chapter Fourteen

113. "The number of huge companies doing big, billion-dollar deals fell in the wake of the financial crisis": Antonio Capaldo, David Cogman, and Hannu Suonio, "What's Different About M&A in This Downturn," McKinsey Insights & Publications, January 2009.

113. "and hadn't yet recovered": Helen Thomas and Anousha Sakoui, "M&A Volumes for 2011 Set to Disappoint," *Financial Times*, September 29, 2011.

114. "some of the analysts in Ricardo's group had procured alertness pills like Adderall and Modafinil": For more on the recreational use of Modafinil by Wall Street workers, see Robert Kolker's *New York* article, "The Real *Limitless* Drug Isn't Just for Lifehackers Anymore" (March 31, 2013).

Chapter Fifteen

121. "had even taken the liberty of reserving the domain name wallstdropday.com, just in case it ever came to fruition": It didn't.

122. "Jeremy went back to his usual spot on the roof of his apartment building, lit up a joint, and broke down": A note on drug use: I'm often asked if young bankers on Wall Street abuse drugs. I can't say for certain, but in my experience, the drug intake for many first- and second-year analysts is limited to heavy drinking, performance-enhancers at work (Adderall, Modafinil, and over-the-counter caffeine pills), and an occasional pot-smoking session on the weekends or at night after work. The financial sector's cocaine use, which was notorious before the financial crisis, seems to be much less prevalent now, or at least is confined to older bankers and traders, who have more free time to go wild anyway.

Chapter Seventeen

135. **"A European debt crisis had been raging"**: For more on the Euro zone crisis, see "Timeline: The Unfolding Eurozone Crisis," BBC News, June 13, 2012.

136. **"Banks were still taking on huge, leveraged positions in opaque and little-regulated markets"**: Dominic Elliott, "Basel Leverage Rules to Put Pressure on Wall Street," Reuters Breakingviews, June 26, 2013.

136. **"The junk bond market...was having its strongest year since the crisis"**: Matt Wirz and Shira Ovide, "Welcome to the Biggest Junk Bond Sale Since the Financial Crisis," *Wall Street Journal* (Deal Journal), July 26, 2011.

136. **"that work lived on under the guise of 'market-making' trading desks"**: Frank Partnoy and Jesse Eisinger, "What's Inside America's Banks?," the *Atlantic*, January 2013.

137. **"traders who had worked in the back and middle offices tended to have deep knowledge of their firm's technical systems, and could exploit them if given the chance to trade on their own"**: John Gapper, *How to Be a Rogue Trader*, Portfolio, 2011.

Chapter Eighteen

141. **"The classic private equity deal was a leveraged buyout"**: In the pro-logue to *Barbarians at the Gate*, Burrough and Helyar describe the leveraged buyout this way: "In an LBO, a small group of senior exec-utives, usually working with a Wall Street partner, proposes to buy its company from public shareholders, using massive amounts of borrowed money. Critics of this procedure called it stealing the company from its owners and fretted that the growing mountain of corporate debt was hin-dering America's ability to compete abroad. Everyone knew LBOs meant deep cuts in research and every other imaginable budget, all sacrificed to pay off debt. Proponents insisted that companies forced to meet steep debt payments grew lean and mean. On one thing they all agreed: The executives who launched LBOs got filthy rich." A kinder description of the private equity business model ("collect money, pair it with debt, and buy a company with the intent of selling it down the line for a profit") can be found in Jason Kelly's *The New Tycoons* (John Wiley & Sons, 2012).

Chapter Nineteen

145. **"the annual earthquake known in the corporatized language of HR as the 'compensation communication period'"**: Kevin Roose and Susanne Craig, "It's Goldman Bonus Day," *New York Times* (DealBook), January 19, 2012.

146. **"bonus season amounts to a combination of Christmas and Judgment Day"**: Every year, banks try to stall their analyst bonus days until after other banks have gone and set their levels accordingly, avoiding paving

Banker A $40,000 while Banker B across the street at UBS gets $45,000 a week later. Nobody wants to overpay or underpay. The whole thing has a whiff of price-fixing to it, and would be funny if all involved didn't take it so utterly seriously.

146. **"Analysts who land in the top bucket are often assured of a third-year offer"**: When bonus numbers emerge, they are invariably leaked to Dealbreaker, the finance blog, where they're posted anonymously for other analysts to kvetch over. One 2010 posting about bonuses at J.P. Morgan that no doubt inspired jealousy all over Wall Street read: "first year IB analyst top bucket $65K, second bucket $60K (first year base is $70K). JPM told analysts they 'want to pay at the top of the market.' People are generally happy with the numbers." (Bess Levin, "Bonus Watch: JPMorgan," July 30, 2010.)

Chapter Twenty-One

155. **"tacked posters of Warren Buffett and George Soros on their walls"**: I don't know if such posters actually exist, but they should.

156. **"Black Diamond is Harvard's most exclusive student-run hedge fund"**: Mercer R. Cook, "Exclusive Investment Club Asks Student Members for $1,000," *Harvard Crimson*, September 14, 2012 (note: Black Diamond has changed its membership and investment rules since the *Crimson*'s report).

159. **"But here, you have guys with commonality; everyone is going into finance, everyone has a background in finance, everyone is interested in making profits"**: After my visit to Harvard, Patrick sent me a list of the firms where Black Diamond's alumni have worked. It's a who's who of global finance, and includes Bridgewater Associates, the Blackstone Group, D. E. Shaw, Bain Capital, the European Central Bank, the Federal Reserve, and every big investment bank you can think of.

Chapter Twenty-Two

164. **"Goldman, like many Wall Street firms, gets relatively sleepy in the summer"**: Patti Domm, "Sleepy Summer Markets Could Give Way to Rougher Fall," CNBC.com, August 16, 2012.

165. **"Jeremy had gone in with more than a dozen other first- and second-year Goldman analysts on a house share in Westhampton"**: For an exploration of the annual phenomenon of Hamptons house shares, nothing beats Vanessa Grigoriadis's 1999 *New York* story "Welcome to the Fun House," in which she describes the summer antics at a Bridgehampton house where twenty-odd summer roommates, many from Wall Street, spent their days "reading *Forbes*, gabbing on cell phones, and slathering Coppertone Sport on well-maintained bodies."

Chapter Twenty-Three

172. **"The slow municipal bond markets"**: Lisa Lambert, "US Municipal Market Shrinks for Two Straight Qtrs.," Reuters, September 16, 2011.

173. **"Well, the idea might at least be floated."**: This is a joke.

Chapter Twenty-Four

178. **"Facebook was preparing to go public the following year"**: Shira Ovide, "What We Know About the Facebook IPO," *Wall Street Journal* (Deal Journal), June 13, 2011.

178. **"Apple had become the biggest consumer-facing company in the world"**: Dominic Rushe, "Apple Pips Exxon as World's Biggest Company," *The Guardian*, August 9, 2011.

178. **"A 2011 survey conducted by the consulting firm Universum"**: Cited by Rachel Emma Silverman, "Young Workers Like Facebook, Apple and Google," *Wall Street Journal*, November 13, 2011.

179. **"Between 2007 and 2012, the number of jobs in New York City's tech industry"**: Jonathan Bowles and David Giles, "New Tech City," report by the Center for an Urban Future, May 2012.

180. **"And among MBA programs, Harvard is a financier's paradise"**: For more about Harvard Business School, I recommend Philip Delves Broughton's *Ahead of the Curve* (Penguin, 2008), a memoir about his two years at HBS. Broughton describes how deeply intertwined HBS and the financial sector had been, writing: "It felt as though the consulting firms and the Wall Street banks had buried encampments on campus from which they deployed their fresh-faced recruiters. They made unsolicited calls to our homes offering to describe their work. It was like being badgered by the Church of Scientology" (p. 135).

181. **"He oversaw the growth of a voluntary pledge called the 'MBA Oath'"**: Max Anderson, "Why We Created the MBA Oath," Harvard Business Review Blog Network, June 8, 2009.

181. **"Dean Nohria's efforts to unhook HBS from the financial sector were visible in admissions, too"**: Statistics on the pre-MBA careers of HBS students were provided by HBS.

Chapter Twenty-Five

185. **"It had made the national news the day before"**: Colin Moynihan, "80 Arrested as Financial District Protest Moves North," *New York Times*, September 24, 2011.

186. **"international cities as far-flung as Sydney, Tokyo, and Davos"**: A big list of Occupy protests can be found here: "Occupy Protests around the World: Full List Visualized," *The Guardian*, November 14, 2011.

187. **"The exceptions were people like Vikram Pandit"**: Donal Griffin, "Pandit Says He'd Be Happy to Talk with Wall Street Protesters," Bloomberg News, October 12, 2011.

187. "Later, JPMorgan Chase CEO Jamie Dimon would say": Polya Lesova, "Dimon: Occupy Wall Street Has 'Legitimate Complaints,'" Market-Watch, May 3, 2012.

189. "The cutoff for the top 1 percent of American tax filers in 2010 was about $370,000 in adjusted gross income": Adrian Dungan and Michael Parisi, "Individual Income Tax Rates and Shares, 2010," Internal Revenue Service.

Chapter Twenty-Six

192. "Roughly 20 percent of the Yale graduating class typically goes into business and finance": Beverly Waters, "Yale College Class of 2010: A Study of Activities One Year After Graduation," Office of Institutional Research, Yale University, June 2011.

192. "among Yale alumni in the industry are such heavyweights as Steve Schwarzman": Other Yale graduates in finance include short-seller James Chanos and Robert Greenhill, the founder of Greenhill and Co., a New York investment bank.

192. "folded the results into an essay for Yale's weekly news magazine": Marina Keegan, "Even Artichokes Have Doubts," Yale Daily News Weekend, September 30, 2011.

193. "I wrote to her and asked her if she could adapt it into a short article for DealBook": Marina Keegan, "Another View: The Science and Strategy of College Recruiting," New York Times (DealBook), November 9, 2011.

194. "students at many other top-flight colleges had begun raising questions about the dominance of financial recruiting on their campuses": Kevin Roose, "An Orange and Black Eye for 2 Banks," New York Times (DealBook), December 9, 2011. For full dramatic effect, I recommend the videos of students at Princeton interrupting recruiting sessions by J.P. Morgan and Goldman Sachs, which are available on YouTube. (Search "JP Morgan-Chase Mic-Checked at Princeton University" and "Goldman Sachs Anti-Recruitment Session at Princeton University.")

195. "students at Harvard and other schools protested the recruiting efforts of Dow Chemical": "Students Will Protest Dow Chemical Today," Harvard Crimson, October 25, 1967.

196. "In the early 1970s, Stanford University banned Goldman Sachs from recruiting on campus for five years": William D. Cohan, Money and Power: How Goldman Sachs Came to Rule the World, Doubleday, 2011.

196. "And after the Iraq War in 2003, students at many top-tier schools protested Lockheed Martin, Halliburton, and other military and weapons companies": Nicole Dungca, "SDS Protests CIA, Raytheon Recruiters," Brown Daily Herald, September 24, 2008; Peter Schworm, "Students Switching Activism to Boardroom," Boston Globe, August 13, 2007.

196. "At Harvard, a young alumnus named David Weinfeld wrote an op-ed": David A. Weinfeld, "Boycott Wall Street," *Harvard Crimson*, October 11, 2011.

197. "At Stanford, two student columnists called for the school": "Op-Ed: Stop the Wall Street Recruitment," *Stanford Daily*, October 11, 2011.

197. "at Duke, another finance feeder school, a majority opinion of the student editorial board added its voice": "Pass the Buck," *Duke Chronicle*, December 1, 2011.

197. "Morgan Stanley CEO James Gorman emphatically denied that the financial industry's massive unpopularity made an impression on incoming recruits": Michael J. Moore, "Morgan Stanley Said to End Ban on Junior Banker Job Hunts," Bloomberg News, April 16, 2013.

198. "At Harvard, the percentage of seniors with jobs at graduation who went directly into financial services fell from 28 percent in the class of 2008 to 17 percent in the class of 2011. At Princeton, where 46 percent of seniors with jobs at graduation were once Wall Street–bound, that number shrunk to 35.9 percent in 2010": Again, these numbers reflect only students who had jobs as of graduation.

198. "But the moral and reputational fallout of the crisis had also had an impact": Kevin Roose, "At Top Colleges, Anti-Wall St. Fervor Complicates Recruiting," *New York Times*, November 28, 2011.

Chapter Twenty-Seven

This chapter is an expansion of a story I wrote for the *New York Times* on January 20, 2012, "A Raucous Hazing at a Wall St. Fraternity."

206. "I'd heard lots about the existence of Kappa Beta Phi": Matthew Karnitschnig and Susanne Craig, "A Wall Street Frat Parties On, Singing, 'Bye, Bye to My Piece of the Pie,'" *Wall Street Journal*, January 16, 2009; Max Abelson, "Wall Street Secret Society Kappa Beta Phi Adds Dealmakers With Lehman Rite," Bloomberg News, January 17, 2011.

211. "Novogratz, who wrestled at Princeton before going into the military": Lynnley Browning, "Wrestling's Private Equity Champion," *New York Times* (DealBook), April 5, 2013.

212. "Alexandra Lebenthal—a bond-investing socialite": In addition to her duties with Kappa Beta Phi and her bond firm, Lebenthal is also the author of *The Recessionistas*, a 2010 novel about the post-crash affairs of the financial elite.

212. "Just leave out the vulgar stuff, please": The day after the dinner, Ross defended the group's activities again. "This is not a political convention," he told me. "It's a group of people that are friendly with each other trying to have an enjoyable evening, mostly at each other's expense."

215. "the idea of a reporter making those views public had caused them to throw a mass temper tantrum": I had hoped that my reporting on

the Kappa Beta Phi induction dinner would give the group some moral pause; instead, I was told by a member of the group that the following year's dinner went on as scheduled, except with "Fort Knox–like" security at the entrance.

Chapter Twenty-Eight

219. "They pulled this off through the use of leverage, and a financial engineering tactic known as a 'dividend recap,' or recapitalization, which involved loading a company with more debt in order to pay out the private equity firm and its investors": Dan Primack, "Dividend Recaps Are Fine, But Don't Pretend They Add Value," *Fortune*, November 11, 2010.

220. "private equity—an industry that had been attacked as a form of 'vulture capitalism' during Mitt Romney's 2008 presidential run (and that would soon taint his 2012 run)": See, among many other articles assessing Romney's career at Bain Capital, Mark Maremont's *Wall Street Journal* story, "Romney at Bain: Big Gains, Some Busts," January 9, 2012.

221. "The supremacy of Wall Street's intellect was, in many ways, the financial sector's founding myth": Ho writes: "The culture of smartness is not simply a quality of Wall Street, but a currency, a driving force productive of both profit accumulation and global prowess" (*Liquidated*, p. 40).

222. "But, on the whole, they weren't *brilliant*": To be fair to financiers, there aren't that many brilliant journalists, either.

Chapter Twenty-Nine

229. "he'd spend hours a day reading the *Economist*, the *Atlantic*, and the *New York Times*": This is actually a fairly highbrow media diet, by young Wall Street standards. Many of the first- and second-year analysts I interviewed spent their downtime reading sites like Barstool Sports and BroBible, with the occasional glance at ESPN.com.

229. "the oil market was still fairly active that fall": Chris Kahn, "Oil Soars, But Don't Worry Yet at the Pump," Associated Press, November 9, 2011.

Chapter Thirty

231. "The policy, known as 'block leave,' had been instituted not to give burned-out employees a week away from the grind, but to catch traders who were engaged in irresponsible or illegal activity": Heidi N. Moore, "Credit Suisse Makes Life a Little Harder for Aspiring Rogue Traders," Marketplace, December 15, 2011.

234. "the firm had been forced to lay off some employees": Lauren Tara LaCapra, "Layoffs Sweep Wall Street, Along with Low Morale," Reuters, August 21, 2011.

Chapter Thirty-One

239. "Bank of America Merrill Lynch reduced the size of its cash bonuses by 75 percent": Gabriel Sherman, "The End of Wall Street As They Knew It," *New York*, February 5, 2012.

239. "Morgan Stanley capped cash bonuses at $125,000 for everyone, even the cigar-chomping executives at the top": Kevin Roose, "Morgan Stanley Is Said to Cap Cash Bonuses at $125,000," *New York Times* (DealBook), January 17, 2012.

239. "And at Goldman Sachs, the amount set aside to pay compensation and benefits was $12.22 billion, or $367,000 per employee, down 21 percent from the year before": Peter Eavis and Susanne Craig, "New Normal on Wall Street: Smaller and Restrained," *New York Times*, January 19, 2012.

240. "Dodd-Frank, which was signed into law by President Obama in July 2010, was the most sweeping piece of new regulation on the financial industry since the Great Depression": For more on the intended (and actual) effects of Dodd-Frank, I recommend Jesse Eisinger and Jake Bernstein's "From Dodd-Frank to Dud: How Financial Reform May Be Going Wrong," published by ProPublica on June 3, 2011.

241. "Next came Basel III": For the backstory on Basel III and what it was meant to accomplish, I recommend Jack Ewing's "A Fight to Make Banks More Prudent," published in the *New York Times*, December 20, 2011.

241. "That winter, JPMorgan Chase reported fourth-quarter profits that were 23 percent lower than the previous year's": Ben Protess, "Weak Quarter Weighs on JPMorgan's 2011 Profit," *New York Times* (DealBook), January 13, 2012.

241. "Goldman Sachs's profits for all of 2011 fell more than 50 percent from the previous year's levels. The net income earned by Bank of America's investment banking division, which includes Merrill Lynch, dropped by 53 percent, and Morgan Stanley's earnings fell by 42 percent for the year": Peter Eavis and Susanne Craig, "New Normal on Wall Street: Smaller and Restrained," *New York Times*, January 19, 2012.

241. "The new regulatory framework will undoubtedly make Wall Street less valuable than it was before": Kevin Roose, "A Blow to Pinstripe Aspirations," *New York Times*, November 21, 2011.

242. "the number of employees in the securities industry in New York City between ages twenty and thirty-four fell by 25 percent from the third quarter of 2008 to the third quarter of 2011, whereas the overall decline in workers of all ages was only 17 percent": Ibid.

245. "In an economic climate where nearly 20 percent of people under twenty-five were unemployed": "Employment Status of the Civilian Noninstitutional Population 16 to 24 Years of Age," Bureau of Labor Statistics, July 2010–2013.

245. "The British economist Roger Bootle has written about the difference between creative and distributive work": Roger Bootle, *The Trouble with Markets*, Nicholas Brealey Publishing, 2009, p. 86. Bootle's chapter also touches on the special problems with the financial sector, which he says are not only the propensity for distributive work, but for their "natural tendency to take up too many resources" and for being "prone to bubbles that, when they burst, can endanger the stability of the whole financial system."

Chapter Thirty-Four

261. "a waitress carried out a wooden alpine ski with five shot glasses built into it": Shot-ski.com claims to be "North America's leading supplier of liquid courage," and sells shot-skis for $69.95 and up, if you're curious.

262. "Associate jobs weren't laid-back by any stretch of the imagination": The pseudonymous author of *Damn, It Feels Good to Be a Banker* says: "Associates are technically one rung above Analysts, but in general, they're less intelligent and worse off" (p. 21).

265. "Even the lowliest back-office manager at a major investment bank earns more than the leading practitioners in many other industries": Salary information from Glassdoor.com suggests that banking compliance officers, who sit pretty low on the totem pole, can expect to command salaries well into the six figures. (http://www.glassdoor.com/Salaries/compliance-officer-salary-SRCH_KO0,18.htm.)

Chapter Thirty-Six

273. "In *Liar's Poker*, Michael Lewis wrote": Michael Lewis, *Liar's Poker*, W. W. Norton & Company, 1989.

276. "One out of every six Ivy League seniors now applies to Teach for America": "Teach for America Fields Largest Teacher Corps in Its 20-Year History," May 24, 2010, via teachforamerica.org.

276. "in 2011, the program recruited more seniors than Goldman Sachs at schools like Brown and Columbia": John Gower, "A Closer Look at Top Employers of College Graduates," Nerdwallet.com, June 20, 2012.

Epilogue

281. "In March 2012, Greg Smith, a vice president at Goldman Sachs, quit his job at the bank with a highly publicized resignation letter": Greg Smith, "Why I Am Leaving Goldman Sachs," *New York Times*, March 14, 2012. Later, Smith would tell me, in an interview for *New York*, that the ensuing media frenzy caught him off guard: "I had no idea what to expect," he said. "Part of me worried it would be ignored. But literally, both my British and my American phones rang constantly for five hours."

281. "the workers were simply 'bailing out with no Plan B'": Leslie Kwoh, "Taking Early Exits Off Wall Street," *Wall Street Journal*, October 26, 2012.

281. "Goldman Sachs president Gary Cohn announced in 2013 that the bank received 17,000 applications for 350 summer intern spots—an acceptance rate of 2.1 percent": Liz Moyer, "At Goldman, You Start Among the 2%," *Wall Street Journal* (MoneyBeat), May 30, 2013.

282. "At Yale, the career center's 2013 student survey found that 'there is no one industry that attracts Yale graduates as a critical mass'": "First Destination Report: Class of 2013," Yale College, Undergraduate Career Services.

282. "A *Harvard Crimson* survey found that the percentage of Harvard seniors with jobs at graduation who were headed to Wall Street fell to 9 percent in 2012, then ticked up to 15 percent in 2013": Julie M. Zauzmer, "Where We Stand: The Class of 2013 Senior Survey," *Harvard Crimson*, May 28, 2013. Harvard's career services center also conducts an annual survey, which shows a flatter trend of graduates going into finance: 12 percent in 2011, 11 percent in 2012, and 12 percent in 2013.

282. "The crisis had shrunk Wall Street tremendously; as of 2013, only 30 percent of the more than 28,000 New York City financial sector jobs lost during the crisis had come back": Susanne Craig, "Wall Street Pay Rises, for Those Who Still Have a Job," *New York Times* (DealBook), February 26, 2013.

282. "Meanwhile, the growing technology industry kept picking off many of Wall Street's recruits": Terry Duffy, "Wall Street Is Losing the Best and Brightest," *Wall Street Journal*, September 29, 2013.

282. "no longer the beacon of high pay and innovation it once was": Suzanne Kapner, "Late Shift: Foosball Over Finance," *Wall Street Journal*, April 28, 2013.

282. "A 2013 study conducted by a recruiting firm found that 89 percent of financial executives were having problems with recruiting, and 83 percent were worried about losing their employees to other opportunities": "Robert Half Global Survey Reports on Financial Services Hiring Environment," April 30, 2013.

282. "Harvard Business School saw the share of its graduates going into the tech sector rise from 8 percent in 2010 to 18 percent in 2013": John Carney, "The Best and Brightest Are Turning Away from Wall Street," CNBC.com, October 31, 2013.

282. "Wharton—that fabled training ground for high finance—revealed that applications to its MBA programs had declined 12 percent since 2010": Melissa Korn, "What's Wrong With Wharton?," *Wall Street Journal*, September 27, 2013.

282. "Goldman Sachs formed a task force": Michael J. Moore, "Goldman Pushes Junior Investment Bankers to Take Weekends Off," Bloomberg News, October 28, 2013.

282. "announced it was ending its "two and out" analyst programs in the investment banking and investment management divisions": Liz Rap-

paport and Julie Steinberg, "A Bump in Path to Wall Street," *Wall Street Journal*, September 14, 2012.

283. **"average wages earned by workers stagnated"**: Robert Pear, "Median Income Rises, but Is Still 6% Below Level at Start of Recession in '07," *New York Times*, August 21, 2013.

283. **"The Dow Jones Industrial Average and the S&P 500 both reached new nominal all-time highs in late 2013"**: JeeYeon Park, "Dow, S&P 500 Post All-Time Highs as Fed Maintains Stimulus," CNBC.com, September 18, 2013.

283. **"housing prices across the country continued to rise"**: Anya Martin, "Real-Estate Rebound Buoys Borrowers," MarketWatch, July 5, 2013.

283. **"U.S. banks made $141.3 billion in net income in 2012, according to the FDIC, their best year since 2006"**: Jesse Hamilton, "U.S. Banks Had Second-Best Earnings Ever in 2012, FDIC Says," Bloomberg News, February 26, 2013.

283. **"In the summer of 2013, a twenty-one-year-old summer intern in Bank of America Merrill Lynch's London office dropped dead"**: Shiv Malik and Ben Quinn, "Bank of America Intern's Death Puts Banks' Working Culture in Spotlight," *The Guardian*, August 20, 2013.

285. **"Marina Keegan, the Yale senior who provided me with a glimpse into the campus recruiting culture after Occupy Wall Street, was killed in a car crash"**: Marina's obituary was written by William Alden and published in the *New York Times* on May 29, 2012.

INDEX